A TIME OF TERROR

A TIME OF TERROR

A Survivor's Story

James Cameron

3RD EDITION

ILLUSTRATED AND ANNOTATED

Foreword by James W. Loewen

life
writes
PRESS

MILWAUKEE, WISCONSIN

LifeWrites Press
11933 W. Burleigh Street, Suite 100
Wauwatosa, Wisconsin 53222
permissions@atimeofterror.info

Ordering Information:
Quantity sales. Special discounts are available on quantity purchases by schools, associations, and others at sales@atimeofterror.info.

Proceeds from the sales of this book benefit the nonprofit Dr. James Cameron Legacy Foundation.

Bibliographical Note

This LifeWrites Press paperback edition published in 2016 is an annotated, illustrated, and expanded 3rd edition of the work published by T/D Publications, Milwaukee, in 1982 and Black Classic Press, Baltimore, in 1994. This edition includes previously unpublished chapters by James Cameron. The Foreword by James W. Loewen, Introduction by Fran Kaplan and Robert S. Smith, and Afterword by Reggie Jackson were written especially for this edition. Edited by Fran Kaplan.

Publisher's Cataloging-In-Publication Data
(Prepared by The Donohue Group, Inc.)

Cameron, James, 1914-2006.
   A time of terror : a survivor's story / James Cameron ; foreword by James W. Loewen. -- 3rd edition, illustrated and annotated.

   pages : illustrations, map ; cm

   Originally published: Milwaukee, Wis. : TD Publications, 1982, ©1980.
   Includes bibliographical references.
   ISBN: 978-0-9965769-0-1

   1. Cameron, James, 1914-2006. 2. African Americans--Indiana--Marion--Biography. 3. Lynching--Indiana--Marion. 4. Marion (Ind.)--Race relations. I. Loewen, James W. II. Title.

F534.M34 C35 2016
364.1/34

CONTENTS

FOREWORD

M any years ago, in Mississippi, I had an "aha" experience that showed me the importance of history in educating our young people and readying them to be citizens. Perhaps I should call it an "Oh, no!" experience, since I witnessed the result of learning history solely from textbooks.

I asked a group of college students, "What was Reconstruction?"[1] All but one told me, "Reconstruction was right after the Civil War, when blacks took over the Southern states, but they were too soon out of slavery, so they messed up, and whites had to take back control again." Except for the first seven words, everything they told me was completely wrong. Worse, it was hurtful to them as black students to believe that the one time they were center stage in U.S. history, they "messed up."

---

[1] Reconstruction was a brief and complicated period (1863-1877) after the Civil War in which the 13th, 14th, and 15th Amendments to the Constitution were adopted. They abolished slavery, granted black Americans citizenship, civil rights, and the right to vote. The Freedmen's Bureau was established to help the former slaves (and poor southern whites) get needed food, clothes, fuel, and negotiate paid work agreements with their former owners. Northern teachers came south to establish schools and vocational training programs for the freedmen. For the first time, black men were elected to local, state and national offices–though never in significant numbers.

Another goal of Reconstruction was to bring the Confederate states back into the Union and establish "normalcy" again. This period also saw the rise of the Ku Klux Klan and other white supremacist groups, whose nightriders terrorized the black population. Lynching, rare during slavery, became common. The South instated Black Codes that effectively abolished the gains made by the freedmen and instituted "slavery by another name." Most historians of the period consider Reconstruction a failure, a first but very flawed attempt to establish a multiracial democracy in our country.

My students were good students–they had simply learned what they had been taught in high school, from textbooks written from a white-biased viewpoint. The textbooks also misled white students to infer that African Americans must not be given equality, lest they mess up like they did last time. Thus I saw that accurate history is crucial to promote children's mental health and understanding of society as they become adults.

Unfortunately, even today and even in the north, high school history textbooks still reflect a white-biased viewpoint. I should know, because for my critique of those books, *Lies My Teacher Told Me: Everything Your American History Textbook Got Wrong*, I read eighteen! Their overall storyline can be summed up in two words: unrelenting progress. We started out great, and we've been getting better ever since, more or less automatically.

This fixed idea allows their authors to assume that the arrival of Europeans (and Africans) into what is now the United States was a development to be cheered rather than examined. Progress lurks beneath their dismissal of our wars against American Indians—they had it coming, goes the unstated assumption, because they were simply not progressive enough. Indeed, progress legitimizes underplaying anything bad that Americans ever did, because in the end American history led us to *here*, the most progressive nation in the history of the world.

To be sure, slavery–and the racism that arose to legitimize it–do form a bit of a wart on the otherwise splendid physique of our body politic. So U.S. history books and popular culture responded by emphasizing that this was mostly a far-away Southern phenomenon; moreover, we fixed it long ago.[2] More recent racism was mostly the product of quirky losers like the three white supremacists who dragged African American James Byrd Jr. to death behind a truck in Jasper, Texas, in 1998.

Unfortunately, this storyline is too simple. At times, whether in foreign policy, equality of opportunity, or even medicine, our nation has moved backward. This retreat is most obvious in the area of race relations.

Here is where James Cameron's memoir comes in. It offers a welcome corrective to the narrative of unbroken progress. This man, who lived and breathed just a few years

---

[2] In the twentieth century, our popular culture and our high school history textbooks further minimized this blemish by idealizing slavery. The movie "Gone With the Wind" showed that the biggest problem enslaved people faced was worrying about their "w'ite folks." However, recent films, notably "Twelve Years a Slave," portray slavery more fully and accurately.

ago, had a lynch mob's noose around his neck. His story shows that racism–vicious, murderous, gut-wrenching, lynch-law racism–was hardly confined to the long ago. On the contrary, lynchings were rare in slavery times. Between 1890 and about 1940, they rose to their all-time high. This period is called the "Nadir of race relations."[3]

Devotion to the idea of progress makes textbook authors incapable of discussing the Nadir. It also makes history textbooks boring. As a result, survey after survey show history to be the least-liked subject in high school. As a further result, most students never take another course in history after they leave high school. Again, Cameron's book is the antidote, because no reader will find it boring. Moreover, after a student has read Cameron, s/he can be convinced to read other books about the past–from truly accurate historical novels like R. A. Lafferty's *Okla Hannali* (1972) to analyses of foreign policy like Jonathan Kwitny's *Endless Enemies* (1984).

Cameron's story also shows that lynch mob participants were hardly limited to idiosyncratic losers. In Marion, Indiana, where his story took place, ministers, business people, and leaders of the community participated or looked on. Indeed, a lynching can be defined as a public murder, done with considerable support of the community. When done by whites to people of color, it is a particularly scandalous expression of racism because the entire community knows that the perpetrators will likely get away with it. What is so compelling about the best-known photographs of lynchings is that they record murders *not* committed by deviants at the margins of society or in the dark of night. Rather, they show upright members of the white community happy to have their images captured in the commission of a felony because they believe that they will be commended, not prosecuted, for their act.[4]

The Nadir was not limited to the South, where it was systematized as "Jim Crow." Writing of the day-to-day interactions of whites and blacks in neighboring Ohio, Frank Quillen (1913, 120) observed in 1913 that race prejudice "is increasing steadily, especially during the last twenty years." Cameron's story takes place in Indiana, "the heartland" of America, in the words of Indiana historian James Madison (2003), who wrote a book about it.

Northern states probably had as many lynchings of African Americans, *per black capita*, as southern states. Lynching statistics don't show this, owing to their origin. The

---

[3] Nadir: the lowest point.

[4] To be sure, not all lynchings were of racial/ethnic minorities, although perhaps two thirds were. Nor were all lynchings by hanging, although perhaps two thirds were.

main list was assembled by a librarian at Tuskegee Institute in Alabama and her successor. They amassed their count of 4,743 mainly from southern weekly newspapers, to which Tuskegee subscribed. Naturally, those newspapers rarely covered lynchings outside the South.[5]

Northern communities also contributed to the development of "spectacle lynchings"–announced in advance, drawing hundreds and even thousands of bystanders. Sometimes these were orchestrated with special trains carrying spectators from nearby towns and with souvenirs given to the participants afterward.

Three of the most famous lynching photos stem from northern spectacle lynchings: the burning body of William Brown with well-dressed white men posing behind it in Omaha, 1919; two black circus workers hanging from a utility pole in Duluth, 1920, a third lying on the ground beneath, with young whites crowding to get into the picture from either side; and the bodies of Thomas Shipp and Abram Smith, James Cameron's friends, hanging from a tree in Marion, Indiana, on August 7, 1930, above a crowd of people in summer dresses and straw hats, including one man pointing toward a body. Ironically, these images have often been used to illustrate stories about southern lynchings.[6]

Not only did lynchings take place in the North; so did sundown towns. These are communities that for decades were–and some remain–all-white on purpose. Sundown towns are *common* in the North. They take their name from the signs that some communities displayed at their city limits: "Nigger / Don't Let The Sun Go Down On You In Elwood," for example, a town 25 miles southwest of Marion.[7] Hundreds of towns in Indiana drove out their African Americans or decided, formally or informally, not to let any in.

Before I began researching sundown towns in 1999, I had no idea how abundant they were. Having grown up 200 miles west of Marion, in central Illinois, I knew I would do more research in Illinois than in any other single state. I thought I would uncover maybe ten sundown towns in Illinois, fifty across the nation. Not so. The

---

[5] In 2013-15, several researchers have been working to broaden the lynching database, but as of this writing, no comprehensive list has yet emerged.

[6] For example, "The Chamber," a Hollywood film, uses the photo of the Marion lynching, dubbing it "Mississippi lynching."

[7] The term "sundown town" was used mostly in the Midwest, Appalachia, and the Ozarks, but intentionally white communities formed across Oregon, Pennsylvania, and many other states.

number now stands at 506 sundown towns *in Illinois alone,* which turns out to be about 70% of all incorporated towns in Illinois. A similar proportion went sundown in Indiana and various other northern states.[8]

During my full-time research on sundown towns, colleagues would ask me what I was working on. When I told them, they replied, "Oh, yes, in Mississippi, right? In Alabama?" Well, no. Sundown towns are rare in the traditional South. Having lived for eight years in Mississippi, for example, I tried to locate every sundown town I could in that state. I uncovered just three.

Hollywood perpetuates the stereotype that lynchings and sundown towns mark the Deep South. I know of four feature films that treat sundown towns. Three are set in Mississippi, one in Georgia. In fact, placing a sundown sign at the edge of town is one of the ways Hollywood *indicates* Southernness. Conversely, the most famous feature film ever set in Indiana, "Hoosiers," treats a basketball team from one sundown town, defeating a team from another sundown town, in a tournament game played in yet a third, Jasper. It covers over this racial reality by inserting African Americans–a black cymbal player in the band, spectators in the stands– where they would never have been allowed. As one Indiana resident wrote me in 2002, "All southern Hoosiers laughed at the movie called 'Hoosiers' because the movie depicts blacks playing basketball and sitting in the stands at games in Jasper. We all agreed no blacks were permitted until probably the '60s and do not feel welcome today."

Sundown towns were so prevalent in Indiana that we must note that race relations in Marion, bad as they were, were unusually *good* for that state and time. Many towns around Marion flatly barred African Americans, including Bluffton, Gas City, Hartford City, Huntington (home of former vice-president Dan Quayle), and Tipton. Mentone, an hour north, bragged, "With a population of 1,100, Mentone has not a Catholic, foreigner, Negro, nor Jew living in the city." When Wendell Willkie kicked off his 1940 campaign for the presidency in his hometown of Elwood, he had the town take down its sundown signs, but after he lost, they went right back up, remaining until the late 1960s. Nor did their eventual removal signal an end to Elwood's sundown tradition.[9]

---

[8] For more information about sundown towns, read Loewen (2005).

[9] Elwood's sundown tradition did more or less end around 2008 when its mayor led a brotherhood march on Martin Luther King Day.

During the Nadir, the Ku Klux Klan (KKK)[10] reached its high point. Again, James Cameron's memoir provides a way in to this shadowy chapter in our past. The first Klan had been southern and had engaged in widespread violence against African Americans and white Republicans during Reconstruction, in the 1870s. The second rising of the Klan was national. Its heyday was from 1916 to 1929, and it briefly controlled four states: Georgia, Oklahoma, Oregon, and especially Indiana. The KKK flourished in towns that had already gone sundown, but as Cameron tells, it also heightened the level of racial terror in interracial Indiana towns like Marion as well.

As his title implies, Cameron's eyewitness account of his near-murder gives us a way to understand the apprehension and uncertainty that always lay just beneath the surface of race relations in the Midwest. After the double lynching in Marion, race relations grew worse. Cognitive dissonance[11] and the need to give a good reason for what they had done caused white residents to claim that African Americans were inferior and more likely to be criminals. Otherwise, why would "we" (Marion) have lynched them? White residents brandished photos of the lynching to intimidate African Americans as late as the 1970s.[12] Even today, in some midwestern communities, African Americans do not know for sure whether it is wise to sit down in the local restaurant, let alone try to rent or buy a home.

However, *A Time of Terror* tells of much more than terror. Its pages teem with kind and competent people of all races, along with con artists and drunkards. It offers a rich source for understanding the everyday life of working class Americans of all races in the first half of the twentieth century. I found it compulsively readable and finished it within twenty-four hours. It will interest high school students, roughly the same age as Cameron when he was almost lynched. They can handle it, especially if they have a wise adult with whom to discuss it. And they will be better and more informed citizens as a

---

[10] A hate group still active today.

[11] Cognitive dissonance: the mental stress or discomfort that results when people hold two contradictory beliefs at the same time. This often happens when people are confronted with new information that conflicts with their existing beliefs, ideas, or values. To ease this stress, people tend to either justify their old behaviors or ignore any new information.

[12] Cynthia Carr (2006) makes this point in her interesting memoir about coming to terms with Cameron and Marion. Even more recently, in March 2015, a black Marion firefighter had a noose thrown at him at work. His wife is a cousin of Abram Smith, one of the teenagers lynched in 1930 (Lowery, The Washington Post online, 2015).

result. Americans cannot achieve the "one single and sacred nationality" that James Cameron seeks in his Epilogue, until we face our past honestly. We must learn that racism was *not* long ago and far away, it was *not* regional but national, sundown towns still exist, and history textbooks are still white-biased. Reading Cameron is one important step toward reaching those understandings.

Jim Loewen
Washington, D.C.
January 5, 2015

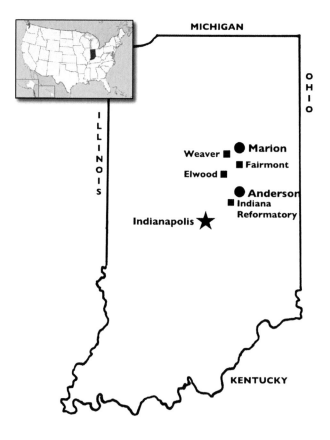

Figure 1. Map of Indiana with important locations in James Cameron's story.

INTRODUCTION

Growing Up Under Jim Crow

You hold in your hand a one-of-a-kind book: the only eyewitness account of a lynching in the United States written by its survivor.

•

On a sweltering August night in 1930, over ten thousand white men, women, and children gathered in the small town of Marion, Indiana. Many had traveled from around the state to witness a great spectacle. Three black teenagers were to be brutally beaten and hanged from a tree on the courthouse lawn. A photographer would be called to record the event for posterity on souvenir postcards.

Jimmie Cameron–a short skinny sixteen-year-old–was dragged to the tree where his friends Tommy Shipp and Abe Smith had already died. But with the noose already tightening around his neck, Jimmie was–suddenly, miraculously–spared. He would spend a year in jail before going to trial, then the next four years in a harsh adult prison. There he wrote this memoir,[13] the first step in his long life as a writer.

In this book, Cameron begins with the events leading up to the Marion lynching. He ends with his release from prison in 1935 at age twenty-one. The lynching certainly shaped his life, but Cameron recounts many other formative experiences as well. A talented storyteller, he presents a richly detailed portrait of a working-class black family during the Jim Crow Era in the North and South. Here are all the elements of great literature: betrayal, violence, risk, despair, hate, love, courage, compassion, redemption, and forgiveness.

---

[13] A memoir is a type of autobiography that focuses on an especially vivid time in the life of the writer.

This book should take its place alongside the works of other African American memoirists, such as Frederick Douglass, Booker T. Washington, Richard Wright, Maya Angelou, and President Barak Obama. Like Anne Frank's *The Diary of a Young Girl*, James Cameron's *A Time of Terror: A Survivor's Story* is a unique historical treasure. Like Anne's diary, this memoir should be required reading for all Americans in school.

Why Read This Introduction

You may be reading this book for a class in middle school, high school, or college—or just for your own interest and enlightenment. You may find yourself discussing it at a book club meeting or in the barbershop. No matter. Reading this introduction will help you more fully appreciate James Cameron's life. You will be able to have richer discussions about the book with others.

The introduction should also help you better understand why *A Time of Terror* deserves your attention today. It shows us how far we have come in one man's lifetime—and how far we still have to go to repair our racially divided society. Like James Cameron, the authors of this introduction are optimistic. We believe that when we face our past honestly, we will see how to heal our future.

The introduction has two main sections:

• *Born Into Jim Crow:* The stories in this book took place between eighty and a hundred years ago, during the period of American history known as the Jim Crow Era.[14] This section describes the world Jimmie was born into. It will help you understand what life was like then for an African American teenager and young adult.

• *The Great Spectacle in Marion:* This section answers these questions—and more: Why were African Americans lynched in large numbers during Jim Crow? Marion is in the North; didn't lynchings just happen in the South? Why did people pose for pictures at lynchings?

---

[14] The term "Jim Crow" comes from a song-and-dance routine performed first in 1828 by a white man, Thomas Dartmouth Rice, in blackface make-up. He portrayed the black man he called Jim Crow as a lazy fool. This stereotypical, cartoonish performance became popular entertainment for whites. At first, using the term "Jim Crow" became a way to insult black men. Later it was used to describe the entire system of segregation laws and customs in the South from the 1870s to the 1960s. We use it here as general term for the Nadir of race relations North *and* South, as described in this book's Foreword. For more information about the Jim Crow Era, visit the Jim Crow Museum of Racist Memorabilia online and www.abhmuseum.org.

Born Into Jim Crow

After America's Civil War,[15] white Southerners found ways to keep the power over black people that they had enjoyed during slavery. This system of white supremacy, known as "Jim Crow," was maintained through a combination of laws, social customs, and mob violence. Baby Jimmie was born in 1914 into a country shaped–both South and North–by slavery and Jim Crow.

In the South: Looks Like Slavery

By the end of the Civil War in 1865, millions of African Americans in the South had been officially emancipated. [16] However, southern states immediately set about constructing a legal system that looked a lot like slavery. In just ten years they succeeded so well that the US Congress issued a civil rights act[17] to stop these racial segregation laws–to no avail. Then, in 1896, the U.S. Supreme Court decided, in the famous *Plessy v. Ferguson* case, that racial segregation was acceptable if blacks and whites had "separate but equal" facilities. The "equal" part of that decision was not seriously enforced. In fact, making segregation legal around the country provided the basis for the rest of the Jim Crow structure. Legal segregation was just one part of a system that also included political, economic, and social oppression.

---

[15] A "civil war" is a war between citizens of the same country. When the Civil War began in 1861, the United States consisted of thirty-four states. Seven slaveholding states declared independence from the U.S. and formed their own country, the Confederate States of America. The Confederacy grew to include eleven southern states. The states that remained part of the U.S. were called the Union. The fight started over the issue of slavery and whether it should be legal in the southern states and western territories. Four years of combat left over 600,000 Union and Confederate soldiers dead. In the end, slavery was officially abolished and much of the South's infrastructure destroyed.

[16] Freed from slavery.

[17] *The Civil Rights Act of 1875* stated, "all persons within the jurisdiction of the United States shall be entitled to the full and equal enjoyment of the accommodations, advantages, facilities, and privileges of inns, public conveyances on land or water, theaters, and other places of public amusement…" The Supreme Court ruled this law unconstitutional in 1883. This Act represented the last congressional effort to protect the civil rights of African Americans for almost a century.

Politically, almost all African Americans in the South were deprived of the right to vote. By the 1890s, America's very brief experience with racial equality had ended. Southern white politicians rewrote their state constitutions to remove blacks from the voting rolls. They claimed that "Negroes"[18] were not qualified to choose representatives and that allowing them to vote would lead to corruption in politics. Some even declared that political equality would lead black men to rape white girls.[19] Politicians from the wealthy planter class used such claims to keep working- and middle-class southern white

Figure 2: The Ku Klux Klan, a large nationwide white supremacist terror organization, marched openly and unmasked in Washington, D.C., September 13, 1926. *Library of Congress*

---

[18] Throughout this book, the terms "Negro" and/or "colored" will be used as they were throughout the Jim Crow Era. Today, however, the appropriate terms are "African American" and/or "black," depending on how the individual prefers to be identified.

[19] Litwak (1998, 221) provides the following example: "One Atlanta newspaper in 1906 explained in all capital letters that promises of political equality would lead black men to rape white girls: 'POLITICAL EQUALITY BEING THIS PREACHED TO THE NEGRO IN THE RING PAPERS AND ON THE STUMP, WHAT WONDER THAT HE MAKES NO DISTINCTION BETWEEN POLITICAL AND SOCIAL EQUALITY? HE GROWS MORE BUMPTIOUS ON THE STREET, MORE IMPUDENT IN HIS DEALINGS WITH WHITE MEN, AND THEN, WHEN HE CANNOT ACHIEVE SOCIAL EQUALITY AS HE WISHES, WITH THE INSTINCT OF THE BARBARIAN TO DESTROY WHAT HE CANNOT ATTAIN TO, HE LIES IN WAIT, AS THAT DASTARDLY BRUTE DID YESTERDAY NEAR THIS CITY AND ASSAULTS THE FAIR YOUNG GIRLHOOD OF THE SOUTH....'"

voters separate from blacks.[20]

Lack of voting power meant that black people had no say in making the laws they had to live by. They could not obtain government services for their neighborhoods, such as paved roads, better schools, garbage collection, and streetlights. Some southern black people were able to remain politically active during those years, but they did so at immense risk to their lives and property. In order to vote, they had to maneuver through legal obstacles like grandfather clauses, poll taxes, and literacy tests.[21] They faced violent intimidation, attacks on their families, and assassination by white supremacist groups and militias like the Ku Klux Klan and the Knights of the White Camellia.

The economic oppression of Jim Crow also looked like slavery. After the Civil War, only a small percentage of the former slaves were given land, tools, or money. Most freedmen were penniless and largely uneducated.[22] They had few options for supporting their families, so many were forced to stay on the plantations to work as farm laborers.

---

[20] Before the Civil War, few working- and middle-class whites owned slaves. The war devastated the South's economy, and many white working families suffered economically. But, they thought, at least they were not black! Whites understood that being black meant being even more disadvantaged. However, white supremacy prevented many whites from seeing what they had in common with blacks. When politicians encouraged poor and middle-income whites to feel superior to blacks, they did not notice that their governments were corrupt and their taxes unfair. Racism allowed upper-class whites to take advantage of working-class people–both black and white.

[21] Poll taxes were fees paid to register as a voter. The fees were high enough to prevent many poor citizens–black and white–from voting. White election officials administered literacy tests to blacks only. They consisted of questions like "how many bubbles are in a bar of soap" or "draw five circles that one common inter-locking part (sic)." The white election official administering the test decided whether the black citizen passed the test. To avoid having uneducated poor whites fail the test, they were "grandfathered in" if they had voted previously, were veterans or descendants of veterans, or were of "good character" (Onion, "Taking the Impossible Literacy Test," slate.com).

[22] During slavery it was illegal and dangerous for most slaves to learn to read, write and do arithmetic.

Figure 3: Black men, women, and children pick cotton, monitored by a white overseer on a horse, in 1917–fifty-two years after the end of slavery. *Library of Congress*

They became sharecroppers or tenant farmers.[23] So did many poor whites after the war. This labor system led to a great deal of abuse of the farmers. Owners could easily cheat croppers by charging them more than they owed in crops and credit. If they protested, white farmers would get a threatening visit or hauled into court. Black farm families would be attacked by "night riders"–or lynched.

During Jim Crow, many African Americans were also forced to work without pay–like slaves–through the convict leasing system (Blackmon, 2008). Southern states passed Black Codes, a series of laws that restricted black people's right to own or rent property and to move around freely. Many forms of behavior were considered a crime called "vagrancy." African Americans could be arrested as vagrants for not being able to prove

---

[23] In sharecropping, plantation owners assigned a plot of land to a family and provided a plow and mule. The sharecropping family then needed to buy seed, fertilizer, food, clothing, and tools on credit from the owner. At harvest, they owed the owner half the crop (usually) plus whatever they had purchased on credit. Tenant farmers possessed their own plow and mule. At harvest, they owed the plantation owner about a third of their crop, plus whatever they had bought from him or her on credit.

their employment, failing to pay a tax, or just hanging out on a street corner. Blacks could be arrested on the simple word of whites, since blacks were not allowed to testify against whites in court. The southern criminal justice system then "leased" the black prisoners to white-owned private businesses at very low cost. This raised large amounts of money for local and state governments.

The prisoners were paid nothing. They were often beaten, starved, and worked to death in dangerous mines, railroads, lumber camps, and factories. All African American adults–and children–lived under the constant threat of ending up as one of these slave laborers. This "slavery by another name" lasted for *eighty years* after Emancipation!

Figure 4. Guard and convicts in Georgia, 1941. *Library of Congress*

Figure 5. The side entrance for "colored" at the Crescent Theater in Belzoni, Mississippi, 1939. *Library of Congress*

The social and personal effects of Jim Crow laws and customs on everyday African American life were also devastating. Segregated educational programs and buildings for blacks were generally of lower quality than for whites, as were the separate rest rooms, railroad cars, waiting rooms, and balcony sections of movie theaters. White swimming pools, parks, hotels, restaurants, and many other businesses refused entrance to blacks. Those few that served black people humiliated them, making them go to the back door for service.[24]

---

[24] Dr. Martin Luther King, Jr. described some of his experiences living under Jim Crow this way: "…you suddenly find your tongue twisted and your speech stammering as you seek to explain to your six year old daughter why she can't go to the public amusement park that has just been advertised on television, and see tears welling up in her eyes when she is told that Funtown is closed to colored children, and see ominous clouds of inferiority beginning to form in her little mental sky…you take a cross county drive and find it necessary to sleep night after night in the uncomfortable corners of your automobile because no motel will accept you; …you are humiliated day in and day out by nagging signs reading "white" and "colored…" (King, 1963).

The Jim Crow system taught even the lowest-status white American that he was superior to any black person.[25] A white child never need address a black adult as Mr. or Mrs., but could call a black man of any age "boy" or "uncle" and any black woman "auntie." Blacks were expected to tip their hats and step off the sidewalk to allow whites to pass. It was dangerous for blacks to make and sustain eye contact with whites. White employers often raped black women and girls who worked in their homes. Their husbands and fathers could not defend them without the risk of being beaten, jailed, or killed. If a black boy or man accidentally bumped into or even glanced at a white girl or woman, he could be lynched.

Figure 6. "Colored" water cooler in a streetcar terminal, Oklahoma City, Oklahoma, 1939. *Library of Congress*

---

[25] For some 200 years, many European and white American scientists tried to show that people of African descent were naturally inferior to people of European descent. Modern genetics has proven this "science" wrong. Still, this false idea became embedded in American society, because it supported slavery and segregation. Many people believe it to this day. The truth is that *no* genes distinguish all members of one "race" from all members of another. There are genes for skin color, but they have nothing to do with the genes that influence intelligence, athletic ability, musical talent, or character (Adelman, 2003).

In the North: Let Him Know His Place

We think of Jim Crow as a southern phenomenon, but black Americans were the targets of frequent racial violence and discrimination throughout the country. In fact, even slavery existed in the North for almost seventy-five years after the Declaration of Independence![26] Alexis de Tocqueville, a Frenchman who famously toured and wrote about the United States in 1831, observed that racial prejudice "appears to be stronger in the states that have abolished slavery than in those where it still exists" (Litwak, 1961, 65). Another visitor, a Scottish journalist, summed up race relations in the North this way:

> "We shall not make the black man a slave; …but we shall not associate with him. He shall be free to live, and to thrive, if he can, and to pay taxes and perform duties, but he shall not be free to dine and drink at our board–to share with us the deliberations of the jury box–to sit upon the seat of judgment, however capable he may be–to plead in our courts–to represent us in the Legislature–to attend us at the bed of sickness and pain–to mingle with us in the concert-room, the lecture-room, the theatre, or the church, or to marry with our daughters. We are of another race, and he is inferior. Let him know his place–and keep it."
> This is the prevalent feeling, if not the language of the free North.
> – Charles Mackay, *Life and Liberty in America: or, Sketches of a Tour in the United States and Canada in 1857-1858* (quoted in Litwak, 1961, 1).

Jimmie Cameron's family moved from La Crosse, Wisconsin, to Indiana when he was a baby. When he was five, they moved to Birmingham, Alabama. Jimmie's mother brought her children back to Indiana when he was twelve. Indiana was one of several

---

[26] "By 1804, all northern states had voted to abolish the institution of slavery within their borders. In most of these states, however, abolition was not immediate. Instead, gradual emancipation laws set deadlines by which all slaves would be freed, releasing individuals as they reached a certain age or at the end of a certain work period. This situation left some African Americans lingering in bonded servitude. Pennsylvania passed its Act for the Gradual Abolition of Slavery in 1780. Yet, as late as 1850, the federal census recorded that there were still hundreds of young blacks in Pennsylvania who would remain enslaved until their 28th birthdays" (Boston and Hallom).

states in the North and West that actively tried to prevent blacks from settling there. In fact, this restriction was written into the state constitution, though it was only occasionally enforced. The law existed to remind African Americans of their inferior position in society and to excuse white harassment and mob violence against them (Litwak, 1961, 72). As Loewen (2006) describes in the *Forward* in this volume, many communities in Indiana were "sundown towns" where whites drove blacks out or did not allow them to settle in the first place. Still, millions of black southerners migrated to the North hoping to escape Jim Crow's terrible violence.

Along with fleeing Jim Crow oppression, black southerners also sought better working conditions and better pay than they received as sharecroppers. At the same time, farmers were starting to use machines in the fields. This was the beginning of the end of sharecropping. Countless sharecroppers left for the industrial cities of the North to find jobs in factories. Others became migrant farmworkers in the West. This era is known as The Great Migration.

Figure 7. A family newly arrived in Chicago from the rural South in 1922. *Schomburg Center, New York Public Library*

Seeking the American Dream in the Promised Land

From the early years of the twentieth century to well past its middle age, nearly every black family in the American South, which meant nearly every black family in America, had a decision to make. There were sharecroppers losing at settlement. Typists wanting to work in an office. Yard boys scared that a single gesture near the planter's wife could leave them hanging from an oak tree. They were all stuck in a caste system as hard and unyielding as the red Georgia clay, and they each had a decision before them. In this, they were not unlike anyone who ever longed to cross the Atlantic or the Rio Grande....

Historians would come to call it the Great Migration. It would become perhaps the biggest underreported story of the twentieth century. It was vast....It would transform urban America and recast the social and political order of every city it touched (Wilkerson, 2010).

The Great Migration of African Americans occurred in two waves. The First Great Migration was during the World War I Era (1910s-1920s). The war stimulated the rapid growth of industry in North. At the same time, young white men were being sent off to war, creating a labor shortage. Prices for Southern crops were going down, and farm machines were reducing the number of workers needed on farms. The sharecropping system began to collapse. The promise of well-paying jobs drew hundreds of thousands of rural black folk to the cities of Chicago, Detroit, Philadelphia, and New York.

When they arrived in the so-called "Promised Land," the migrants found that Jim Crow had made the journey too. In fact, the Great Migration sparked further racism across the country. Whites who had immigrated to America from Europe in recent years found themselves having to compete with blacks for jobs. Northern factories actively recruited black workers from the South. They sometimes used them to break strikes and keep white workers from forming unions. There had been plenty of jobs during World War I, but when the war ended, the government did nothing about jobs for returning soldiers. The competition for employment stirred up racial hatred among working-class whites. This was part of what led to the 1919 Red Summer riots.

Figure 8. Will Brown, circa 1919.
Nebraska State Historical Society

Jimmie Cameron was just five years old during the Red Summer of 1919. That year white mobs in cities in the North and South attacked black neighborhoods, vandalizing, looting, and burning homes and businesses. In Chicago, Illinois, the attacks lasted for thirteen days, and some one thousand black families lost their homes. During 1919, at least forty-three African Americans were reported lynched in these widespread "race riots," including Will Brown. Mr. Brown, aged 41, was a black packinghouse worker in Omaha, Nebraska, who was accused of assaulting a white woman. He was taken by a mob of young white men from the courthouse where he was held. They beat and hanged him. Then they riddled his body with bullets and burned it before setting off through the city to attack black neighborhoods. Federal troops had to be called in to restore order. Just eleven years after Willie Brown's murder, Jimmie would also be dragged from a jail and brutally beaten by a large northern lynch mob.

Soon, however, the returning white servicemen replaced black industrial workers. White men controlled the labor unions, and the 1935 Wagner Act permitted them to

Figure 9. The burning of Will Brown's body on September 28, 1919, during the Omaha race riot. *Nebraska State Historical Society*

exclude nonwhites. Black workers were mostly segregated into the lowest paying and most dangerous jobs—without benefits like healthcare, paid vacations, or job security. When Social Security was created to provide a safety net for retired workers, it did not cover housekeepers and farm workers. Most of these domestic and farm workers were African American.

In the Second Great Migration (1940s to 1970s), many of the black migrants were from southern cities, where they were confined to segregated low-skill, low-paying jobs. The Second World War had created another labor shortage, and many of the available jobs paid high wages. Millions headed for the western states, especially California, where there was a large defense industry. Others sought their fortunes in the smaller industrial cities of the North, such as Milwaukee, Wisconsin, where James Cameron would settle in 1952.

Black migrants were also immediately segregated into ghettos. They were allowed to settle only in the oldest, most rundown neighborhoods, where the European immigrant populations had once lived. White residents fled to suburbs or the regions of the cities with better housing. In the 1930s-40s the federal government set up the FHA (Federal Housing Administration) program and made home ownership affordable for millions of average Americans. However, property values and eligibility for loans were tied to race, so blacks got almost none of the loans. There were also written covenants and informal "gentlemen's agreements" between realtors and sellers to exclude blacks from white neighborhoods. Owning a home in a valued neighborhood is how most average Americans save money and pass it on to their children. This critically important method of building family security and wealth[27] was denied to most African Americans.

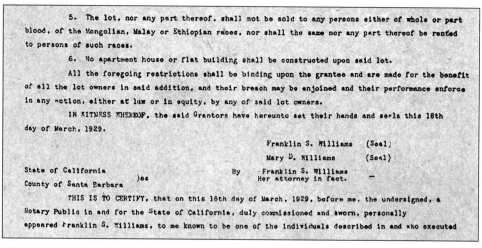

Figure 10. Portion of a 1929 covenant between a buyer and sellers of a lot in Seattle, Washington, in which the buyer agrees not to sell or rent to nonwhites. *Seattle Civil Rights and Labor History Project*

---

[27] Wealth is the value of a family's financial assets, including their home, other property, savings, and investments.

And Still We Rise!

As we have seen, the Jim Crow system supported white supremacy in every part of society. This made day-to-day life for black people shaky at best, life threatening at worst. But African Americans did not take this lying down. They created black communities and towns. They built black businesses and a host of black institutions. When the new opportunities pulled black people north and west, they already had a history of relying on themselves and each other. This helped African Americans survive and even thrive under the harsh Jim Crow system.

Once free of enslavement, black people formed many self-help and advocacy groups: the Black Women's Club Movement (1890s), the National Association of Colored Women (1896), the National Association for the Advancement of Colored People (1909), the Urban League (1910) and by the 1920s, the New Negro Movement (also called the Harlem Renaissance) and the Garvey Movement. Hundreds of newspapers were written, published, and read by African Americans around the country.

These organizations, movements, and newspapers fought back against racist stereotyping and assaults on the "Negro" presence. Their leaders stood for pride in their race and redefined black identity on their own terms. They used art, literature, and music to challenge the racist notion that blacks were inferior intellectually, culturally,

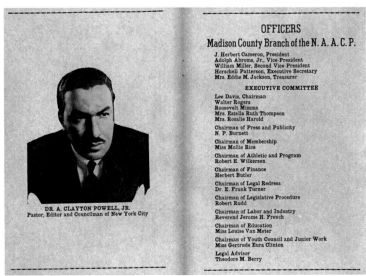

Figure 11. The March 1944 program booklet of the NAACP branch in Anderson, Indiana. They brought to town the well-known and charismatic advocate, Dr. Adam Clayton Powell, Jr. Cameron, the branch president, introduced him. Powell was the first African American on the New York City Council. He would later represent Harlem in the U.S. Congress for twelve terms. *Cameron Family*

and socially. They also challenged lynching and the other abuses of Jim Crow through protest and political movements. These movements laid the foundation for the Civil Rights Movement of the 1950-60s.[28]

The End of Jim Crow?

Jim Crow is said to have ended in the mid-1960s when two important national laws were passed. The 1964 Civil Rights Act outlawed segregation in public places like schools, workplaces, hotels, theaters, and restaurants. The Voting Rights Act of 1965 outlawed discrimination in voting. Since then, conditions have improved for some African Americans, but many of the economic, political, and social patterns established during Jim Crow remain today.

For example, most white people in this country live in all-white communities and neighborhoods, attend all-white churches, and do not know a single black person well. Residential segregation still makes it hard even for middle-class black people to escape the ghetto. When the white working and middle classes fled to the suburbs and exurbs,[29] most industries and businesses moved there too. The bus systems used by the inner city poor do not go to these communities. This has left many African Americans and low-income whites unable to get family-supporting jobs. In 2013, white households had thirteen times the wealth of black households—and the gap is growing (Kochnar and Fry, 2014).

Most schools are still racially segregated, and those serving primarily black children are often underfunded. These schools struggle to educate many children who are chronically stressed by the racism and poverty their families have suffered over generations.[30] These super-stressed children often receive harsh punishments for petty misbehaviors, like throwing a lollipop ("battery"), tapping a pencil on a desk ("destruction of property"), and talking back ("disturbing the peace"). Students of color are punished more frequently and more harshly. For every white student suspended

---

[28] Leading black intellectuals and activists in this era included W.E.B. DuBois, James Weldon Johnson, Marcus Garvey, and Mary Church Terrell. Among many leading literary figures were Zora Neale Hurston, James Baldwin, and Langston Hughes. Towering figures in music included Paul Robeson, Billy Holiday, Ella Fitzgerald, and Louis Armstrong.

[29] Small towns that ring large cities.

[30] DeGruy (2005) explains how the effects of racism are passed down across generations.

from school, four black students are pushed out. The increased presence of police within schools has resulted in the handcuffing and arrests of children as young as five. These conditions have created a "school-to-prison pipeline."[31]

As we write this, a national conversation has developed about the "New Jim Crow." Witnesses with camera phones are now recording the too-frequent killings of unarmed black teens and adults by policemen. Their videos, plus protests in many cities, are shedding light on a biased justice system. The white press and public have begun to take notice of problems that black communities have known for a long time. Blacks are more likely to be mistreated at every point in the system—from frequent "driving while black" stops to receiving inadequate legal defense to getting longer prison sentences than whites for the same offenses. White people tend to perceive black people as criminals much more often than is the case (Ghandnoosh, 2014). This reminds us of the Jim Crow era when the idea that blacks were, by nature, criminal "brutes" was used to excuse race riots and lynchings.

The Great Spectacle in Marion

A lynching is an "extralegal" execution[32] performed by community members who appoint themselves judge and jury. We use the word "performed" on purpose. Lynchings of black people in the Jim Crow Era, whether staged publicly or privately, were rituals meant to intimidate the black community. African Americans could be brutally executed without a trial on the word of a single white accuser.[33] Lynchings

---

[31] See the Advancement Project, "Ending the Schoolhouse to Jailhouse Track," online.

[32] "Extralegal" means "outside of the law," i.e., illegal.

[33] Here are some examples: Anthony Crawford was lynched in 1916 in South Carolina for being "insolent" and "too rich for a Negro." Born enslaved in 1865, he grew up to become an educated black landowner. He had argued with a white man about the price for his crop. His entire family was then run out of town and off their land (Memorial to the Victims of Lynching, ABHM).

In Duluth, Minnesota, in 1920 three circus workers were lynched on the rumor that they had raped a sixteen-year-old white girl. When a doctor examined the girl, he found no evidence that she had been attacked or raped. The three black men had already been killed. Warren Read, a teacher whose great-grandfather was active in the lynch mob, writes about it in an ABHM exhibit: *Shaking the Family Tree.*

clearly demonstrated that white people could do anything to blacks for any reason without fear of punishment, so blacks better stay "in their place."

Many people think that the word "lynching" means a tree and a noose, but these illegal community executions were carried out by many means aside from hanging. Victims were beaten to death, drowned, shot, burned, stabbed with knives or hot pokers, and dragged behind cars.

Figure 12. The lynching of three circus workers–Elias Clayton, Elmer Jackson and Isaac McGhie–in Duluth, Minnesota, on June 14, 1920.
Minnesota Historical Society

An American Tradition

Lynchings took place most frequently in the South, beginning during Reconstruction and continuing through the Jim Crow Era. Paramilitary organizations, such as the Ku Klux Klan, Knights of the White Camellia, and the White League,

---

In 1935 during the Great Depression, Rubin Stacy, a homeless worker in Ft. Lauderdale, Florida, knocked on the door of a white woman to ask for food. Seeing a black face, she screamed and he was arrested. She then claimed he attacked her with a knife. After the lynch mob murdered him, she took back her story.

John Carter, a black man in Little Rock, Arkansas, was lynched in 1927 by a mob that was angry because they could not catch the man actually accused of the crime.

organized right after emancipation. Their purpose was to reclaim white control over the South by terrorizing the black population.

We know the most about southern lynchings, because they were generally publicized in the newspapers–sometimes even before they occurred. The Tuskegee Institute collected these reports and counted nearly 5000 lynchings between 1882 and 1968. The vast majority of lynching victims were black men and boys. Some were black women. Others were Mexicans, Chinese, and Native Americans, as well as Jews, Italians, and other European immigrants who were not yet considered "white."[34]

But lynching was not a purely southern custom. There were also lynchings in the old West and the North. The Ku Klux Klan and similar violent white supremacist organizations had spread across the country. During Jimmie Cameron's childhood in Indiana, that state was a KKK stronghold. The Klan was not a secret organization. Voters elected men to local and state government *because* they were Klan members.[35] Members of lynch mobs were almost never brought to court, because lynching was seen as an acceptable, even healthy, community tradition.

Spectacle Lynchings

When the lynch mob came for Jimmie, Tommy, and Abe, the teenagers already knew what to expect. From the early morning, they watched as a crowd gathered around the county jail where they were being held. This was to be a "spectacle lynching."

Spectacle lynchings had a festival-like atmosphere. Entire towns and nearby communities would take part. If law enforcement officers were not actively involved in the planning and execution of these events, they often would not or could not stop

---

[34] The American definition of who is a member of the "white race" has changed over our history. Before World War II, most people from southern or eastern Europe–Italians, Greeks, Poles, and Jews–were considered to be of distinct, non-white "races." These groups were thought to be unfit, unskilled, ignorant, and inferior to the "white race." English and French immigrants were considered "white," but the Irish were not. After World War II, the definitions of who was "white" began to include all people of European heritage. Genetics has now shown that "race" is not a biological fact. "Race" is a purely social, cultural and political idea that changes over time. "Whiteness studies" is an examination by scholars of these ideas and their impact on our society.

[35] Throughout his life, James Cameron was a fierce foe of the Klan. When the KKK held a rally or parade in the Midwest, Dr. Cameron would often march in opposition–even into his eighties.

them. News of the upcoming festivities was spread by word of mouth or advertised beforehand in the newspapers. When the time came, the lynch mob would, forcibly if necessary, capture and take the victims to the public lynching site. The crowd would brutally beat and drag victims along the way. If death did not come by beating, victims would be riddled with bullets, hanged with ropes, and/or burned alive. Some victims were castrated.[36]

Lynching spectators would collect and often sell souvenirs. These included such objects as body parts (fingers, ears, genitals); pieces of the lynching rope or the victim's clothing; bark from the tree; and photographic postcards. James Cameron would later be given a piece of the rope that hanged one of his friends by a Marion man whose father had been there. The souvenir photograph of the Marion spectacle is the most famous lynching picture in the world.

"Dear Mom, Wish You Were Here"

Thousands of photo postcards of lynching were openly bought, collected, and sent to friends and family as souvenirs. For example, in 1915 a young man in Temple, Texas, sent his parents a card showing the burnt corpse of William Stanley, with the note, "This is the barbecue we had last night. My picture is to the left with a cross over it. Your son, Joe" (Allen et al., 2010, 26).

Lynching parties often took "selfies" with the bodies of their prey.[37] Professional photographers would be called to the scene, usually once the victims had died. Occasionally, though, they were able to take pictures right from the beginning, during the exciting capture and transportation of the victims.

---

[36] Their testicles were cut off.

[37] As have many other tormentors and executioners since photography was invented. The Nazis extensively photographed themselves and their victims in ghettos and concentration camps in the 1930s-40s. So did U.S. Army and CIA personnel in Iraq's Abu Ghraib prison, acts that came to light in 2003. The camera phone and social media now send real time videos of atrocities like Islamic State beheadings around the world. In most of these images, the perpetrators are seen smiling in satisfaction, pride, and amusement.

The photographer[38] might set up lights to better illuminate the scene. Tree limbs might be cut away so he could get a better shot. He might ask that the spectators and victims be arranged a certain way. The group that performed the tortures and execution would then pose around their victim. Often onlookers jostled their way into the frame, into that esteemed circle. Frequently there were small children in the crowd, learning from their elders to see the victims as vermin–bugs or rats that must be done away with to sanitize the community.

When we look at lynching photographs, our eyes are drawn first to the spectators, because they are usually looking directly at us. They are not repulsed by the horror of what they or their neighbors have done. On the contrary, they look proud and happy, even celebratory. Looking at them, most of us feel disgusted, outraged, and bewildered. But it is easier to look more closely at the perpetrators than at the victims.

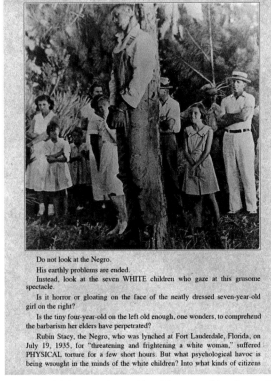

Do not look at the Negro.
His earthly problems are ended.
Instead, look at the seven WHITE children who gaze at this grusome spectacle.
Is it horror or gloating on the face of the neatly dressed seven-year-old girl on the right?
Is the tiny four-year-old on the left old enough, one wonders, to comprehend the barbarism her elders have perpetrated?
Rubin Stacy, the Negro, who was lynched at Fort Lauderdale, Florida, on July 19, 1935, for "threatening and frightening a white woman," suffered PHYSICAL torture for a few short hours. But what psychological havoc is being wrought in the minds of the white children? Into what kinds of citizens

Figure 13. This NAACP anti-lynching pamphlet shows the murder of Ruben Stacy. It points out how white children were taught to accept this type of murder as normal, natural, even healthy. In the background, her face turned away, there is a black maid who was likely required to bring the children in her care to this scene. *Schomburg Center, New York Public Library*

---

[38] In Marion, professional photographer Lawrence Beitler was called to the scene after Thomas and Abram were hanged. He carried his heavy view camera, tripod, and flash powder from his studio. Members of the crowd turned and posed for him, including a young couple, a pregnant woman, and a man with a tattoo on his arm pointing towards Tommy's body. The flash captured two young women in front holding pieces of dark cloth, probably souvenirs of Tommy's clothing. Thousands of other spectators were hidden by the darkness beyond the flash's reach.

Often a victim has been partly or fully stripped–of his clothing and his dignity. Sometimes blood runs down his thighs. Even if his lower body has been covered with a sheet (as was Thomas Shipp's in Marion), we can see the castration. We can see where beatings or bullets have lacerated his body. We can see how fire contorted or destroyed his arms and legs. We can see the aftermath of awful suffering. But can we see the victims as real people?

Figure 14. August 7, 1930. Marion, Indiana. Some of the lynching spectators, in a crowd estimated at ten to fifteen thousand, posed on the courthouse lawn under the mutilated bodies of Abram Smith and Thomas Shipp. Jimmie Cameron would soon be brought to stand between them with a noose around his neck. *Indiana Historical Society*

Each of these victims was once a living human being with feelings and families. For us, the trauma of their visible deaths overshadows their unseen lives. Though heartrending, when we look at lynching, we must honor its victims by seeing and remembering.[39] *A Time of Terror* by one of lynching's few survivors can help us do that.

Many of us would like to forget about the perpetrators. Some of us are their direct descendants, but all who live in this country are shadowed by their legacy. We cannot erase the past, but by looking at it honestly we can find ways to repair the future. Around the country, descendants of the lynched and descendants of the lynchers have recently begun to remember and heal together.[40]

Jimmie Cameron grew up in a time of terror for African Americans. In his book, you will learn how he managed nonetheless to survive and thrive, supported by his mother's faith and love and by the guidance of some surprising adult mentors.[41]

As an adult, Dr. Cameron told his story and showed lynching photographs in lecture halls, in films, on television, and in the museum he founded.[42] It was painful for him to do this repeatedly; he would often cry during the retelling. But he persisted because he saw his listeners open their hearts and minds. This courageous man is no longer with us, but he has bequeathed this book to us, his countrymen, as a precious legacy and call to action.

How to Get the Most from This Edition–and Beyond[43]

When he left prison at age twenty-one, James Cameron vowed to "pick up the loose ends of my life and weave them into something beautiful, worthwhile, and God-like." If

---

[39] You can pay your respects at America's Black Holocaust Museum's *Memorial to the Victims of Lynching* and view an art exhibit, *The Stories Behind the Postcards* (Scott), that reminds us of the pain of families who had to retrieve their loved ones' bodies once the spectacle ended.

[40] Take an online tour of activities for racial repair and reconciliation at ABHM.

[41] A recently published book includes an examination of Dr. Cameron as one of the world's "supersurvivors" who transform their lives and achieve extraordinary things after terrible trauma. (Feldman and Kravetz, 2014.)

[42] You can watch Dr. Cameron tell his story in the short video, *Sweet Messenger* (Ferraro and Kaplan, 2012).

[43] Our goal in editing this edition was to maintain the integrity of Cameron's text as a historical document, while keeping it easy to read. Scholars can find an explanation of edits made at www.atimeofterror.info.

you wonder what this survivor made of the rest of his life–whether he kept that vow, you'll want to read the *Afterword* by his protégé, Reggie Jackson, at the end of this book.

You will notice many footnotes in *A Time of Terror*. These annotations provide brief explanations that will help you understand and appreciate Cameron's story even more. Most relate interesting parts of the story that do not appear in Cameron's account. Some give you historical and other background details. A few provide definitions of unfamiliar words, such as the slang of Jimmie's times.

To read more about James Cameron, Jim Crow, The Great Migration, lynching, lynching photography, and related matters, we have provided a bibliography of print books, films, and online resources at the back of this book. You will also find exhibits on these topics online at the America's Black Holocaust Museum (ABHM).

Lesson plans for educators and a reading guide for book clubs are available at this book's website, www.atimeofterror.info.

We hope these resources, along with the many photographs we included, provide you with a rich and satisfying reading experience. Now, step into the world of young Jimmie Cameron.

Fran Kaplan and Rob Smith
Milwaukee, Wisconsin
June 15, 2015

PROLOGUE

Have you ever watched one man die and then another, knowing that your turn was next? Have you ever looked into ten thousand angry faces whose open mouths screamed for your blood? Have you ever felt yourself in the hands of such a mob whose sole purpose was to destroy you?

All of these things and more happened to me several years ago. This I acknowledge not boastfully but humbly, for the fact that I am alive to tell this story is due to a power greater than myself or any man.

It is an established fact that people learn a great deal quickly when caught in traumatic events. The things I believed I learned, as well as the unforgettable events themselves, are the reasons why this book has been written. It is just as I remember living every word of it. The story is true in every detail. It is a matter of record.

I had heard of white people lynching black people all the days of my life. My mother, relatives, and friends used to tell me some hair-raising factual stories about this enigma to us black people. I had read in the newspapers and magazines and heard about the practice over the radio. To me, it was a strange way of avenging real or imaginary wrongs committed by that lunatic fringe of our population who advocate white supremacy.

Little did I dream that one day, one horrible night filled with stark terror, I, too, would fall into the hands of just such a merciless mob of fanatics; that they would be my judge, jury, and attempt to execute me to carry out their diabolical scheme of death because of the color of my skin. This whole way of life was and is still a heritage of black slavery in America. Every black person knows the routine, the ritual.

How did I act when it came time for me to die? This question has been thrown at me countless times. It is impossible to explain the impending crisis of sudden and terrifying death at the hands of people I had grown up to love and respect as friends and neighbors. The words I am putting down on this paper can only give an idea of the big emotions involved. Only God knows the agony of such a trial. Man's inhumanity to man is especially terrifying to a black man who has experienced the fury of white mob violence.

I remember, I remember, I remember the mobsters breaking into the jail. They surged forward in one great lunge, knocking and trampling the black prisoners around me. Some of them got their hands on me, right away, three on each side, and then the merciless beating began. I tried to break out of their grasp, but there were too many of them. They beat and kicked me in the corner of my cellblock for several minutes before dragging me out of that part of the jail. Their grips were like bands of steel. They knew, now, how to hold a captive because they had just lynched Tommy and Abe, my two buddies. I was in the clutches of the same murdering hands who had lynched them on a tree on the courthouse lawn.

All the way down the corridor outside my cellblock, all the way down the steel stairway, the angry pounding continued. So many clubs and hands were aimed and swung at me, they got in each other's way. Now and again, one of the men holding me would cry out in pain, but they never released their holds on me. Somehow, not because I wanted to, I remained dimly conscious. Through a maze, a thick haze mixed with my own blood, I saw the crowd come to life as we emerged from the jail.

"Here he comes!" the crowd shouted. "It's him! They got Cameron!"

"We got him!"

"We got him!"

"We got him!"

The people pushed and shoved for a chance to get close enough to hit me. Only a few were successful, it seemed, because of the press [of the crowd] around me. I was too weak to fight back anymore. The cruel hands that held me were like vises. I sagged and reeled lifelessly, but I still did not pass completely out. More fists, more clubs, more bricks and rocks found their marks on my body. Only the strongest and the biggest were able to get in close enough to inflict inhuman pain. The weaker ones had to be content with spitting on me and throwing things at me. Some of those holding me caught spittum in their faces as much as I did. Little boys and girls, not yet in their teens, but being taught by their elders how to treat black people, somehow managed to get in close enough to bite and scratch me on the legs.

And over and over the thunderous din rose the shout:

"Nigger!"

"Nigger!"

"Nigger!"

Again and again the word rang out until it seemed as if this was the only word in the English language that held any meaning in their lives.

A crowbar thumped against my chest. A pick handle crashed down against the side of my head.

"I haven't done anything to deserve this," I heard myself mumbling weakly.

My voice was barely audible coming through bruised and swollen lips. I barely heard myself. No one else could hear me. I was too numb by this time to feel the excruciating pain anymore. The cruel and merciless blows that continued to fall no longer had any meaning. Once or twice I thought I saw a kind Christian face, someone who was civilized, in the press near me. To each of these I cried out for some kind of help while, at the same time, I gave others a pitiful look, mutely imploring mercy. But nothing happened. The mob mauled me all the way up to the courthouse lawn. Not once did they stop pounding on me.

Many uniformed policemen helped the mobsters to clear a path through the swarming thousands of people so they could get me all the way up to the tree where Tommy and Abe were hanging in shredded clothing.

"Where's the rope?" somebody yelled out the question.

At this, I felt my stomach shrinking. My whole body felt as if it was encased in ice packs. I was shocked into something approaching full consciousness. What a way to die! I screamed as loud as I could above the din and the roar of the crowd that I had raped no woman or killed any man.

Rough hands grabbed my head and stuffed it into a noose. The rope was handled so roughly that it seared my neck. For a moment, I blacked out. I recovered in a second, though, as they began shoving and knocking me closer to the tree and under the same limbs weighted down with the torn and mutilated bodies of Tommy and Abe. Now it was my Judgment Day! All my days and nights seemed to flash before me in my mind's eye. I remembered what my mother had told us children about sinners facing death, about the thief on the Cross. She told us the Lord will forgive and have mercy on their souls if the sinners will only call on Him.

I knew I had nothing to lose, everything to gain. I couldn't be any worse off than I was at that moment.

"Lord," I mumbled through puffed lips. "Forgive me my sins! Have mercy on me!"

I stopped thinking then. In my own mind and body and soul, I was already dead and was glad to be leaving a world filled with so many false and deceitful people.

But what brought me there to that spot under the death tree? What business did I, a sixteen-year-old, have for being in such a condition and situation? How did it all begin?

CHAPTER ONE

In the Beginning

I was one of a family of four. My mother's name was Vera. I had two sisters, Marie and Della. Marie was the eldest by five years. I was four years older than Della. In 1930 all of us lived at home with our Mother and Grandmother, in Marion, Indiana.

My mother had been raised to fear God. She was born in the state of Kentucky in a little town called Mayfield. The year was 1891. She was the fourth daughter of Jerry and India Carter.

In those days when people mentioned the word "family," they usually meant a very large family. Mother came from just such a family. She had ten sisters and one brother. It was just as trying raising a large family then as it is today, although the value of the dollar was worth considerably more at the neighborhood grocery store. The fact was that raising twelve children on a weekly salary of eight dollars posed no simple managerial problems. That was why Grandmother India took in all the washing and ironing she could handle to supplement the family budget.

At that time, people had to be very poor before they "stooped" to such money-making chores. Grandmother India kept a whole room full of other people's clothes to be washed and ironed. Mother could recall many a day spent over an old-fashioned wooden barrel that had been sawed in half and made into two washtubs. She had scrubbed away on a washboard until she felt faint.

Mother used to talk to me about Grandmother India:

"Mom never told us children about herself. She never told us much about ourselves either," she told me one day. "Even when she died, none of us children could supply all the necessary information for filling out her death certificate. All we were able to find out was that she was the daughter of some white man and a Cherokee Indian woman." Grandmother India was light enough to pass for white if she chose to do so. Frequently she did, but she was fiercely proud of her mixed ancestry.

At any rate, Grandfather Jerry was extremely dark in complexion. To say that he was jet black left no grounds for an argument. He was a mortar-maker by trade. During the course of his entire life he worked for a building contractor who went all over the United States erecting government post offices. While his family was in the process of growing by leaps and bounds, almost yearly, he moved his family to Indianapolis, Indiana. They took up residence in a suburb named Washington. Mother graduated from Washington High School.

Grandfather Jerry had his favorite butchers scattered all over town. They were glad to donate "scraps" to him. He would take the meats and bones home to Grandmother who knew just what to do with them. The scraps in those days were much different than those found in our markets today. He used to receive whole hog heads, pig feet, pig tails, pig ears, pig snouts, chitterlings,[44] lights,[45] livers, neck bones, backbones, and ox tails from his butcher benefactors. Nowadays such scraps are made into various kinds of luncheon meats.

Mother had to perform a task she always dreaded when Grandfather Jerry was working nearby. She had to take his dinner to him when he was on the job. He was one of those men who didn't believe in carrying a lunch to work. Mother would get on the electric trolley car with a large wicker basket under her arm. It would be loaded to the brim with steaming foodstuffs for him. Her embarrassment knew no bounds whenever she had to carry cabbage and other loud-smelling victuals to him in that fashion. It seemed to her that everybody riding on the trolley would look at her and the large wicker basket she was struggling with. With a twinkle in her eyes, she told me "You could smell cabbage all over the streetcar!"

The old-time flour sack, the one with the Indian head stamped on it, served as bloomers or panties for the Carter girls. As Mother grew into adolescence she rebelled at the sight of those itchy drawers.

"Whenever Mom had to whip one of us girls," she told me, "she used to make us roll up our dresses over our ears as if we were going to take them off. Then, while the

---

[44] Pig intestines. Also called "chitlins."

[45] Lungs.

dress was up like that, Mom would grab it and hold it in a vise-like grip, pinning our arms up around our heads, holding us like a cat caught in a bag. There was no way to see out or duck to escape a swift blow from a buggy whip, the horse reins, a sapling switch, or whatever Mom could get her hands on to knock the daylights out of us. And all the while it seemed like the Indian head on our panties was laughing at what was taking place!"

Mother was denied the clothes that appealed to a young, beautiful, unattached woman. No matter how hard she worked, there seemed no end to her plight. But she would always end up turning over her earnings to Grandmother.

Grandmother hesitated to let any of the girls go out with boys, and it was a long time before some of them gathered enough courage to marry and leave such a stern, yet Christian-like, home. Never was there any knowledge of sex imparted to the girls, my mother told me.

"Mom used to tell us girls that a buzzard had dropped us on a rock, and the sun had hatched us! I was silly enough to believe this version of life until I was almost ready to get married. Most of the old folks were like that. 'Don't tell the children anything, they'll find out soon enough' was the way they looked at the picture."

Mother was now eighteen years old and as pretty as a picture on a magazine cover. She was still living at home with Grandmother and Grandfather. It was in the city of Indianapolis that Mother met her husband-to-be, James Herbert Cameron. The meeting came about at a church function, a great meeting place for black people.

In those days, there were signs all over the town reading "Colored Only" and "White Only." Even if the signs were not up for all to see, it was generally understood that there be a separation of blacks and whites, and any black person ignoring what was considered "gentlemen's agreements" and "an unwritten law" were subject to the mob for getting out of "place."[46]

So it became a habit for black people, through enforced segregation laws, customs and habit, to congregate among themselves. Whole Sundays were spent on church grounds in Christian fellowship with one another. The preacher was the people's

---

[46] A "gentlemen's agreement" is an agreement that is either verbalized or simply understood between two or more parties. Gentlemen's agreements were—and sometimes still are—tactics used to keep "undesirables" (such as Jews and African Americans) from buying homes in certain neighborhoods, getting certain jobs, playing on certain sports teams, and so forth. This unspoken and unwritten type of discrimination is often difficult to prove.

marriage counselor, employment office, psychiatrist, psychologist, spiritual advisor, schoolteacher, and trusted friend. It was the black preachers who held the people together and gave them "hope for a better day."

For a while Mother and my father-to-be regarded their acquaintance as mere members of the same parish. He was very light-skinned in complexion, and passed for white on many occasions. To Mother he appeared as a dashing and romantic young man come to life from the tales of some faraway mystic land of her many dreams. He swept her off her feet like a hurricane. He always seemed to know just what to say and when to say it. Of all the young men who sought her company, he stood out so far in front it wasn't even a contest.

Mother began thinking about him both night and day. In a very short while, there was nobody in this big wide wonderful world quite like him to her. She began to build her dreams around him in her every thought. He sensed her helplessness and when he popped the age-old question to her, he felt he didn't stand a chance of being rejected. Mother welcomed the chance to become mistress of her own household.

She hesitated to tell her parents about her plans for the future. There seemed to have been a generation gap between children and parents then as it is today. She bided her time. The opportunity presented itself when her parents moved to Winchester, Indiana. Immediately, she and Herbert Cameron were married in Indianapolis. This done, they sat down and wrote a long letter to Grandmother and Grandfather, informing them of the marriage. Grandmother was furious and didn't like the news, but there was nothing she could do about it. After she had gotten over her pouting, she and Grandfather sent the newlyweds their blessings.

After a two-week honeymoon in Indianapolis, Dad returned to his home in Champaign, Illinois, gathered up his belongings and returned to Indianapolis. Mother trailed along with Dad, hoping his family would approve of her. It was on that trip to Champaign that he and Mother encountered difficulty in purchasing train tickets.

Mother told me, "We walked into the Union Terminal and had to get into a long line of people who had formed in front of the ticket agent's window and await our turn to purchase tickets. The delay at the head of the line was caused by an old black woman about seventy or eighty years old. She had a little boy about five years old with her.

She had walked up to the ticket window and told the agent, 'Ah wants a ticket gwine and comin.' 'You want a ticket gwine and comin'?' asked the agent, his brow knitting into a puzzling frown. 'Yassuh, dat's right,' answered the old lady. 'Gwine and comin'.' 'You mean you want a round-trip ticket, don't you lady?' the agent asked her. 'Nawsuh, ah wants a ticket gwine and comin'–jist lak ah done tole yuh!' the old lady answered in a tone of voice that was becoming peevish.

The agent stood there looking at her. He reasoned it would be useless to attempt to explain anything to her. He didn't give up, though. He sensed that the old lady was unlearned and meant good in the only way she knew how. 'Yes, ma'am,' he said. 'where to?' 'To gwine and comin', dat's where,' the old lady insisted in a very serious mien.

The little lad with the lady, evidently, had heard enough of this talk going back and forward. Perhaps he knew, at the rate they were going, it would be some time before she was straightened out about how to purchase tickets to ride the trains. At any rate, he turned around and looked up at the old lady. In a loud voice he said: 'Aw, Grandmaw, you want a roundtrip ticket to Chicago, Illinois. That's what the man wants to know!'

As sudden as a summer storm and as quick as a trip-hammer, the old lady spun around on the heels of her buttoned-up shoes and with her open hand, slapped her little grandson off his feet. It was one of those old-fashioned backhand licks, and it knocked the daylights right out of the little fellow. 'Shuddup ya mawth, youngin!' she hollowed at him. 'Dat's why dese white folkeses knows all about us colored folkeses. Yuh talks too much!'"

The following year, a beautiful brown-eyed girl was born to Mother and Dad. They christened her Marie Juliet Cameron in the A.M.E.[47] church in Naptown [Indianapolis]. This birth seemed to mark the beginning of real misunderstandings between Mother and Dad.

Dad wanted to drink all the time. This was a trait Mother didn't know he had before they got married. Perhaps due to the short courtship and hasty marriage, Mother was not aware of his problem. In that regard, my mother was like a lot of married women today. Some women are married for years before they find out their mates are alcoholics. The well-kept secret is revealed when the husband makes a mistake and comes home sober!

---

[47] African Methodist Episcopal Church. A Methodist denomination formed in 1816 by free blacks who had left a predominantly white Methodist congregation due to discrimination. "Episcopal" refers to the church's hierarchal structure in which bishops are the highest local authorities. The AME Church is not part of the Episcopal (Anglican) church. Today the AME church serves around 2.5 million predominantly African Americans. It has been a leading provider of higher education for black students. Wilberforce University in Ohio is one of the church's twenty colleges. Jimmie was raised in the A.M.E. Church.

"Whenever your Dad was in one of his drunken moods, he would express his thoughts to me and rue the day he tied himself down to one woman," Mother told me.

She began to sense a tragic mistake in her haste to get away from her Mother's home. She prayed to God for the success of her marriage and did whatever she could to make it so. Life at this stage held many moments of joy, happiness, frustration, confusion, and sorrow for her. I gathered from my mother that my father was always restless, and there were times when he evidenced no concern at all whether Mother had food in the house, or money to pay the rent. Mother held on doggedly, hoping for some sort of a miracle to change Dad and save their marriage.

I was born February 25, 1914, in La Crosse, Wisconsin, the second child in the family. Heavy snow had fallen for a whole week and huge drifts were piled everywhere. But that particular day no snow was falling. The sun was shining and there was a crisp sting in the air. It was a beautiful February day, typical for Wisconsin. The weather thermometer read twenty-five degrees below zero. It was a quiet day, save for the occasional whistle of a train engine at the roundhouse.

The people who lived in the town were accustomed to the cold weather. Life went on as usual without a murmur. Children ran along in the middle of the streets en route to school and back home. Here and there small boys could be seen tossing a snowball at a playmate or wrestling in the deep piles of snow. Occasionally, a bully would pick up a large rock packing it around with snow and throw it at someone. Girls talked noisily and would once in a while gather a handful of the cold, moist, powdery snow and toss it at some boy. Horse-drawn sleighs loaded with fuel glided along the streets.

During the afternoons, people found immense pleasure ice-skating, skiing, and sleigh riding. On the frozen surface of the swirling waters of the Mississippi River that flowed through the town, separating Wisconsin from Minnesota, all sorts of winter festivals were held. It was always a winter wonderland.

Farmers who lived nearby attended their herds. They busied themselves making regular milk rounds and other deliveries in the city. Even our white minister could be seen making the rounds of his parish with his heavy black wool coat with its great fur collar pulled around his ears, and a raccoon cap on his head.

The house my parents lived in was a rambling shack built in the rear of a large house that fronted on Mill Street (Copeland Avenue now). One could open the front door of Mother and Dad's shebang[48] and see all the way through the three little rooms and right on out the rear door to the alley. It was a real shotgun type house[49].

The people who lived in the front house were white. They were wonderful landlords, neighbors, and friends. Mother would never forget them. They would remain a bright spot in her memories of people. They were Mr. and Mrs. Octavius Ostrowski, Polish immigrants. Mrs. Ostrowski had already made several trips to the house in the rear to try and make her tenant and friend as comfortable as possible. The whole neighborhood knew that Mother was expecting an addition to her little family. An air of busy activity could be discerned at our house during the early morning hours.

Mother said, "I had awakened early that day, as was my habit, to prepare your father's and Marie's breakfast. But I started having fainting spells and had to go back to bed. You were the kickingest baby I ever had."

Another one of our white neighbors, Mrs. Marilyn Brown, who was married to a black man, kindly prepared breakfast for my sister Marie and my father. Dad was in no mood for eating, though, because several of his white friends had stopped by the house and offered him some liquor of which he had eagerly partaken. He was in a drunken mood and didn't care who knew about it. At the same time, he tried to look sober. Mother said it was the darndest act he could have put on. He kept walking all over the house in a quiet manner offering to help the womenfolk. But he was more of a hindrance than a help. He was finally talked into the kitchen to take care of Marie.

Marie was nearly five years old and the prettiest and sweetest little lady in the whole neighborhood. The neighbors had already spoiled her by lauding her beauty, and long coal-black hair that fell way past her shoulders in neatly braided pigtails, decorated with glorious pastel silk ribbons. They called her a little heartbreaker! Mother used to act like she was piqued at such lavish praise heaped upon Marie, who would giggle until tears

---

[48] An old term for a hut or shack.

[49] Shotgun houses were a popular style of housing in the old South following the Civil War, but they can also be found in the Midwest and California. Shotgun houses are long and narrow, with no hallway; one room simply opens into the next. They were initially built around manufacturing centers and railroad hubs during periods of rapid industrialization as cheap rental housing for workers. Recently, in some southern cities, shotgun houses and neighborhoods are gentrifying. Some scholars believe that this architectural style arrived in New Orleans from Africa by way of Haiti and that its name comes from the Dahomey Fon word "to-gun," meaning "place of assembly."

rolled down her pretty little cheeks. Maybe that was the woman in her, the part that thrived on pure flattery. And a funny thing, too, Marie never had much time for the women neighbors. She displayed all the wiles of the feminine species to the menfolk in the neighborhood. This, and only five years old!

That day Marie felt that something was wrong. The day hadn't started out as usual. She knew that Mother was doing a lot of sleeping and crying. When Mother got back into bed, and the neighbors started bringing in all sorts of presents, Marie got real curious. She tried to understand what was about to take place but the mystery was too deep for her. She let the grown-ups know, though, that even if she didn't know what was causing all the commotion, she knew something was going to happen. When Mrs. Brown served her breakfast, Marie told her in a matter-of-fact tone of voice "Y'all up to something!"

Mrs. Brown told Mother about the remark. Though Mother was not in the mood for laughter, when she heard what Marie had said and how she said it, she laughed so hard until I was almost born during the fit. The neighbors made Mother as comfortable as possible. The small pot-bellied, cast iron stove standing in the center of the front room was red-hot. The coal was burning with a mighty roar. It was as if the stove itself was aware of the tenseness of her condition and was doing its share to lend comfort and ease.

Dr. Callahan was called. He was a young white doctor who possessed a gentle, paternal touch in making his patients feel that he was eager to serve them. He enjoyed a very lucrative practice among the people of La Crosse and the surrounding areas. Mother was glad to see him because her waterbag had just burst.

"And you were born to us, son. You made us all very happy. Your father had gone back into the kitchen where Marie was playing. When he heard you cry out for the first time, he rushed to the door of our bedroom to look in. Marie asked him 'What was that? I thought I heard a baby cry!'

"Your father told her that it was you she heard and that she now had a baby brother. She jumped up and down with joy and much excitement. 'I got a little brother! I got a little brother!' she kept hollering all over the house."

Dr. Callahan set up his scales on top of the dresser and weighed me right there in the room where I was born. I weighed over ten pounds. Mrs. Ostrowski and Mrs. Brown cleaned me up, rubbed me down with olive oil, dressed me, and then tucked me alongside my mother in bed.

With the gentle and tender care of a mother and a father who had promised to do better, I grew and thrived on love. They christened me James Cameron. In a few months I was a plump little baby with large brown eyes and brown hair.

Figure 15. Baby James (center) held by his mother Vera and surrounded by female relatives, in La Crosse, Wisconsin, in 1914. His sister Marie stands in front of their mother. Grandmother India is to Vera's left. *Cameron Family*

CHAPTER TWO

Life With—And Without—Father

Things went along fine until I reached the age of six months. I had the world in a jug and the stopper in my hand. People would come over to our house and say "Oh, whew! What a pretty little boy!" "Ain't he the cutest thing?" Then they would toss me up in the air and pinch my cheeks (on both ends) and put pennies and nickels in my piggy bank. It was during this wonderful time in my life that my sister Marie showed signs of jealousy because of the attention given to me, which had formerly been given entirely to her. She had stood about enough of that stuff. Enough of anything was enough! The time had come to do something about the situation before it got completely out of control.

One day, in her childish way, she decided to put an end once and for all to my kind treatment. She had gotten hold of a standard size claw hammer and was on the verge of knocking my brains out! She raised the hammer high in the air, loaded with potential energy, but before she could reach the height of her upswing, Mother came into the room and prevented her from carrying out her plan. My life was yet to experience more brutal and senseless attacks far more advanced than childish whims, which would be meted out by peers and elders.

Providence at this juncture was not very kind to me. Scarcely had I reached the age of seven months when I contracted bronchial pneumonia, which was followed by a wracking whooping cough. But I survived these ordeals to have my parents discover, several months later, that my intestines had become strangulated. In order to remedy this condition, a major operation was necessary.

I was now fifteen months old. My intestines had ruptured through my abdominal wall and dropped into the pelvic region. They were knotted up like knuckles when the fist is clenched. An added aggravation was that a piece of flesh had caught around the intestines. This condition caused me to have spasms. The fits kept coming one after another.

I was rushed to the Saint Francis Hospital in La Crosse for an emergency operation. Dr. Callahan was the surgeon. When he had made an incision into my abdominal wall he was shocked to find my appendix ready to burst. The appendix had to come out first before my bowels could be worked on. Having finished this operation, Dr. Callahan then drew my intestines out of my abdomen and into a washbasin where they were untangled and cleaned. Gently, the intestines were placed back inside my abdominal cavity and the operation was completed.

Before the hospital attendants could transfer me from the recovery room back to my private room, I had begun to come out from under the effects of the ether anesthetic. I was looking around to see where I was and trying to sit up in bed!

Back in my room I continually cried for water. Dr. Callahan and the nurses and attendants told me I couldn't have any. But I kept right on crying and yelling my head off for some water. I raised so much sand they had to send for my father. Dad came and told me the doctor and nurses were the boss in my case. He told me they knew I wanted some water and they wished they could give me some, but I had just undergone a very serious operation and I couldn't have any water and there was nothing he could do about it. I then turned over and went to sleep.

The following day I suffered a relapse. Everyone was apprehensive thinking I was going to die. Some of the attendants thought I was already dead. Dr. Callahan rushed into my room accompanied by a nurse. They agreed that there was a faint pulse, barely detectable. They placed their heads on my bosom to hear my heart. Dr. Callahan applied his stethoscope to my chest. When he finished, he ordered one of the aides to give me an enema at once. This order was hurriedly carried out. And you know what? Almost immediately I revived and showed signs of improvement! Dr. Callahan, on observing the favorable reaction that resulted from the enema, turned around to my mother and said, "What in the hell did you make this boy out of–pig iron or what?" Mother laughed until the tears ran down her cheeks.

I had been the first black baby ever admitted as a patient in the Saint Francis Hospital. Visitors who came to see their relatives and friends ended up by coming past my room to see me, too. A whole roomful of toys was accumulated from these people. I was really their object of curiosity. Finally the hospital was forced to place a NO VISITORS sign on the door of my room to hold back the crowd.

Mother and Marie remained in the hospital with me for two weeks in order to keep me in bed. Dr. Callahan, though very skilled in his profession, was amazed at my recuperative ability but doubted my longevity. He told my mother, "If James lives to be twenty-one years old, I want to see him. I'll buy him a brand new suit of clothes, overcoat, shoes, hat. In fact, I'll buy him an entire new outfit when I see him." Mother did not place much credence in the doctor's remarks and made me a small truss to wear to strengthen my weak abdominal wall.

I came out of this ordeal and developed into a rather healthy child save for the fact that I was bowlegged, so much so that my mother described my legs as looking like pot hooks! But the neighbors outdid her. They said I was so bowlegged, a three-hundred pound hog could run between my legs and wouldn't brush up against either one of them! I was only two years old at the time. Mother worked diligently with me and got my legs straightened out by washing them in warm left-over dishwater and seeing to it that I wore braces on my legs, like a polio victim.

My life at this stage seemed to have had its share of superstition. Several months later spasms recurred. A neighbor lady told my mother whenever these attacks commenced she should cover my head with a black shawl. Dr. Callahan's advice, however, was very different. Mother followed the doctor's advice.

First, she placed a teakettle of water on the stove and heated it to boiling temperature. Then she got some mustard from the kitchen cabinet, ground it up into powder and sprinkled it in a foot pan. Next she poured the hot water into the pan, then cooled it with some cold water. Even then the water was still hot enough to blister my feet, causing the skin to peel off. I had to place my hands in the water, too. I thought I was going to die and that my mother was trying to scald me to death! But, as the circulation began, the reflex was instant. I let out a lusty yell. After several treatments, I ceased to have those awful spasms.

My parents moved their place of residence from La Crosse back to Naptown, Indiana. There they lived for a very short while. Then they moved over to Marion, and then on over to Muncie [Indiana]. It was while we were living in Muncie that I met with a near fatal accident.

One day while running in and out of the house chasing my sister Marie, I tried to tear the front door of our house off its hinges with my head. As a result the whole left side of my face, from the temple down to my chin, was ripped wide open, leaving a large gaping wound. I was just four years old. Save for a scar that requires close scrutiny, I outgrew the ugly disfiguration. Then, my parents moved from Muncie to Wabash

[Indiana]. We lived there only a short time before returning to Marion. My father's trade was cutting white people's hair. Dad often moved from place to place to find employment. Either he was never satisfied or the boss was not. Marion, Indiana, was always an ace in the hole. My maternal grandmother, India Persley Carter, lived there.

On or about my fifth birthday I was on my way to Birmingham, Alabama, with my parents and sister Marie. My paternal grandmother was living in that hustling city. It seems to me that her house was the first place we stayed after arriving in "Bama." She had a very beautiful and spacious home. The only thing wrong was that this Grandmother didn't like my mother.

Quickly, my father found a house for his little family on Avenue F, across the street from Hill's wholesale and retail grocery store. There Mother and Dad set up housekeeping.

The breaches of misunderstanding began to widen between my father and Mother. It seemed as though he had stopped caring, despite the fact that Mother was pregnant again, the first time in over three years. He had taken to heavy drinking again. He would stay away from home all night long. Sometimes he would listen in wild-eyed wonder to Mother pleading with him for support money.

At mealtime he would sit at the table and pick over his food, hardly eating any of it. Most of the time he wouldn't even touch it. He would just sit there, not uttering a word, reach across the table, grab a bottle of milk and drink it himself. It made no difference to him that the milk had been bought for Marie and me. If he didn't drink all the milk, he'd pour off the top and drink that. This was in the days before milk was homogenized. Whatever amount of cream was in the milk would rise to the top. About a cup of cream almost always rose to the top of each bottle. He always liked his food rich. Sometimes he had the nerve to complain about his stomach being upset. The blame would be placed on some peaches and cream or some other highly seasoned delicacy he had bought and eaten–away from home.

Such carrying-ons would burn Mother up with anger. Her cooking wasn't good enough for him anymore. He had to eat out and suffer stomach disorders. She would cook black-eyed peas, fat back, and corn bread for her family to eat while he was away in some fine restaurant enjoying juicy beefsteak with all the trimmings.

Miserable days followed for me, my mother and sister. Many days we had nothing to eat but dandelions. Marie and I would help our Mother gather these from some vacant lot or field. This would be supplemented with hunks of cornbread fried in a skillet. Over half the time Mother never knew where the next penny was coming from.

Dad never knew, let alone cared, what we had to eat. All the time Mother kept praying for a miracle, a change in Dad to make him realize his responsibilities. She kept praying to God for strength.

Father changed all right–from bad to worse. The seeds of destiny were sprouting by leaps and bounds for Mother as she struggled with fate. At this time my father was working at his trade in the Union Terminal Station in Birmingham. He soon tired of this job and accepted another one in Tuscaloosa [Alabama]. He told Mother that she could go with him or stay in Birmingham; it made no difference to him. Mother decided to stay in Birmingham. She got a job to help care for me and Marie. She couldn't hold onto it because of her pregnancy.

In Tuscaloosa my father worked for a white man named John Wright. He hadn't been employed there over two weeks when he called Mother on the telephone and told her that he was in trouble with the law.

"I just got into an argument with a white man and had to kill him!" he told Mother.

Mother took this announcement with a grain of salt. She had a feeling Dad was lying to her. She could sense the insincerity in his voice. He told her, "John Wright is helping me leave town and get to my sister Frieda's place in Washington, D.C. I won't have time to stop by and see you and the children before I go, so I want you to send me their sizes and I'll send them something when I get a chance."

Mother hung up the telephone on him and was very thoughtful for a moment. Then she went and confided in one of her lady friends. It happened that this lady had a Tuscaloosa telephone directory in her home. In it they found John Wright's telephone number. Mother called him right away. Knowing Dad as she did, she had a strong suspicion that he had run off to live somewhere in common-law with some other woman. Wright answered the telephone.

"Do you have a barber working for you by the name of Herbert Cameron?" Mother wanted to know.

"Why, yes, I do," came the answer. "Who is this wanting to know?"

"Just a friend of his. Is he working in your shop right now, at this very moment?"

"Yes. He is. Would you like to speak to him?"

"Oh, no! That's all right!" Mother assured him. Then she broke down and cried over the telephone. She told Wright why she had called him, who she was, and also her suspicions.

Wright exploded over the telephone. "Why that lying, low-down, good-for-nothing scoundrel! Deserting his wife and children for another woman–and a damn whore at that! He's the most worthless nigger I have ever had working for me, and I've had plenty of them in my shop!" He was really angry with my father.

Dad was actually living with some mulatto[50] woman in the town, and she was calling herself Mrs. Cameron!

Mother tried not to worry about him and his many lady-friends. A month later she gave birth to a girl named Della. Afterwards she vowed she would rather have bastards than to have any more children by him.

I was the proudest big brother in the world of my new baby sister. Whenever Mother would let me push her in the baby carriage, I was acting like a chicken who had just laid her first egg. I'd tell everybody I met on the street: "Look, look, look! I got a little white sister! Look, look, look! I got a little white sister!"

I finally reached the Alabama school age of seven. Mother enrolled me in an all-black school on Sixteenth Street. Blacks and whites did not attend the same schools. This particular school had been named in honor of a great American ex-slave and abolitionist, Frederick Douglass.

Very shortly Mother moved her little family out to a suburb of Birmingham named Tittusville. It was about seven or eight miles away from where we lived. I liked living in this community, because it was there that black people had some of the most beautiful homes in the world! They were the types of houses seen in fashionable real estate magazines. A feeling of great contentment came over me and I felt like somebody for the first time in my life. To think I was able to live in a house with a large front yard and backyard in which to play! That was really something! There had been so many times in my life before when the plain and simple comforts of a really nice home were lacking. Mother had picked out a beautiful little bungalow with a wooden picket fence running all the way around the lot. White people with a lot of money didn't live in houses any better than we were living. Every time I thought about it I grinned.

One day Mother took me with her to visit a friend of hers, Mrs. Perrin. I fell in love with the woman at once! It was a pure and simple childish love. She had two sons, Hugh and Jack, who took up a lot of their time playing with me. Both of them were employed at the Birmingham Malleable Iron Works. At first I thought Mrs. Perrin was a

---

[50] A term for a child with one white and one black parent, it was used as a racial category from the first census conducted in the United States until the census of 1930. Some people now consider "mulatto" an offensive term. These children are usually referred to today as "biracial," "multiracial," or "mixed."

white woman. She wasn't though. It was only that her family tree was riddled with white blood, like the Camerons'. She was slim-built and blond. She was tall, about six feet, with the prettiest blue eyes I had ever seen. She was about forty years old.

Right away I noticed that she always kept plenty of cakes and pies on hand for her boys, and after awhile she began to include me. That was how Mrs. Perrin began to put rings in my nose. She was one of those ladies in life who have a way of putting a ring in a little boy's nose to cause him to think of nobody but her! It is a kind of hypnotism that works on a sweet tooth. Every neighborhood has one of these sweet angels who go around putting rings in little boys' noses!

Every time I'd call at her house–which was every day after I found out about the cakes, pies, puddings, ice cream, syrup and bread–I always found plenty of sweet tidbits. I soon became so enamored until my every thought, asleep or awake, was of Mrs. Perrin, and Hugh and Jack! A Texas bull could not have been ringed more completely than was I!

The neighbors, especially Mrs. Perrin, were most kind to my mother and us. Had it not been for their loving goodness and concern, there is no telling just what might have happened to us. Their sympathy and words of encouragement gave my mother strength to carry on, to stay in the battle for survival. This was coupled with my mother's inexhaustible leaning on God, her unshaken belief that He works in many ways to aid people whose backs are to the wall, people who do not know which way to turn in their quest for a decent living.

During this rocky period on the road of my Mother's life and her struggle to raise her children, she gave out many times and had to stop by the wayside for rest and contemplation, but she absolutely refused to give up the battle! If, as she believed, she had a hand in her destiny, it was up to her to carry on through faith and good works to back up that faith in God. God would help her if she helped herself. This was the foundation of her life.

I remember one day my father drove up to our house in a big, black, shiny new automobile. I was in the front yard playing with my sisters, Marie and Della. Dad had a couple of real pretty women in the car with him. They appeared to be dressed in the very latest styles. And they looked as if they had plenty of money too! Mother wouldn't let him into the house, so they stood out on the porch and talked for a while.

On the way back to his car, Dad stopped and gave me, Marie and Della a nickel apiece. Mother ran out into the yard, snatched the money away from us, and flung it into Dad's face. He laughed at her as he drove off with his high-toned company.

CHAPTER THREE

Life Is Like A Mountain Railroad

My sister Della was nearly four years old. She had just been tucked into her bed for the night. When Mother had finished with her, she came into the room where Marie and I slept together in a large double bed. She laid across our bed and began to talk to us about the love of God: how it passes all understanding; how we must learn to love God and trust in Him each and every day of our lives and thank Him every day for each day; how we must learn to treat people as we would want them to treat us; how we must live for something and be somebody in this life of ours on earth.

Suddenly, like a frightening tornado, without any warning whatsoever, who should walk into the house, boldly, uninvited, as if he lived there, as if he was paying the rent, and as drunk as he could be? There was not even a knock on the door, just an abrupt entrance. Mother was caught in the midst of singing one of her favorite hymns to me and Marie as we nestled closer to her. I can never forget her favorite song. It was "Life Is Like a Mountain Railroad." It seems to me she had sung that song a thousand times to us. We heard it again that night. Each time my Mother sang it, it sounded more beautiful, more spiritual than the last time. It all had to do with the way Mother rendered it. And always the tears in her eyes gave constant evidence of the feelings in her heart of confusion, pain, sorrow, and despair. Now here was my father standing in the doorway, defiant, drunk, domineering, and demanding!

He staggered slowly toward the bed. His face was puffed with raging anger. Mother didn't like the look in his eyes. He leaned over and spoke roughly, insultingly, to her. She placed her arms around Marie and me drawing us closer to her.

Dad wanted her to leave us in the room and go with him, but Mother wouldn't—and screamed her protests. She refused to leave the room. The neighbors heard them arguing and knew that he was up to no good. After many attempts to entice Mother to join him, he became desperate. He just had to have his way with her, whereupon, he snatched out a small double-barreled derringer from his vest pocket. He threatened to kill her if she didn't heed his command. Mother cried like a baby but she stood her ground, firm in her conviction. She told Dad to go ahead, pull the trigger, shoot her, kill her; anything would be better than going to bed with him!

At this point I stood up in the middle of the bed and stepped in front of my Mother, between her and the gun. I looked him straight in the eyes and pointed my finger at him and said, "Don't you shoot my mama!" He lost his nerve, turned around and walked out of the house.

When he got outside, a crowd of black men grabbed ahold of him and turned him every way but loose. They were angry because he had created such a ruckus in their quiet community. They took his gun away and gave him the thrashing of his life. When they had finished, they chased him out of Tittusville, running for his life. My father was my first example of man's inhumanity to man!

My father returned to Birmingham and got another job at his trade. Mother heard about it and had him served with divorce papers. At the Domestic Relations Court in Birmingham, he did not show up for the trial. A white attorney represented him. Mother was not able to afford an attorney. The presiding judge asked Dad's attorney if he desired custody of his children. The answer was an emphatic no. But the attorney did inform the court that his client's sister, Frieda in Washington, D. C., or even his mother in Birmingham, might want the children if Mother didn't want us. Mother wanted us.

"That's all right," said the judge. "I just wanted to know how he felt about his own children."

Mother was granted a decree of absolute divorce from my father and full custody of her children. She also received a permit to carry a revolver in the event that Dad tried to molest her again. The judge told my Mother to "Shoot the shit right out of him and you won't have to do a day for it!"

Since Della was large enough for me to be her babysitter, it seemed like I had to stay with her all the time. That did not make me happy—having to stay home and play with her all the time. The pies, cakes, ice cream, puddings, syrup and bread at Mrs. Perrin's was all that I could think of! Anytime Mother found me missing from home, it was natural for her to assume that I was at Mrs. Perrin's house. And she would be right. So completely had that lady taken over my life that upon awakening as early as five o'clock in the morning, all I wanted to do was to go to Mrs. Perrin's for breakfast! I was her little fool!

It was always life at its best when Jack and Hugh would take their .22 caliber rifles and shoot down dozens of English sparrows. They would show me how to hold the gun and let me shoot too. Then we'd gather the batch and take the birds home to Mrs. Perrin, who dressed them just like you dress a chicken, and cook them with mouth-watering dumplings! Man alive! That really was a feast fit for a king! I never tired of eating sparrows and dumplings!

Mother got a job in downtown Birmingham at some restaurant where they served two old-fashioned cinnamon rolls and a large glass of root beer for a nickel. The place was owned by a white man who catered only to black people. She made a few tips on this job. This, coupled with her salary, caused her to do for a while.

I remember that as soon as Mother got this job she bought me a brand new pair of shoes. I had been barefooted for some time. The bottom of my feet had become so tough until I could run over broken glass and not draw blood. Mr. Harris, a neighbor, also had a small boy. His name was Henry. When Henry found out that my mother had bought me a pair of shoes, he became unreasonably jealous because his mother didn't buy him a pair too. While no one was watching, he took one of my shoes away from me, ran away, dug a hole in the ground, and buried it. This act of mischief caused me no end of consternation. To lose a new shoe! My mother gathered all of my playmates together and offered a reward of twenty-five cents to anyone who found my shoe. The hunt was on! Soon, Henry made a beeline to a certain spot of ground. He dug up my shoe while being spied upon by his mother. To his chagrin, the reward was something else. Mrs. Harris, his mother, administered a generous portion of "Mr. Switch" on his rear end.

A character named Lester used to come around every day where Mother worked. He'd order his cinnamon rolls and root beer. After being served, he would sit around and attempt to woo her with his old-fashioned, plantation-style romance. He was about sixty-five years old or older, bald-headed, toothless, skinny to the point of looking like he was suffering from consumption, and he had a flushed-red complexion. He didn't have sense enough to leave Mother alone and quit pestering her. So it happened one day that he kept after her until she showered some choice sentences upon his wrinkled head. She had been trying to act like a lady during the whole ridiculous ordeal but now he had gone too far. He forgot she was a lady. She told him off in words that were unmistakably clear to Lester. She angered him. Despite his bruised pride, he hung around the place until later that day when the owner came in to check on the day's receipt. Lester called him over and whispered in his ear that Mother told one of the customers the cinnamon rolls were stale and suggested that he go around the corner to spend his money.

The owner took Lester at his word. Walking over to a small safe in the corner of the place, he counted out the amount of money my Mother had coming and fired her outright. Mother was speechless! The whole circumstance upset her terribly. She went home that day crying all the way. The three of us cried too.

The Methodist minister delivered his sermon that Sunday morning and directed his remarks to the children of the parish. His text was "Suffer the little children to come unto Me, and forbid them not, for such is the Kingdom of God." The words of that inspiring sermon sent me soaring on clouds of celestial joys to another world, a world where sorrow and rain was no more, a world where my Mother wouldn't have to cry because of any wrongdoings, a place where one could glory in the Lord!

In my fairyland mind, I could see Jesus placing His arms around me and blessing me. When the preacher gave out the altar call at the end of his sermon, I was the first one up to the railing surrounding the pulpit, to be saved. I wanted to know more about this good man called Jesus, the Savior of the world! What a nice man to know! Everybody should love Him, because He loves us! He loves little children! He wanted me for a sunbeam! I was a little boy and I wanted Jesus to love me so much. As I stood in front of the pulpit, facing a church full of people, I could feel thrills running through my body, causing so much happiness within my bosom that tears of happiness and peace began to roll down my cheeks.

My sisters, Marie and Della, had looked at me in a strange sort of way and doubted the sincerity of my answering the altar call. But when I carried through my intention they were the most surprised members in the church! I told the minister I wanted to live for Christ, for Jesus–just like my Mother was doing. He baptized me then and there by sprinkling water on the top of my head. What a blessing was mine! Oh, how sweet it was!

As soon as we returned home that day, Marie ran into the kitchen and told our Mother, who had just returned home from work, "Jim's got religion, mama! He got it today! Jim's got religion, mama, and joined the church! The preacher baptized him, mama! Jim's got religion!" She was so excited and happy for me she could hardly talk. Della was standing there beaming with pride.

I had to tell Mother all about the experience and my conversion. When I finished telling her about how Jesus worked on me, her eyes were overflowing with tears of joy. She gathered all three of us into her loving arms and reminded us that, "Life is like a mountain railroad!"

All the people at the church seemed to take special notice of me after this episode in my life. My Buster Brown suit and shoes and large bow tie were my distinguishing Sunday outfit. I would thrill to the sound of pennies jangling in my pockets that many churchgoers gave to me.

Mother got a job working in a bakery shop. I used to go out and help her with the many chores she was expected to do, during my school vacation days. She would draw up a large rack of freshly baked bread alongside a wrapping table. I would wrap the loaves in wax paper. After wrapping the bread, I would shove it through a trough no wider than a loaf of bread and no higher. The trough had places on each side and on the bottom where there were small, electrical hot plates. They didn't have bread-wrapping machines and slicing units in those days. When the wax paper reached the hot plates the wax melted and sealed the ends and bottom together. The packaged loaves were pushed off the trough into huge bread baskets. Then I would place them back on the racks and wheel them out on the dock where they were loaded onto trucks for delivery.

I liked that job of wrapping bread. I don't think anything can smell as good as freshly-baked loaves of bread in a bakery. When I finished there were always plenty of sweet tidbits, cakes and pies for me to eat to my heart's content. A delicacy known as a George Washington pie captured my attention and held me spellbound every time I ate one of them. It was the largest piece of pie in the world for a nickel. I never tired of wrapping my palate around a piece.

My Mother worked with a young lady named Judy Miljohn. She liked Judy very much. They got along like two doves. Judy was a happily married woman. I noticed that Mother always seemed to take on a new lease on life in company with Judy. Life held many satisfying smiles for her and Judy. Such a beautiful friendship was too good to last. A tragic fate ended it all.

It was reported that Judy had gone into a lavatory and sat down on the commode. Someone had sprinkled invisible powder on the seat. People said it was some kind of witchcraft. At any rate, Judy was stricken at once and went mad. Doctors attended her at her home but there was nothing anybody could do for her. For three days and three nights, Judy neither ate a bite of food nor drank a drop of water, or slept a wink of sleep. Only blubberings and whimperings came forth from her foaming mouth. She was beyond the aid of modern medicine and died a horrible death. It was rumored that another woman had gotten rid of her because she wanted to make a play at Judy's husband.

When nature had healed the hurt in her mind and the sadness in her heart, Mother met and became very fond of a Mr. Fred Ewald. He became very affected by her too and liked us a lot. We liked him, because he acted like we thought a father should act. But just when something serious was about to happen between them, Ewald contracted pneumonia and died.

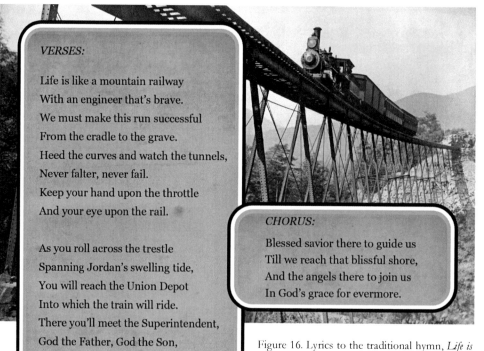

VERSES:

Life is like a mountain railway
With an engineer that's brave.
We must make this run successful
From the cradle to the grave.
Heed the curves and watch the tunnels,
Never falter, never fail.
Keep your hand upon the throttle
And your eye upon the rail.

As you roll across the trestle
Spanning Jordan's swelling tide,
You will reach the Union Depot
Into which the train will ride.
There you'll meet the Superintendent,
God the Father, God the Son,
With a hand of joyous greeting,
Weary pilgrim, welcome home.

CHORUS:

Blessed savior there to guide us
Till we reach that blissful shore,
And the angels there to join us
In God's grace for evermore.

Figure 16. Lyrics to the traditional hymn, *Life is Like a Mountain Railway*. Photograph: The Frankenstein trestle in the White Mountains. *Library of Congress*

CHAPTER FOUR

Knives, Guns, Fists and Switches

One day a large, whiskey-drinking woman, who always carried a switchblade knife, threatened to "beat the hell" out of my sister Marie. Marie had been skating on the sidewalk in front of the woman's house. When Mother came home from work, we told her all about the mannish-looking woman. We said that we were afraid to go out of the house because of that "mean old woman."

The woman's name was Helen Simpson. She had the appearance of a man masquerading as a woman. She was very out-of-shape and real bulgy. She stood about six feet or more in height and weighed about two hundred and fifty pounds. Her complexion was a real sooty black, and her hair was close cropped, like a man with a crew-cut.

This made her look like a muscle-bound veteran wrestler. Her countenance was real mean looking, and the only time she was ever known to smile was when someone was bending her ear with an ornery joke, or she was holding someone spellbound with one of hers. She lived only a few houses from us in the same block.

When we finished telling Mother all about Mrs. Simpson's threat to beat Marie, she got up from the davenport and took out of her purse a small key. She walked over to the dresser in her bedroom and inserted the key into the lock. Reaching inside the drawer, she pulled out a .32 caliber revolver. She broke it open, checked it and snapped it back in place. Satisfied that it was loaded and in working order, she slipped it into her purse. It was the same gun the court had granted her permission to carry since her divorce from my father. We children didn't know what to expect or what to think. We became very apprehensive.

Mother walked to the front door, placed her hand on the knob and turned around and looked at us. "I'll be back in a minute. Be good children," she told us.

She opened the door and stepped out into the darkness. She walked to Mrs. Simpson's house as straight as she could go. It was generally understood that Mrs. Simpson was somewhat of a character in the city of Birmingham. Besides being low-down, she had beaten up half a dozen women around the town and cut up several men with her flashing blade. It seemed it made no difference to law officials as long as her victims were black. This was the notorious woman of the neighborhood my mother was calling on.

She walked up to Mrs. Simpson's door and knocked. Mrs. Simpson opened the door. It was obvious she had been drinking because her breath smelled like it. "What in the hell do you want?" she blared at Mother.

Mother remained calm, refusing to be antagonized. Looking Mrs. Simpson straight in the eyes, she answered, "My children tell me that you threatened to beat the hell out of one of them for skating on the sidewalk in front of your house. I have come to ask you if that is true."

"Hell, yes, it's true. That's just what I said and I meant every goddamn word of it, too. I don't like nobody's damn children and they'd better not play in front of my house anymore."

Mother continued to hold Mrs. Simpson's eye while, at the same time, opening her purse. "Why you must be crazy, Mrs. Simpson. You don't own the sidewalks. My children will play on the sidewalks as long as they please. You better not lay a hand on any one of them, either."

"And just what in the hell do you think you can do about it if I do?"

"Just this," replied Mother, as she whipped out her revolver and leveled it steadily at Mrs. Simpson's head. The barrel of the gun was pointed straight between her eyes. She gasped in horror at the sight of the gun, and stepped back as if to brace herself or to duck an oncoming bullet. She was cringing like a cat caught in the middle of a dog pack!

"If you ever bother any one of my children, I'll take this gun and blow your damn brains out, that's what I'll do about it," Mother told her in a deadly calm voice.

Convinced that Mrs. Simpson had taken her point real well and that they had now been formally introduced to each other, Mother returned home. As soon as she got inside, she broke down and cried, more in sorrow than in pity. She told us children that she started to pull the trigger on Mrs. Simpson but that something had stayed her hand.

After that incident, news circulated all over the neighborhood that Mother was kind of touched-in-the-head and "You'd better not mistreat any one of her children because she is just as liable to shoot you as look at you." And "If her children do any wrong, just tell her about it and she'll punish them. She is one woman who doesn't believe in sparing the rod!"

I was well aware of this fact. So were Marie and Della. It was a dreaded fact, a bone-dry knowledge, that simply because our Mother took up for us when we were in the right, she also lowered the boom on us whenever we failed to do what was right.

Several weeks later, Mrs. Simpson met a bloody and violent death in a running knife and gun battle with one of her many men friends who didn't like the stuff she was putting down. Marie and I had been playing almost in front of her house when we heard this awful frightening racket, the start of a great commotion inside her house. We stopped playing and stood there listening, watching, expectantly, wondering, petrified! The front door of the house was opened with a force that almost ripped the casement from the setting. Mrs. Simpson ran onto the porch with blood dripping from the blade of a huge knife she held in her right hand. A fierce-looking man staggered to the door after her. He still had enough strength left to raise the large revolver he held in his right hand. He pointed the barrel of the weapon at her. He was standing only about six feet away when the gun went off with the sound of a clap of thunder! The shot knocked her off her feet, off the porch. She fell as if released from the force of a raging hurricane and landed almost at the feet of me and Marie. We just stood there, transfixed with horror and fright at the sight of seeing someone killed by another person. The shooter leaned against the railing on the porch, and five more shots went off in erratic succession. Each bullet found its mark in the crumpled body lying on the sidewalk before he, too, collapsed and died.

I remember one day something came up and Mother told me if I didn't stop clowning around she was going to tear my behind up. The worse part of this incident was that my mother was entertaining company in her front room. Three ladies had stopped by the house and they were all talking women business. I proved I was a real show-off, a professional exhibitionist. I had the nerve to stick out my little behind and said to her "Here's my little ass, whip it!" But five fast and furious minutes later, with my behind glowing like charcoals ready for barbecuing fresh meats, I was sorry, oh so sorry indeed, that I had ever thought of saying and doing such a thing to my mother. It had to be a case of temporary insanity.

As I look back on these childhood days, I cannot recall a single whipping I received from my mother that was not well-deserved or well-earned. Mother wasn't the only one who made me toe the line. All the neighbors were on the look out for juvenile delinquents and issued summary punishment according to the mischief.

I finally got enough syrup, and it was my own fault. One day while over at Mrs. Perrin's house, I was nosing around places I should not have been when I overturned a gallon of Karo syrup all over the top of that lady's nice clean kitchen table. She caught me syrup-handed! Whereupon she got a whole loaf of bread out of her cupboard and made me eat every drop of that spilled goody. I never dreamed there was that much syrup in the world! I ate so much until I wanted to puke my guts out. But Mrs. Perrin was adamant and stood right there beside me in the kitchen, holding a large switch in her hand that looked more like a heavy-duty mop handle than anything else I could describe, daring me to vomit! I knew she meant business. I showed her I meant business, too! I stuffed and stuffed and stuffed....

On still another occasion, I had slipped into Mrs. Perrin's kitchen and pulled the oven door open on her stand-up gas range–just looking around. I looked into the bread box, the cupboard, and wherever I thought there might be a piece of cake or pie laying around that could stand some of my special attention. It began to look as if Mrs. Perrin had caught on to me, I thought, as I continued my search. Suddenly, I heard someone coming and started running back into the front room. It was Mrs. Perrin! In my haste to make a clean getaway, I forgot all about the oven door being open. I ran into it full force, fell, and almost tore my tongue out of my mouth.

The doctor was called to attend me and had to sew my tongue up. Then he prescribed soft foods for me. I knew that wouldn't do–not for me anyway, because eating was my specialty. It was paradoxical that I would come to the dinner table and sit there, trying to eat meat and other hard foods, looking more like a dog eating persimmon seeds than anything human.

After I recovered from my tongue injury, some of my small buddies and I strayed away from our home in search of adventure and excitement. We wandered over to the railroad tracks where we began to have all sorts of fun, singing all kinds of songs as small boys often do. We were singing a song that day that went something like this:

"Honey, honey, honey, don't wear no black,

Cause if you do my spirit will come wandering back.

I'm gonna lay my head on the railroad tracks,

And when the train comes along I'll jerk it right back!

I'm gonna lay my head on the railroad tracks,
And when the train comes along I'll jerk it right back."

The crack express of the Alabama Southern was due to pass along the right-of-way where we were playing. Me and my little buddies were cutting up like a bunch of monkeys turned loose on a banana plantation. We were actually placing our heads on the railroad tracks and jerking them back as we lustily sang our songs.

As luck would have it, Mrs. Perrin just happened to walk past the tracks where we were playing. She surveyed the situation in the twinkling of an eye. She knew the "Flyer" was due to pass our spot any minute. She had already heard its warning whistles. Me and my buddies were unaware of this fact. Hurriedly, she ran over to the spot where we were playing and immediately began tearing up little behinds. I had not been swift enough to escape her wrath. She had a special interest in me. A quick and sure hand reached out, like the tongue of a hungry South American lizard, grabbed ahold of me, and my scrambling was over. Every man was for himself when the chips were down.

Mrs. Perrin marched me home with her and stood me on top of her nice clean kitchen table–the same table I had spilled all that syrup on–and tore my behind up! She didn't know it at the time, but if she hadn't stopped trying to kill me when she did, I was just about to mess up her tabletop again! When she had exhausted herself, she marched me to my home still in a furious mood and told my mother everything that had happened, how I almost got run over by a train. And you know what? They were in complete accord with each other's views. They understood each other quite well. So, before Mrs. Perrin could get through talking and telling on me, my mother finished trying to kill me right there in front of her!

It didn't take me long to get the idea that both of them were picking on me because I was smaller than they were. That was an awful feeling. Why a fellow couldn't do anything around the old town without being slapped down and half-killed at every turn!

By the time I was ten years old, I thought I was pretty good with my dukes. I had already worked my bluff on one of the larger boys at school. When school dismissed every afternoon, I always ran this big boy home. I loved to see how many minutes he had in his feet! Sometimes, I could hardly wait for school to let out.

My plan of attack was to run up from behind, land a hard jab into this boy's rib section, then dare him to fight back. All the other boys and girls would egg me on and I gloried in the encouragement they offered. This made the cheese more binding. Like the bully I tried to be, it also made me feel much larger than I was. But I got such a thrill out of running this big boy home every day. The boy's name was Rufus Davis. He was only twelve years old but looked like he was sixteen. He was fat and weighed about twice as much as I did. He was very timid. But as all roads have turns in them, so did the table turn on me one day after school.

I remember I had run up to Rufus and struck him in the back. He took off like a rocket shot to the moon. I took out after him in merciless pursuit. After a spirited chase to the next corner, Rufus stopped, suddenly, and refused to run anymore. I should have known that something was wrong. This was not the way things were supposed to be; this wasn't what had been happening. I ran up to Rufus, still not thinking clearly and said, "So, you wanna fight, huh?"

"You better go on and leave me alone. I ain't bothering you," Rufus answered in a quiet tone of voice.

I struck him in the chest. "You better quit hitting me!"

I jabbed him again. "Aw right. Just keep on!"

I then lashed out with a swift rendition of an uppercut for my fourth blow.

"Now, you just hit me one more time!" Rufus raged at me. There were deep pools of fire glowing in his eyes. He was bristling with anger, more and more each moment.

No sooner said than done. I fired another lick at Rufus. But now the cake was all dough. Rufus lashed out at me like a wild creature, striking me everywhere but the bottom of my feet. There was no controlling him. He had lost all reasoning. I didn't know whether I should ask him to go ahead and kill me and get it over with, or what. Only one thing stood out very clearly in my mind: I didn't have any business there the way Rufus was manhandling me! I was knocked down as fast as I could get up. I signaled Rufus that I gave up, and he quit trying to kill me. I had been so terribly beaten up in front of the other children until I was actually ashamed to attend school the next day. Rufus and I became the best of friends after this formal introduction.

For the next two years I settled down and made wonderful progress in school. I was skipped twice.

Then Mother left Birmingham with her little family and moved to Kokomo, Indiana, some six hundred miles north. There we lived with my maternal aunt, Marion Dupee, at 901 North Bell Street. It was about four blocks from the local Frederick Douglass School, another all-black institution. Marie, Della and I attended this school. Marie and I graduated. I was a center on the city championship basketball team that Douglass won in 1928. We lived in Kokomo for about two years.

CHAPTER FIVE

Apples Meets the Klan

After our stay in Kokomo, my mother moved over to Marion, about 58 miles northwest. My maternal Grandmother was still living in Marion. I was fourteen years old when we moved in with Grandmother India. Because of my work as a bootblack at the interurban station in Marion, I came to know most of the people who lived in that town, especially those who frequented the downtown part.

During the month of May that year, my widowed Grandmother India and I had gathered some apples from her orchard on a lot next to where her house stood and stored them in barrels for use during the winter months. Each day I would fill my pockets with those delicious apples before setting out for school, a distance of about a mile from where I lived on Popular Street. Grandmother did not know that I was fiercely robbing her of apples every day I left for school. I would fill the inside of my shirt with apples and distribute them to my schoolmates. One day at school while class was in session, the principal, Mr. Herbert Terry, a black man, was explaining a mathematics problem to us. He had just finished clearing up a point and had turned around to write on the blackboard. As soon as his back was turned, I reached into the compartment of my desk, took out a large apple from the many I had put there, and took an enormous bite out of it. The other children in the room began to snicker and whisper to one another. Their behavior caused the quiet in the room to be replaced by a twittering buzz, a rippling sound. At the same time they were telling on me on the sly. Mr. Terry turned around from the blackboard and looked at us. My face was radiant with guilt. All the children laughed at my being caught. I had to tell Mr. Terry what I had in my mouth. When he said, "Bring those apples up here, Apples!" the children laughed until they nearly rolled on the floor. Mr. Terry escorted me to the back room and wore my behind out with a large switch. The instrument of punishment was really too large to be called a switch. Sometimes, if there were not switches in the back room, which served as a coal-bin, Mr. Terry would make us go out into the woods and pick a whole armful ourselves. And they had better be of the right size, too, or we had to give up more behind. When Mr. Terry gave a student a name it stayed with him for life. I still answer to the name of Apples.

Figure 17. "Apples" in a class photograph at the D.A. Payne School in Marion, circa 1928, when he was 14 years old, two years before he would be lynched. *Cameron Family*

During a history discussion about the strategy of Hannibal, a black general, in crossing the Alps with a herd of elephants, Mr. Terry called on a student named John Hawkins to explain how it was accomplished. John's explanation was, without a doubt, one of the most masterful and clearly understood explanations ever witnessed in our history class. When he had finished amid loud applause from the students, Mr. Terry said, "Thank you, General Hawkins!" And from that day for the rest of his life, John was known as General Hawkins.

One day, during school vacation, I happened to be standing on a street corner in downtown Marion. I was near a public drinking fountain across the street from the courthouse square. I saw something I had never seen before in my life. It was a parade of the Marion chapter of the notorious Ku Klux Klan.[51] Klansmen had gathered from all parts of the state and were staging a membership drive parade through the downtown streets. This was their state convention and Marion was the host city!

Figure 18. A Ku Klux Klan parade at New Castle, Indiana, in 1922. *Indiana Historical Society*

The Klansmen were dressed in white regalia from head to foot. Many of them walked over to the drinking bubbler[52] where I was standing nearby, tossed their cone-like headdress and mask to one side, and got a drink of water. I recognized many of those Klansmen. Lots of them knew me, too, but before that day I had not the faintest idea that they were members of the bigoted Ku Klux Klan.

---

[51] The Ku Klux Klan (KKK) is the name for a series of violent white supremacist organizations. The first KKK formed in the South during Reconstruction to terrorize and control the formerly enslaved black population. The second KKK was a nationwide group made up of white Christians who were anti-Catholic, anti-Semitic, and anti-immigrant, as well as anti-black. They flourished from the 1920s to 1940s and claimed membership of over four million men. This was the Klan that Cameron saw marching in Marion. The third manifestation of the KKK is actually many small independent groups that arose to oppose desegregation and the Civil Rights Movement. Today the Klan is viewed as part of the numerous hate groups and domestic terrorist organizations around the country.

[52] This story may have been added to the present book after 1952, when he moved to Milwaukee, Wisconsin. Only in Wisconsin is the term for drinking fountain a "bubbler."

A fat bald-headed man was among the members of this order of hoods and sheets who came over to the fountain to get a drink. He was the neighborhood grocer from whom my Grandmother India had purchased foodstuffs for years! Immediately after the parade, I went home and told my mother and grandmother all about what I had seen. It appeared to me that all of the white men I knew in Marion were in that parade, dressed in the robes that are still the shame of freedom-loving Americans! Marion, Indiana, at that time, was a hotbed of concentration for the varied activities of these cowardly nightriders.

Figure 19. David Curtis Stephenson, the Grand Dragon of the Indiana KKK. *Indiana Historical Society*

The state had recently sentenced one of the nation's Klan leaders to life imprisonment in the state penitentiary for second-degree murder. He was D.C. Stephenson, a Grand Dragon,[53] who had been accused of murdering a young white female secretary. During a blackout in a drunken orgy, the state contended, he had performed all sorts of perverse acts upon the young lady's body, eventually driving her to take poison. The young lady's name was Madge Oherholtzer. She was 28-years old. She accused Stephenson of raping and mutilating her in the act. The state contended he had abducted her and, on a train ride to Hammond, had attacked her all the way there from Indianapolis.

According to court testimony, she took poison the very next day. Stephenson and several of his aides escorted her back to Indianapolis, where they kept her overnight in the living quarters over a garage instead of taking her to a hospital. She was taken to her home the next day. Several months later she died of infection and aggravated bites on her breast that had been chewed by Stephenson. In a dying statement by the young lady, corroborated by witnesses, the Klansman had been accused of causing her death.

---

[53] At that time, a Grand Dragon was the commander of a Realm in the Ku Klux Klan. A Realm was made up of Klan members in a state. Stephenson was the head of the Indiana Klan, under the command of the Imperial Wizard, who ruled over the entire KKK.

After a month long trial that covered 2347 pages of transcript, Stephenson was convicted of second-degree murder in 1925 and sentenced to life imprisonment in the Indiana State Penitentiary at Michigan City.

David Curtis Stephenson did not take the stand in his defense. If he had, the state was prepared to put on the stand eleven other young ladies Stephenson had been accused of fiendishly ravishing in sex orgies! He is reputed to have earned over five million dollars ($5,000,000) as his fees for selling memberships and Klan paraphernalia to hate mongers. He received four dollars out of every ten-dollar membership fee. He was such a super salesperson of racial hatred until he was placed in charge of a 20-state area, and became the second in command of all the Klan organizations in America. His strongest sphere of influence was in the state of Indiana, whose people bought all he had to sell about hatred of people, places, and things. In three year's time, from 1922-1925, he made his fortune with spellbinding oratory. In the Hoosier state, under his super salesmanship, Klan membership skyrocketed to 500,000 during the Roaring Twenties!

Stephenson was so gloated with Klan influence until he boasted, publicly, "I am the law!" To add glitter to that belief he called himself "Power!" He even aspired to become President of the United States.

Sneering at the prospect of life imprisonment, he was confident the newly-elected Governor Ed Jackson would pardon him, for the Klan having brought about his victory at the polls. He was confident of a pardon from that governor. Jackson had been Stephenson's choice for governor. The Klaverns[54] all over the state had worked to that end. When Jackson refused to be drawn into the maelstrom and denied the Grand Dragon a government pardon, Stephenson did a flip-flop and began telling all about the machinations of the Klan, the anti-black, anti-Catholic, and anti-Jewish racial and religious propaganda, the murders and political corruption throughout the state in cross-burnings. If he couldn't continue in power and influence in the state, no one else would enjoy the fruits of his labors! He even revealed all about the Klan's vicious campaign planned against Al Smith, Governor of New York, who was certain to get the Democratic nomination for President in 1928. The Klan had planned for Herbert Hoover, the Republican nominee, to be President. They got their desire, and America suffered one of the greatest depressions in the history of our country!

---

[54] Local Ku Klux Klan chapters.

Stephenson's spilling of his guts was the beginning of the disintegration of Klan membership in Indiana. Local, state, and judicial officials all over the state were being jailed and/or resigning from public office as a result. Those public officials who had refused to go along with Klan philosophy—the mayors, sheriffs, city councilmen, prosecutors, and judges—were wooed by women of loose morals whom the Klaverns kept in harems for just such purposes. They were the weapons used in conversion methods. All sorts of trumped-up charges were levied against recalcitrants in efforts to force them into the folds of the Klan organization. And that is why the Klan was able to get away with their deliberate and planned disregard for the laws of our land—because they were the law! They are still the law in many sections of our country. [55]

When William Joseph Simmons, a founder and deposed leader of the Klan, fell, as did Stephenson, because of murders and political crimes, it escalated the downfall of the Klan all over America!

In March of 1950, Stephenson was granted a parole by Governor Henry F. Schricker. But, before the year was out, he was back behind the walls of the state prison at Michigan City [Indiana] as a parole violator. He had refused to report to a parole officer! He still lived in a world of his imagination when he was the king of the hill, when he was "the law" and his name was "power!"

He stayed locked up until paroled without a requirement to report to a parole officer by Governor George Craig, a Republican, in 1956. The condition was that he leave the state and never return!

In Independence, Missouri, in 1961 Stephenson was arrested and convicted of assaulting a sixteen-year-old girl. He denied the charge. He was found guilty and given a four-months jail term plus a $300 fine, which were suspended on condition that he leave the state!

This then was the type of leadership the people of Indiana had chosen to lead them in the Roaring Twenties! I did not know it then, but standing there near that drinking bubbler in downtown Marion in the spring of 1930, I was witnessing the remnants of a once-powerful Invisible Empire![56] Some of the people were still espousing the hatreds and teachings of D. C. Stephenson.

---

[55] As of 2013, there were more than one thousand documented neo-Nazi, Ku Klux Klan, and other extremist hate groups active in the United States (Southern Poverty Law Center, Spring 2014).

[56] A name the Klan called itself.

CHAPTER SIX

The Crooked Path

J ust twenty-four hours before I would stand under the death-tree with a rope around
my neck awaiting what I thought was certain death, I had arrived, breathless, at the
clapboard shack I called home. It was a hot, suffocating August night in 1930. I was
gasping for breath. The house was actually a barn that had been converted into living
quarters. It stood exactly one block away from the [Grant] County line, leaning like the
Tower of Pisa, and appeared to be ready to collapse with a strong gust of wind, sooner
or later. But no matter how hard the elements beat against the barn-house, it stood like
the Rock of Gibraltar. The outside of the dwelling was covered with black tarpaulin
roofing paper to aid in lessening the heat from the rays of the sun in the simmering days
of summer, and to keep out the cold wintry blasts. It stood where it had been built, on a
lonely and desolate [edge of Marion], surrounded by hundreds of acres of cornfields and

mixed farming ventures. It
was the sixth day of the
month.

My mother, Vera, was
waiting up for me as usual. It
was well past 10 o'clock at
night, but she was sitting in
her favorite rocker, the only
one in the house, the one
which creaked and groaned
with a protest of many years
of usefulness, each time it

Figure 20. Cameron's childhood home as it looked in 2006. *Fruit of
the Tree Productions*

came forward or was pushed backward. She was sitting in the front room sewing a patch on a pair of my freshly laundered overalls by the dim light afforded by the kerosene lamp on the battered end table at her elbow. That's how my mother was. She never slept until all three of her children were safely home.

"James, I wish you wouldn't stay out so late at night," she said automatically, as she opened the door to let me into the house.

Then, looking at me for the first time, a deep, penetrating, searching look, she gave out with her feelings. She felt that something was wrong. In fact, she knew something was wrong!

Standing there in the piercing stare of my mother, panting and sucking in my breath as if each gulp would be my last, I tried desperately to hide my paralyzing fright. A cold, naked fear gripped me tighter and tighter and tighter. My mother knew. She always knew! I stood there swallowing my Adam's apple, wondering what direction her probing questions would assume.

"Look at your shirt," she exclaimed, her eyes widening with a growing curiosity. "You're wringing wet with sweat!"

She laid aside her sewing and studied me more closely. She was now in her early forties, her straight black hair beginning to show streaks of gray. She wore it swept back severely in a neat bun at the base of her small neck. She was dressed in one of her plain calico dresses, blue and black in color. She had an air about her, a way of carrying her shoulders or sitting on a chair, that made her look every inch a great lady—which she was.

I told her that I had been playing football in a vacant lot about a mile and a half down the dirt road from where we lived.

"You're lying to me, son," Mother told me, patiently, as if she knew how to coax the truth out of me. "Now, tell me what's the matter. Are you in some kind of trouble?"

I felt a surge of relief, as I always did, when she saw through my lies. I wanted to get down on my knees and lay my head in her lap and tell her everything. I wanted to tell her how my soul was deeply troubled. All of these things were on the tip of my tongue as I stood there and looked into her kind and understanding brown eyes. But I couldn't. I was sixteen years old, her only boy, and the head of the family, so to speak. My sister Marie was twenty-one years old, and Della, my other sister, was thirteen.

I felt that to break down and cry in my mother's lap would be somehow letting her and my sisters down. I was the man of the household even if I did have a boy's head on my shoulders.

A black man with more Indian blood in him than white, named Hezikiah Burden, came around sometimes. He was my stepfather. But he was not cut out to bear responsibility. He spent most of his time hunting and fishing all over [Indiana] and sometimes as far away as Oklahoma and South Dakota!

All of these things were racing through my mind as I debated whether to tell my mother the truth. I decided I couldn't–not then. My fright was too near. Although my fear had begun on a lonely and desolate country road on the other side of town–and I had run all the way home to escape it, the rampaging fear, like uncontrollable flood waters, had matched my every stride, as swift as they had been. That fear kept pace with the fast drawing of my breath and the furious pounding of my heart. It had become a malignant presence breathing hotly on my neck.

"Aw, Mom," I began as casually as I could. "There's nothing wrong with me."

But that was a second lie. Even as I told it I wondered if there was really anything wrong. Perhaps I had imagined the whole scene. Maybe it was just a dream. It couldn't have happened to me! I wanted to believe that. But, then, I remembered the white girl's face, pale and lovely, and very much frightened in the bright moonlit night. And the gun. It had looked more like one of the toys I used to play cowboys and Indians with. But the way the girl looked, the way the man looked when they saw the gun, I'd never forget. I wondered too whether Tommy and Abe were still out there or had they run home, too. Then, too, there were some shots that had echoed through the scary stillness of the night. Who was shooting whom?

"Go on upstairs and go to bed," Mother told me formally. Only a trace of irritation showed in the sound of her voice, but I could sense it was weary. Her face was dark with worry. "I'll talk with you in the morning."

My thoughts raced back to the present. I looked at my mother feeling sorry for her for the first time in my life. She had worked so hard to try and bring up her little brood to a decent maturity. She had washed clothes and cooked and scrubbed floors for white families.

I looked at the scantily furnished room of our home. There were no rugs on the floors of wide, rough, oaken boards. Many traces of the barn could be detected. A large pot-bellied stove dominated the center of the room. A broken-down sofa with the springs showing through in spots, squatted, menacingly in a corner, and a wooden crate–a bottled milk container–occupied the opposite corner. It served as a bookcase for the few discarded magazines and newspapers Mother brought home from the families whose washings and ironings I helped to deliver. The sofa was the bed where my mother slept. A square end table with two of its four legs uneven stood against the window, which looked out on the dark dirt road that ran the length of Western Avenue, the district where most of the black families lived in Marion.

The room, our house, our very lives were not very different from the other black families who lived in Marion. I had no idea that even those meager things might soon be denied me. Neither did I have the presence of mind to consider them precious and part of my life until Abe pulled that gun. I was totally confused in mind. I vaguely understood that that incident would have a lot to do with whatever happened to me for the rest of my life.

I felt like a mechanical man going through the sequences of slow motion as I mumbled goodnight to my mother. I trudged over to the stairway entrance and practically stumbled up the steep and darkened stairway steps, also made of rough oaken boards. I was like a man who had had too much to drink. The steps groaned every time my foot came down. I tiptoed into my cramped attic bedroom, which was divided into three tiny cells by plywood partitions. I could hear the even and untroubled breathing of my sisters. They were fast asleep in cells beyond mine.

I sat on the edge of my bed in the darkness, jerkily removing my clothes like a skillful puppet. I was like a man in a hypnotic trance. As I slipped into the cotton shirt nightgown that Mother had made from bleached flour sacks, I wondered why I wasn't tired. I figured I had run nearly six miles without stopping, without even slowing up! It had been a run laden with deep forebodings. I somehow thought I should still be running. It was soon evident that I was not going to get any sleep that night. I was too keyed up. There were too many questions buzzing around in my head that needed some kind of answer. The veins in my body felt as if they could have jumped through my flesh. I remembered something one of my schoolteachers had once said about what to do when you have a problem. She was Miss Louela Greer. "Try to look at it objectively," she had said. "Get outside the problem and look at it as if someone else were involved."

I tried it. Basically I told myself I had done nothing that could really be called bad. I had been foolish, yes, but I had not done anything bad. The trouble was, this was Marion, Indiana, where there was very little room for foolish black boys.

Not that there was a race problem in the town. The 4,000 or more blacks allowed to live in that community, with a total population of 27,000, had their places selected for them by the white power structure and were expected to stay in them. There was no trouble from the whites at all to speak of, other than the fact of a denial of equal opportunities, a condition that was widespread all over the United States. There were the usual menial tasks in Marion, and it was generally understood that black people were the best people available to perform them. The menial jobs provided food and clothing. The fact that most of the black families lived in third- and fourth-generation houses— which were more like shacks—on the other side of the town was not a particular source of trouble either. But always in the background, however, was

Figure 21. Downtown Marion, circa 1930. *Marion Public Library Museum*

the bone-dry knowledge that the place had its limitations. Once the boundary was crossed, anything might happen to the trespasser.

This thought made me more frightened than ever. It sent my head spinning! The realization dawned on me that I had crossed over into the most sacred area of all: the world where white women lived!

At that moment, as if spawned from the depths of hell and my paralyzing fears, I felt the whole house vibrate with an urgent booming, pounding on the front door. I bolted upright in bed. The pounding in my ears and the runaway thumping of my heart seemed as thunderous as was the knocking on the door. Before I heard any voice I instinctively knew who it was. If I could have vanished by simply willing it, or even died, I would have done so gladly.

I could hear the springs of my mother's sofa-bed creaking in angry protest as she got up to answer the door. I jumped out of bed and moved quietly and quickly to a dingy porthole window on the side of the house. I looked out into the streets below. Marie and Della were still asleep.

Cars and trucks surrounded our house, and policemen in blue uniforms, more than I had seen at one time before. They were approaching the house with drawn revolvers. First one spotlight, then two, and finally, a dozen or more, it seemed, began raking the house from every angle. I crouched below the window, cringing, wishing again that I could disappear and start my life over again.

"Who is it?" I heard my mother ask.

"The police," a gruff voice answered. "Open up!"

I summoned what little courage I had left to sneak to the top of the stairs just as my mother opened the door. Light flooded the bottom of the steps. It came from the searchlights outside the house.

"What do you want?" Mother asked them nervously.

"Does James Cameron live here?" the police wanted to know. It sounded more like an accusation than a question.

"Yes," my mother told him. And then, sensing real trouble, she broke into uncontrollable tears that sounded almost hysterical. Words began tumbling out of her mouth, rushing between wracking sobs. "What's he done? What do you want him for? He's a good boy. He's my only son. There must be some mistake!"

The police cut her off. "Where is he?" Mother told them I was upstairs asleep in bed. Then she begged them again to tell her what I was wanted for.

"Oh, Lord, have mercy!" I heard my mother cry out in mental anguish and physical pain. "Give me strength, dear Jesus. Help me." Her voice trailed off, words lost in a fresh torrent of tears.

Without another word, the policemen began moving toward the stairway, their steps as heavy and foreboding as an army of giants invading our world from another planet. I slipped back into the bed–I don't know why–and pretended I was asleep. The heavy footsteps grew louder and louder and louder. Even with my eyelids closed in simulated sleep, I could feel the powerful beams of the flashlights playing all over my body.

"That's him!" I heard someone say, as rough hands reached out and shook me. I opened my eyes wide. The room was jammed with policemen. Every one of them seemed to be ten feet tall and five feet wide. They moved about like the shadowy nameless creatures I had seen in some of my nightmares. For what seemed like a long time no one spoke. Finally, a voice that I recognized said, "Get up out of that bed and put your clothes on!" There was no mistaking that demand.

I did as I was told, hastily pulling on my trousers and my sweater over my nightshirt. I slid bare feet into ragged tennis shoes. The voice I had heard belonged to Officer Harley Burden. But now his voice sounded surly and full of anger. It sounded like the end of the world for me, of everything. It even sounded like a voice from another world. It was nothing like it had been all of those times he had held up traffic for us children at 35th and Washington Streets to let us cross the busy intersection after a high school football or basketball game.

Officer Burden was a genial, round and ruddy-faced black man in his early forties, with a ready smile and usually cheerful greeting. He was one of only two blacks on the force. He was known among the black community as "all right" since he never went out of his way to be nasty or overbearing. He spoke to me as I fumbled with the laces in my sneakers.

"Why didn't you tell your mother what you and those other boys did tonight?" He wanted to know. The other policemen, a roomful of them, were strangely quiet.

I heard myself say in a voice I barely recognized "I haven't done anything!" I had begun trembling and could not stop. I felt cold.

"You haven't done anything?" Officer Burden sneered and stormed. Then he exploded all over the room in a booming voice. "The hell you

Figure 22. Officer Harley Burden. *Marion Public Library Museum*

haven't! You bastards went out in Lover's Lane and shot a white man and raped a white woman!"

His face was flushed with anger. His words were like .45 caliber slugs laden with atomic warheads. I died a little when they hit me and exploded.

"Oh, no!" I managed to reply, weakly. "I didn't!"

It was all I could do to keep from falling on my knees and begging him to believe me.

"Remember, anything you say may be used against you in a court of law," another officer said, dryly. That man was Chaney Boles, a detective. I didn't understand what he meant, but something in his voice told me that he and probably everybody else had already decided on my guilt.

"Let's go," Officer Burden said to me. "The Chief wants to talk with you."

Two of the officers grabbed me by the arms and half dragged, half carried me down the narrow steep stairway. I remember feeling a great sense of gratitude that my sisters, Marie and Della, on the other side of the partitions, had not awakened.

Downstairs, my mother had collapsed on her bed, crying and praying all at once. "Lord, Jesus Christ, have mercy," she moaned over and over and over. "Give me strength!"

In the brief moment I was allowed to mutter a passing goodbye to her, I tried to be brave. Mother's tears always had that effect on me. I will never forget that lonely and tragic figure of my mother, framed in the doorway of our house, wringing her hands in a nervous frenzy, tears streaming down her haggard face. I had no words to describe my own stark, naked terror, but I felt that she was more frightened than I.

Slammed into the rear seat of a big, black, shiny patrol car, a six-passenger touring model (convertible), I was wedged between two grim policemen I did not know. Officer Burden sat in front of me on a jump seat. All the way to the station at Fourth and Booth Streets, he kept questioning me. The other four policemen in the car were strangely quiet. There were three other squad cars in front of the one I was in, and more behind, with private cars and trucks trailing along behind them. It was quite a caravan. Most of the men had been sworn in as a posse. It was an appropriate time for some bank robbers to ply their trade in the town. Every police officer, it seemed, was concerned with getting me downtown to police headquarters.

"You might as well come clean," Officer Burden told me. "Tommy and Abe have told us everything. They said you shot the man and raped the woman!"

I thought I had seen enough gangster movies to recognize a bluff when I heard one. "I don't know anything about shooting or raping anybody," I told him. It was a line I was sure I remembered from some movie.

"The hell you don't know something about it!" Officer Burden thundered at me. "Listen, you little bastard, you are going to tell me the truth if I have to beat the hell out of you to make you do it."

For some strange reason, his outburst calmed me a little. Officer Burden, I guessed, was just acting.[57] He did not touch me all the way to the station.

The police caravan drove on, picking up speed as they left the rough dirt roads in the black district. Officer Burden continued threatening and questioning me, asking the same questions over and over and over. He kept repeating that he was going to knock the hell out of me if I didn't come clean. I gave him the same answer over and over and over. "I don't know anything about it. I don't know nothing!"

My mind kept racing. I was trying to figure out just what had happened back there in Lover's Lane. Suddenly, I grew very tired. My head was buzzing. I remembered hearing shots shatter the stillness of the night about four or five minutes *after* I had run away from the scene of the crime. I had had no intentions of going back there to find out what happened. I had kept on running until I got home.

As the caravan approached the downtown area I was surprised at the amount of traffic at that hour of the morning. The district was a beehive of automobiles moving about. People were already on their way to the 7 a.m. work shift, it seemed, yet the sun had not risen. It was about 2 a.m.

The police hurried me downtown. The squad car I was in came to a screeching stop in front of an old dilapidated residential building that served as police headquarters. The officers hustled me out of the car. I moved like a man on rubbery legs struggling to keep his head above water and hold his breath or drown. There were fifteen or twenty white men and several white women standing on the corner in front of the station. They stared at me with a cold taciturn expression as I was taken up the stairway to the second floor. One of the men was muttering to himself, as if on the verge of a wild rage. The group didn't look friendly nor did they act pleasantly. Hadn't they ever seen a man arrested before? The police took me directly upstairs. A door was opened by one of the uniformed officers, and I was ushered into the booking room. It seemed even smaller than it was with the press of white men and women (civilians) eyeing me curiously. I

---

[57] This is the first of several times that Cameron describes a survival and resistance strategy honed in slavery in which black people put on an act. They behaved as whites in power wanted and expected "their coloreds" to behave. They pretended to go along in the moment, while privately feeling, thinking and behaving quite differently. Even at sixteen, young Jimmie recognized that Officer Burden's harshness was a show. Known as a kind, friendly man, Burden must have needed to protect himself from criticism, since he was just one of two black officers on a white police force.

found out later that they had come in to get first-hand information to relay to the people outside.

I was acutely aware of the sudden quiet that greeted my expected appearance. It was the kind of stillness you could almost hear crashing down with the force of nerve-wracking thunderclaps. There was danger in the air. It seemed to flow from the crowd outside and into the two officers holding my arms. I wanted to cry out in pain as I felt their grips tighten from that anger, their fingers burrowing deep into my arms like the jaws of a vice. Strangely enough, though, it had not occurred to me that that anger might be translated into frightening physical violence. That was something that might happen down in the Deep South, to other people, not to me in Marion, Indiana, a northern town.

I was led before a huge desk set high off the level I was standing on. A sleepy-eyed sergeant in short sleeves sat behind the desk chewing on the stub of a cigar butt. There was a big black book laid out on the desk before him. One of the officers whispered a few words to the sergeant that I failed to catch, partly because I was growing more aware of the undercurrents of intensity and passion of racial hatred I could feel growing out of the silent anger that was filling the room, and partly because, in the awesome hushed silence, my fear was returning.

Presently I was ushered into an even smaller room, a bare cubicle except for a small desk-table and two straight-backed chairs. A single electric light bulb, with a green pan-like shade hung limply from the low ceiling. The county sheriff, Jacob Campbell, was seated at the desk. He was a short-looking man, real chubby, not fat, in his late forties, I would say. He did have a noticeable flabbiness around his mid-section, which appeared to lap about six inches over his tightly drawn leather belt. His face was benign but showed traces of irritation

Figure 23. Officer Jake Campbell, in a 1922 photo. By 1930, he had become the Grant County Sheriff. *Marion Public Library Museum*

caused by the stifling heat in the room. Great rivulets of perspiration rolled down from his damp, sandy-colored hair, and bathed his face.

The interrogation began; it lasted about three hours.

A lifetime later, the sheriff told me that I had been placed in his custody by the police, that I was to be taken to the county jail and locked up to await a hearing. It was several days before I learned that I had been booked on charges of bad associates, armed robbery, criminal assault, auto banditry, rape, and probable first-degree murder!

Officer Burden was one of the four policemen who escorted me to the county jail. It was an edifice one block north of Washington Street and about four or five blocks from police headquarters. On the way over in a squad car he told me, "If that man dies, it's going to be too bad for you, boy!"

I didn't answer him. I didn't know what to say. But I did pray, silently, that the man would live. If he did not survive his wounds, I prayed he would tell the police that I did not shoot him before he passed away. That was the first time I could ever remember praying for a white man. I am ashamed that I had to wait that long to pray for a fellow-human being. I pray for everybody now.

Figure 24. The Grant County Jail in Marion. *Marion Public Library Museum*

The county jail was a large, modern brick and stone building, three stories tall.[58] The jail had six wings, two on each floor. Each wing faced the other with a dimly lit corridor about ten feet wide between them. The officers took me directly up to the second floor and locked me in the south wing of the cellblock.

There were twenty-nine black men and one black boy incarcerated in that wing. All of the men had been caught riding a freight train through Marion's city limits and sentenced to thirty days in jail.[59] The boy was the son of one of the men. Three white men were also in the cellblock.

After the steel-plated, barred door had been shut behind me, one of the men walked up to me and asked why I was being held. I answered as briefly as I knew how, telling them my troubles. When I finished, everybody in the cellblock had crowded around me in stark, wild-eyed wonder.

"Dis your furst time in trubble, son?" somebody, wanted to know.

"Yes, sir."

"What dey got yuh booked fur?" another asked. I didn't know what booking meant at the time. The man rephrased his question. "Ah means what dey got ya charged wid?"

"Oh, I don't know," I answered. Somehow they were all so interested and sympathetic that I felt a little better, but not much.

"How old is ya, son?" asked the man imprisoned with his son.

"Sixteen, sir."

"My boy, Charles, here, is sixteen, too," he told me.

---

[58] This imposing red brick and limestone structure still stands in downtown Marion. The building was used as a jail until 1981. In 2000, the jail was repurposed as the Castle Apartments. The cells were turned into apartments for moderate and low-income tenants. When ABHM Head Griot Reggie Jackson visited in 2003, he found that some of its current tenants had previously been inmates there. When Dr. Kaplan saw Castle Apartments in 2005, the windows still had bars.

A website now advertises the property as more upscale condos and apartments conveniently located in the heart of Marion. There are no longer bars on the windows. In the history section of the website, no mention is made of the infamous lynching that began within its walls (Castle Property, 2015).

[59] During the Great Depression, thousands of unemployed black and white men and youth crisscrossed the country trying to find work. Few had cars, so most hitchhiked or "rode the rails" by hopping onto freight trains. This was illegal, and many were caught, beaten, and sent to jail by the fearsome railroad security guards known as "bulls."

"Aw, come on. Let the kid get some rest. Leave him alone," somebody called out.

But most of the prisoners were too curious, too excited to leave me alone. Then, too, I was anxious to talk to somebody who didn't seem to have decided that I was guilty. The men wanted to know whether the police had beaten me or not, to make me sign a confession.

I told them all that happened in the interrogation room with Sheriff Jacob Campbell.

"What's your name, boy?" the sheriff wanted to know.

"James Cameron, sir."

He handed me a brown felt hat and told me to try it on for size. Luckily, it slid over my ears. He seemed a little disappointed. "What were you doing on the night of July 6, last month, around ten o'clock at night?"

Good Lord, I thought angrily. How in the devil could anyone remember something like that? But all I told him was, "I don't know. I guess I was home in bed at that time of night."

He told me that some black boys had robbed a service station and one of them had dropped that very same hat in the get-a-way. "What do you know about it?"

"Honest, sheriff. I don't know nothing about it!"

While the sheriff was questioning me, uniformed policemen and plainclothesmen kept coming in and going out of the room in a brisk, businesslike manner. Each one of them would stand around for a while, uncertainly, then leave, only to be replaced by others who followed the same nerve-wracking routine. I guessed they were trying to make me uncomfortable. They succeeded.

"Cameron, you may not know it, but you are in one hell of a mess of trouble, facing a lot of time in prison," the sheriff continued. "That is, unless you tell me the truth about what actually happened tonight."

I stared at him, blankly, swallowing hard. I could think of nothing to say. All I could think of was, what in the world happened back there in Lover's Lane, on that lonely stretch of road?

Sheriff Campbell asked me if I knew Thomas Shipp and Abram Smith. I said I did.

"Tonight, just a little while ago, they told me that you shot a white man and raped a white woman. They said they belong to a gang and that you were the ringleader!"

As the sheriff listed the accusations against me, it seemed as if he became angrier and angrier. For a moment, I wondered, fearfully, whether the wounded man was a friend of his or whether the young lady might have been his daughter.

"Now what do you say to that?" he threw at me.

"Oh, no! Not me! I don't know anything about that!"

"Now, look here, son. There's no use in you lying or trying to get out of this trouble. If you did it, say you did. I want to help you all I can." He spoke in a mild tone of voice to me.

This sudden waxing of warmth, a quick switch by the sheriff, more than startled me, but I still held that I did not know anything.

Sheriff Campbell continued. "Thomas Shipp has a 1926 Ford convertible coupe, and you were seen in it last night, or rather tonight. We have all the witnesses we need to prove that point. You boys used that car in the shooting and raping. There's only one other black boy in town with a car like that. He's got an ironclad alibi for his whereabouts. You were with Shipp and Smith tonight, weren't you?"

Figure 25. 1926 Ford convertible coupe.

I swallowed my Adam's apple for the umpteenth time and looked down at my feet.

"Yes, sir," I admitted weakly. "I was with them for a little while."

At this disclosure, the sheriff grew even more friendly, somewhat fatherly.

"Tell me, son. How old are you?"

"Sixteen, sir."

"Are your mother and father living?"

"My mother is living but I don't know whether my father is alive or dead. He and my mother have been divorced for a long time."

"Where do you live, Jimmie?"

"On 31st and Popular Streets, here in Marion."

"How long have you lived in Marion?"

"About two years."

"Where did you come from before you came here?"

"From Kokomo, Indiana."

"Do you go to school here?"

"Yes, sir."

"Which school?"

"I graduated last May from the D.A. Payne School here in Marion. Now I am waiting for September to roll around so I can enter McCullough High."

"What have you been doing all this summer to keep you in spending change?"

"I've been shining shoes in the interurban station[60] on Adams Street."

"How long have you known Shipp and Smith?"

"Me and Tommy went to school together, but I don't know Abe so well."

"What did you boys do last night?"

I hesitated answering him. My tongue flicked out of my mouth to moisten desert-dry lips. I swallowed hard to ease the parchedness in my throat. I took a deep breath. Maybe the sheriff wouldn't understand my side of the story. I looked around the room and every eye I met seemed intent on seeing and hearing whatever I might have to say.

"Well," I began quietly. "We stood around on the corner by old man Hump's place, the candy store, for awhile. Then a bunch of us crossed the street and went to Ogden Weaver's backyard where we pitched some horseshoes."

"In the darkness?" the sheriff wanted to know.

"Oh, it wasn't dark at all. The moon was full and real bright, just like daylight," I hastened to assure him.

"Who were some of the boys pitching horseshoes?"

"Lemme see, now. There was Carl Jordan, Joe Davis, Rufus Jones, Henry Slide, Harold Swanson, Dave Sapp, Pee Wee, Paul Christmas, Gene Smith, Bill Hawkins, Mule, Long John, Buck, Highpockets, Jabbo, and a couple of other fellows."

"How long did you boys pitch shoes?"

"Till about nine o'clock, I guess."

"Then what did you do?"

"Well, I was getting sleepy and had started on my way home when Tommy asked me and Abe if we wanted to go riding for awhile in the car with him."

"Were Tommy and Abrams pitching shoes, too?"

"Yes, sir."

"Where did you boys go?"

"We drove out by Soldier's Home, on over the 38th Street Bridge, and kept right on going until we got way out in the country."

"What happened then?"

"I got scared then because Abe said he wanted to hold up somebody and get some money to buy a new car. I wanted to get out of the car."

"Did you get out of the car?"

---

[60] At that time Marion was well connected by interurban trains to other small and large cities in the region, such as Gary, Indianapolis, and Chicago.

"No, sir."

"Why not?"

I hesitated again. Again my tongue flicked over my bone-dry lips that felt the need of moisture. "I don't know,' I stammered. "'I just couldn't, that's all."

"But why couldn't you get out of the car?"

"Well, Tommy and Abe kept saying there was nothing to it and kept right on driving. They wouldn't let me out of the car."

"You mean to tell me that Thomas Shipp and Abram Smith wouldn't stop the car and let you out?"

"Yes, sir."

"Where were you sitting in the car?"

"I was sitting in the front seat between the two of them."

"What happened then?"

"Abram pulled a gun out of the bib of his overalls. It was a .38 caliber breakdown Iver Johnson special. He said he would be the leader and Tommy and I would be his gang."

"Yes, yes, go on!" the sheriff urged me.

Figure 26. The old River Road outside of Marion that Abe, Tommy, and Jimmie traveled towards the Lover's Lane where Claude Deeter and Mary Ball were parked. *Fruit of the Tree Productions*

He had, finally, won my confidence. I felt he was really my friend. Besides, I wanted to tell somebody and was glad to rid myself of it. It was weighing heavily on my mind. At that moment I was thinking there is nothing in the world that weighs more heavily on a person than a piece of undelivered mind.

"We drove on down a real country road that was rough and narrow. We parked the car behind some tall shrubbery just off the dirt road. We could see the river with the old McBeth Evans Glass factory on the other side. Abe told us to follow him, and Tommy and I got out of the car and followed him."

"Why did you follow Tommy and Abe?"

I told the sheriff I didn't know, but I lied to him. I knew. I was one of that vast army of people who hated responsibility or, at least, did not recognize its true worth. Many times in the past I had found myself doing what someone else with a stronger will had decided for me.

Along the river bank a soft breeze was faintly stirring across the water, bringing welcome relief from the day's sweltering heat, which still hung somewhat oppressively in the air. The road ran parallel to the riverbed and was known as Lover's Lane. Frogs croaked incessantly in the deep stillness of the night. Crickets added their steady soprano to the chorus of nature. Now and then, the quiet rippling of the river was broken by a splash here and there that told me fish were jumping.

But the sound [I heard most] was the pounding of my heart. It seemed to be knocking a steady staccato message, pleading with me on bended knees to beware! The decision between good and evil had to be made at once. There was no response from me. My emotions were a paralyzing mixture of fear, excitement, and utter confusion. Anything could have emerged from the river, or from under some rock in the darkness that lay all around us.

I could feel my flesh crawling as Abe lead the way to the blackest part of Lover's Lane. Something inside me kept crying out: "Go back, go back!" But I seemed to have lost control of my legs, my whole body, my will. I kept plodding onward behind Abe and Tommy as if tied to them.

We came upon a car parked off the road in the bushes. There was a man and a woman in the car. They were too busy talking to one another to notice us. When Abe saw them, he stopped and whispered, "We'll see how much money they got and take it." I hung back, trembling, telling him that I was afraid.

"All you have to do," said Abe, "is throw the gun on people and they stick up their hands. If they don't, you shoot them!"

Then he took the gun and handed it to me. "Here, Apples," he said. "You stick them up and Tommy and I will search them."

"Why did Abe call you Apples?"

"Because that was a name my school principal hung on me for eating apples in school."

"Okay, go ahead."

"I told Abe I was scared and couldn't do it."

"What did Abe do then? What did he do?"

"Abe insisted that I hold the gun. I asked him to suppose the people in the car had a gun, too. What then? But he just ignored my reasoning and shoved the gun into my hand. There was nothing I could think of to say, so I tried to get it over with as quick as I could. I walked up to the car and yanked the door open. The man and the woman jumped up from the backseat. I said 'stick 'em up!'

Then Abe came out of the bushes with his right hand in his pocket, like he had a gun too. He said, 'Awright, come on out of the car and keep your damn hands in the air."

Figure 27. Claude Deeter, age 23, the nice young man whose shoes Jimmie regularly shined, not long before the tragic fatal encounter in Lovers Lane. *Deeter Family*

Abe had done that sort of thing before, I learned later. He had served two terms at the state penal farm at Putnamville.

"The man got out of the car, and then the woman, with their hands high in the air. I didn't get a good look at the lady, but I did recognize the man. He was a young fellow, a white man, whose shoes I had shined dozens of times. He was one of my regular customers at the interurban station where I work and shine shoes, and he always tipped me, too. A lot of times he would wait until I was through with another customer because he didn't care for anybody else to shine his shoes but me. When I saw this man who was so nice to me, that's when I really and truly realized that I couldn't go through with the crime and pushed the gun back to Abe. I told him I was going home and that I was not going to have anything more to do with him and Tommy."

I paused, waiting for the sheriff to say he understood what I was talking about, how I felt. He nodded his head, and I rambled on.

"I started running away from there as fast as my feet could move me. I ran down the road and was almost to the 38th Street Bridge (about four or five blocks away, I guessed) when I heard the sound of gunfire. It was three shots. Bang! bang! bang!–just like that."

"When you heard these shots, Jimmie, what did you do?"

"Nothing. I just kept right on running. I was going so fast I hit a rock in the road and fell down. It's a wonder I didn't kill myself the way I fell. But I got up and ran even faster. A car was coming down the road toward me. When I saw the headlights, I jumped over to the side of the road into some tall weeds, hoping some snake wouldn't bite me. I laid there until the car passed by. Then I got up and kept right on running.

I don't know what happened back there in Lover's Lane, Sheriff, and that's the truth! I only knew I wasn't going to go back there to find out after I heard those shots. I crossed the 38th Street Bridge, circled around past Soldier's Home, doing a mile a minute, and ran down the railroad tracks to Washington and 30th Streets. I didn't stop running until I got home on Popular Street."

I had finished telling him my story. I sank back in my chair as far as the straight back would allow. The sheriff looked at me for what seemed like a long time before he said anything. He had been writing all the time I was accounting for my whereabouts that night. I thought the sheriff probably thought I was telling a lie. He was shaking his head as if to say "Boy, oh, boy, oh boy!" He blinked his eyes and shook his head at me with disbelief.

"Are you sure you didn't rape the girl and shoot the man?" he asked me again.

"Yes, sir. I'm sure I didn't!"

"Didn't you hold the girl's hands while Abe and Tommy raped her?"

"Sheriff, I have told you everything I know. I can't tell you anymore because I don't know anymore!" I was trying desperately to keep the irritation out of my voice. I felt the sheriff was betraying me by doubting my word. He had suddenly become an angry man again, trying to make me say I had raped a woman and tried to kill a man.

"Then who in the hell did it if you didn't!" he thundered at me.

By this time there were at least eight uniformed policemen in the small room. Most of them hovered around me. One of them seemed to be bracing himself on the back of my chair.

Sheriff Campbell looked over my shoulders, and his head went up and down in a nod to a group of officers. "Well, the woman said you did it and that's good enough for me!"

At that precise moment a huge fist exploded with the force of a fully swung wrecking ball against the side of my head, knocking me out of my chair. A blur of a million stars clouded my vision and made me oblivious of landing on the floor. Before I could regain my senses and attempt to get up, a ring of policemen tightened around me as if I were a poisonous snake or a raving, mad dog. The punishment meted out to me could not have been over two or three minutes in duration, or they would have killed me then and there. Nevertheless, to me it seemed like an eternity.

The first kick landed in the pit of my stomach, completely paralyzing me. I could only lie there and take it, gasping for breath like a fish out of water. There was no strength left in me to ward off any crushing blows. No part of my body was able to respond with any kind of a defense. Each vicious kick brought on recurring streaks of unconsciousness. When, at last, I thought I was going to die, that I was going to pass out for good, somebody, Sheriff Campbell, I guessed, hollered out "Hold it!"

Roughly, several officers shoved and pushed and lifted me from the floor and slammed me back into my chair as if I was some kind of an animal too dangerous to handle with the naked hand. I tasted blood, my own blood. I swallowed it. I felt like vomiting. Several teeth had been loosened. My body was one massive quivering ache of pain.

"Now, sign this paper," the sheriff commanded me. His voice was frightening.

Even in my dazed and incoherent condition, I remembered that my mother had always taught us children never to sign anything before reading it and approving the contents. I made ready to look over the paper in front of me. They were sheaves he had filled out while he was questioning me. I leaned forward, squinting at the paper. I did not pick up the pen that lay beside it. One of the officers slapped me up side my head as if he was trying to tear it off my shoulders.

"The sheriff didn't say read it. He told you to sign it!"

I had had enough. I picked up the pen and scrawled my name as hastily as my trembling hand would allow. (Later I found out that it was a confession admitting that Abe raped the woman and Tommy shot the man!)

CHAPTER SEVEN

Say It Isn't So!

When I had finished telling my story to my cellmates, a huge black man in tattered clothing pointed out to me where to get some water, where the latrine was. He was just one of the unfortunate human beings trying to make it as the Depression[61] was tightening all over our land. He was the picture of the typical hobo.[62] Then the men who had grouped around me, hanging on to every word, formed back into small knots of card players.

My cell was dirty and smelled of unwashed bodies. Funky scents seemed to be everywhere the air circulated. The whole inside of the wing had a stench of something dead or decaying. The steel bunks, the kind I had so often seen in the motion pictures, had iron strips that served as springs. There was no give in them. A thin straw-filled tick covered the hard bed. It looked and smelled as if it had been used for a hundred years. How many prisoners, arrested as a result of some fight, had shed their blood on it I had no way of knowing. It was a great effort to lie down on the bunk, but I did.

---

[61] The Great Depression (1929-1939) was a severe worldwide economic downturn. It began with famous Black Tuesday stock market crash in the United States that wiped out millions of investors. Banks were forced to close, businesses and industries had to cut workers' hours and wages, and millions of Americans became unemployed. At the same time, a terrible drought and horrendous dust storms hit the Great Plains. The breadbasket of the nation became the "Dust Bowl," and thousands of farmers lost their land and homes.

[62] "Hobo" is the term used during the Depression for a very poor, usually homeless, person who moved around the country, often by hopping freight trains, to find work.

The cells did not have solid partitions for any kind of privacy. Long rows of steel bars served as walls on all four sides. I looked around, then buried my face in the dirty tick when I thought no one was looking. I cried until no more tears would come.

Some of the tears were for my mother, others were for myself. Shame and mental anguish wracked my whole body. My mother hadn't raised me to end up like this. "Oh God, help me!" I prayed. I could still see my mother standing in the doorway of our shebang, pleading with the Marion police officers, begging them to let her come with me, imploring them to arrest her instead of me. Although I believed I was unjustly accused, I somehow felt I had completely betrayed her. She was the one person in all the world I should have honored with respect and decency. She had been both a father and mother to me. Like a man near death, my whole life staged a panorama before me. In my mind's-eye, many events stood out in startling boldness. I was utterly ashamed of them. It was a cruel reckoning. It had to come, and I had no one to blame but myself!

I thought of the time when I was fourteen years old and had stolen some apples from the neighborhood grocery store; the many slices of cake and pie I had stolen from the cupboard at home and had blamed on my sisters; the time I dipped Alice Mansfield's pigtails in the ink well on my desk at school; and the many times I had "done it" with a girl in a cornfield near the roads or inside the bed of a high-sided wagon some farmer had left in his field overnight. I had been as mannish as I could. There were always girls ready to love.

All of these things seemed so adventurous, funny, and satisfying when they happened. There had been so many escapades and conquests to round out my young life. But, suddenly, crying in the county jail, I realized they had only been the beginning of the trouble I found myself in now. If only I had listened to my mother! If only I could have seen where such a path was going to lead. I guessed that was how every man felt when he found himself in trouble—too late.

At the age of sixteen, I realized a weakling cannot improve the destiny of mankind. Man had to be strong and honest and courageous to arrive at his true fate. That had to be the secret of life! But I had learned too late. I had been only half a man. On the one hand, I had been all ready to supply the material needs of my body. Whereas, on the other, I had neglected the most important thing that people must learn to live by—the spirit. This spirit, or will to do good rather than evil, was the self-same spirit that had pleaded with me on bended knees, had cried out to me, "go back, go back!" I had been given ample time to put under control the ugly side of man's nature.

I thought of the time when I was seven years old. I had found a cigarette butt in some gutter. I carried it to bed with Marie and Della. I puffed away in the darkness as they slept on both sides of me. I fell asleep with the stub still burning in my hands between my fingers! Luckily, for all three of us, Mother had stuck her head into the room to see if we were tucked in for the night. She was just in time to save all of us from burning to death. The mattress was smoldering all around the edges ready to burst into a flaming coffin for the three of us. The whipping Mother gave me was hard, but looking back now, it didn't seem hard enough.

Suddenly, my thoughts returned to the present. I began wondering where Tommy and Abe were. Had they really put all that blame on me or had the police just said that to find out how much I really knew? A shudder went through my body as I thought of the cruel beating they had given me at police headquarters. I prayed the officers would not come in and take me out and beat me again. What seemed a long time later, exhausted in body, mind, and spirit, I drifted off into a troubled sleep.

The next day, or rather later on that very same morning, life started out mildly enough, but before it was over it would prove to be the most turbulent of my young life. It was the 7th day of August, 1930.

At times even now, I awaken in the middle of the night, reliving that whole day–and night. On such nights, I can never return to sleep. I suffer headaches all through the night. I just lie there, thinking, praying, saying my Rosary,[63] hoping, reassuring myself that it all happened a long, long time ago; that I am not the same man, that I am somebody else now; that my family and I are safe in our own home–at least for the time being. I can never be sure of such domestic quiet and security because of the many connotations of evil many whites attach to black people. When will the time ever come when black people can shed this lurking fear?

It was about seven o'clock when I got up that morning. I had been trying to sleep for less than an hour. Leaving my cell, I joined some of the other prisoners in the narrow corridor that circled our cells. Some of the men were busy making up their bunks. Others just stood around and wondered about me, because they had been asleep when the sheriff locked me up. A few of them were washing their faces and hands at the sink. Several fellows were starting the day off right by squabbling with one another

---

[63] Saying the rosary is a form of prayer in the Catholic Church. A rosary is the special string of beads that helps Catholics say prayers in a particular order. Cameron converted to Roman Catholicism in his forties.

in a jocular vein. A couple of them were sweeping the floor of the cellblock. Everybody, it seemed, had some chore to do to keep the wing as sanitary and as livable as possible. The narrow corridor circling our cells was called a "bullpen." I was in that area. It was a vacuum between the rows of cells and the walls of the jail building. There, the prisoners were allowed to walk around for exercise and look-sees into the streets below.

I strolled around the bullpen looking out each window I came to, my mind racing like mad. People were crossing the streets, turning into stores, stopping to look at window displays, chatting with one another. Life seemed to go on without me. The sun was bright as it beamed down from a cloudless sky. It was the beginning of another beautiful Indiana summer day. It was hard to reconcile my troubles with the seemingly carefree world I read in the scenes below.

For a long time I stood looking down into the streets through the window farthest from my cell. I found a curious pleasure in watching the people who seemed to be talking, some of them to themselves. If only I had someone to talk to, someone who would believe me. All of a sudden I was a little boy again, frightened, confused, frustrated and, oh, so lonely. More than anything else in the world, I wanted to talk with my mother.

"Hi, there!" somebody behind me called. I turned around facing one of the prisoners. He was a white man, a tall, lean, hungry-looking fellow, about thirty years old. He had a crooked smile and shaggy blond hair. His voice was soft and friendly enough, and his blue eyes were large and kind. "How ya feeling this morning?" he asked me cheerfully.

"Oh, all right, I guess. Just a little stiff and sore." I heard myself speaking in a voice that sounded small, weak, and uncertain. I felt that I was going to burst into tears. "I want my mother," I told the man, irrationally implying that he could produce her.

The fellow placed his arms around my shoulders and said quietly "Don't worry, son. Everything's going to be all right. Just take it easy." With those few words of attempted encouragement, he turned around and walked back into the cellblock. A few minutes later, somebody yelled:

"Come and get it!

"It" was a good name for it.

I joined the noisy and mad scramble to the door of the cellblock. The way most of the men were rushing forward reminded me of hogs crowding around a slop trough at the sound of the farmer's sooooo-eeeeee!

"Man," one of the men called out, "don't it smell good dis mawning!"

The steel door was opened from the outside and a steaming bucket of coffee was set inside by one of the uniformed guards. At least, it was supposed to have been coffee. Tin plates, cups, and spoons arrived presently on a dumb waiter built in the wall inside the entrance to the bullpen. On the next trip up, the contraption brought up a scalding bucket of watery oatmeal, sugar, and bread that looked as if it was two weeks old. One of the prisoners began ladling the stuff onto plates. I stood looking at my portion, wondering whether I could hold it down if I ate it. I noticed a few others with similar notions giving their plates to less squeamish neighbors. I did the same.

Most of the prisoners sat around wolfing that gruel down as if it was some kind of a delicacy. They speculated about my troubles. That was all they could think to do. They seemed not to know that I was standing nearby, catching every alarming word they said about me:

"If'n dey don't kill him befo he gits a trial, dey will tell all sorts of lies on him and git him electrocuted!"[64]

"Yeah. If dey don't kill him, dey will keep him in prison until he is an old man. Mah boy Charles here will be a grandfudder when de white folkeses turn dat boy loose!"

"It don't make no difference if'n he ain't guilty ob what dey say he is guilty ob. Some ob us is going to hafta pay wid our lives to satisfy some ob dese old mean white folkses!"

"As long as de white folkses purpose is served, dey will let us lib and when dey wants to kill ere one of us, dey will kill us and ain't nothing ever done about it. We's just a bunch ob dead niggers, dat's all!

"De white folkses doos wid us jist what dey wants to do. When ah was a young man, ah wanted to be a doctor, but ah knew it would do me no good to study medicine and surgery cause de only things white folkses would let me work on would be horses, mules, and niggers. And it wouldn't do no good to study to be a lawyer either, cause anytime de white folkses wants to put a nigger in de jailhouse, dey puts him away!"

It seemed that all of the black men had a very disturbing opinion about just what was in store for me.

Just what was going to happen to me?

After the breakfast tins had been lowered on the dumb waiter, most of the fellows dallied around and tried to settle down to their daily games of "Dirty Hearts." A few of

---

[64] By writing the inmates' exchange in dialect, Cameron again lets the reader know that these men, these train-riding migrants, have come up North to Indiana from the South.

them were taking their daily exercises by walking around the bullpen. Several of them stood looking out the windows into the streets below. I tried to interest myself in some of the half-hearted card games. After awhile, I noticed some of the men at the windows beckoning to their friends. In a few minutes practically every card game was broken up! Everybody was crowding around the windows, mumbling and swearing cuss words I had never in my life heard before. I edged forward through the group to see what was going on.

A crowd of white people, at least a hundred of them, were standing and talking in groups of four and five, all around the jail building. Some of the old-timers in the bullpen with me interpreted their presence as a bad omen.

"Dey ain't up to no fuggin good," one of then exclaimed evenly, "and ya can believe dat!"

The prisoners could not hear what was being said down on the ground level below us. They didn't need to. There was no doubt in any of their minds. It was natural to assume that the crime that had been committed in Lover's Lane last night was on everybody's tongue. Occasionally, a white man would point to the windows of the jail. We saw people shaking clenched fists at us.

"Man! Ah shore wish mah time was up so's I could git out ob dis town!" somebody sighed.

"Me too!" came an echo. "Ah don't lak de looks ob dis heah, at all!"

Everybody's nerves grew taut, it seemed. All the card games broke up. The prisoners began to prowl restlessly around in the bullpen, inspecting locks, shaking bars, testing them for strength. At first, not understanding these signs as readily as the older black men, I was not especially afraid. I was just lonely for my mother and my sisters. But the men's fear soon communicated itself to me. It slowly creeped in like the rising sun pushing back the darkness of night.

You could feel the tension in the bullpen grow thicker and thicker and thicker, as small groups of white people, three, then five, then seven, and more, kept coming up the stairs inside the jail outside of my cellblock. They were all white people. They stared at us in the bullpen and cellblock through the bars of the door. They were not police officers, just plain white folks. They would mumble to themselves, then leave, only to be replaced by a similar group!

"Don't worry, son," I heard one of the white prisoners say, the one with the crooked smile. "People in this part of the country wouldn't lynch anybody.[65] Besides, the rest of the black folks in town wouldn't stand for it."[66]

He was standing close to me as he told me of a mob that had tried to lynch a black man in the northern part of the state in the 1880's, in Michigan City, Indiana. He might have made it up to reassure me. It did–a little. It seemed the sheriff had fired one shot into the unruly crowd besieging the jail. The leader of the pack was killed outright. He was the one raising the most hell and crying out the loudest for the blood of the prisoner. The rest of the gang fled before the enforcement power that upheld the doctrine of law and order in the town.

"Ain't never been an attempt to lynch anybody else in this state since then," he concluded.

Yes, I felt decidedly better the more I thought about it. If a mob tried to storm the jail in Marion, all the sheriff would have to do would be to shoot down the leaders, and the rest of them would disperse. My comforter saw that he was gaining my confidence and told me more. "This heah is a northen state, not down in Dixie," he said. "They only pull off stuff like that down in Georgia, Mississippi, and Alabama."

One of the black prisoners came over to where the white prisoner was talking to me. He stood nearby. His name was John. He was a heavily built man about six feet tall, very dark and very wrinkled with age. He was stuck with a sharply receding hairline; his hair was white as pure clouds, and very woolly. The top of his head shone like he had

---

[65] This man expresses the mistaken belief, still held by people today, that lynchings took place only in the South. For example, just eleven years before, Will Brown had been lynched in Omaha, Nebraska. The photograph of his burning body, surrounded by a white mob, became well known. (You can see it in the Introduction to this book.)

In fact, during that "Red Summer of 1919," there were some twenty urban race riots, including in nearby Chicago. In these riots, thousands of whites rampaged through black neighborhoods attacking black people and their property. They shot, hanged, and burned many black men to death. In 1920, three black youth had been famously lynched in Duluth, Minnesota. (See this photograph in the Introduction, too.) Despite the myth of northern civility, hundreds of lynchings took place in the Midwest, according to scholars' estimates.

[66] After the white police refused to intervene in the Chicago and Washington, D.C., race riots, black youths fought back. The NAACP (National Association for the Advancement of Colored People) also fought back by organizing peaceful protests against racial violence and advocating for local and national legislation to curtail lynching.

had a coat of jet-black enameled paint baked on it. He had all sorts of scars and knots (man-made) on the top of his head. He didn't say anything, at first. He just stood there patting me on the shoulders and nodding, sympathetically. Not until the white man left to go to the latrine did John say his piece.

"Dat guy is nuts!" he said then. "Anytime one ob us black folks is accused of raping a white woman, whether it's true or not, I don't care where it is, North, South, East, or West, dere's always some white folks wants to hang us for it. Dey'll go out ob dere way to do it, too, and any black man will do! I sure wish dey would get you boys out ob heah and down to the state capitol for safekeeping."

I swallowed hard. My eyes widened. My head literally spun around in slow motion. It took me a few seconds to find my voice. "Do…do…do…do you think they'll try to lynch us, John?"

"Dey will try it even if'n dey don't gitaway wid it. The police done said a white woman's been screwed. People will believe de police before dey will believe you."

"But, John, wouldn't the sheriff stop them or shoot them to keep them from taking us away?"

"Maybe, maybe not. Most ob de sheriffs don't care where you and me is involved. It's his duty all right. Maybe the police won't stand still for a mob. Maybe and maybe not. Dey usually do stand still, though. Besides, you is not a police prisoner now. Dey turned you ober to de custity ob de sheriff."

All of the confidence the white prisoner had built up inside me vanished before John's grim predictions. I slumped to the floor, feeling weak, helpless and lost. There was nothing for me to do but wait, hope and pray.

John reminded me that Marion had a Ku Klux Klan klavern and was only twelve miles from Noblesville, the Klan state headquarters. "Hell, for all we knows, de sheriff might even be a member ob de Klan in good standing!"[67]

"Holy smokes! I never thought of that!" I exclaimed.

"Ob course, it don't make no difference whether you boys is guilty or not. Dey thinks you is and dat's all dey wants to think. On de other hand, if de boys hadda been

---

[67] The prisoner was correct. In that era, Ku Klux Klan membership included community leaders, such as lawmakers, educators, police chiefs, and businessmen. Indeed, about a quarter to a third of all white men native to Indiana were Klan members in 1925. In some places, a man could not be elected or appointed to important community roles if he was not Klan, so people in Marion could fairly assume that Jake Campbell was a member.

white and dis heah woman and dis heah man was black, it would'da made all the difference in de world! De police wouldn't have to think about a mob. Dey'd probably laugh it off as a huge joke as dey always do when a white man screws a black woman.

"De only way any mob can take a prisoner away from de law is fur de law to cooperate wid de crowd. De police hab a notorious habit of cooperating wid de white folks when dey gits together and wants to kill ere one ob us!"

In the past twelve hours, I had been as scared as I thought humanly possible and still retain my sanity. But the feeling that came over me as John made these grim predictions was stronger than fear or utter futility. It was indescribable. It simply left me without hope. I tried to get my mind off the matter. But the more I tried the more my mind kept racing back over the countless stories about Ku Klux Klan treatment of black people, stories that every black person knows by the time he or she is five years old. By the time you were sixteen, you were well versed in what a "nigger" was in America.

Klansmen were experts in inventing deaths too horrible to be conceived by rational minds. This has been demonstrated over the years of their existence. The fact that I was a black man, a hated "nigger," came to me in full force. The impact left me breathless.

These were my thoughts as I looked out the window of the Grant County Jail in Marion, Indiana, and witnessed the mob growing in number in the street below. While my mind was busy racing with frightening thoughts, one of the jail's trustees, an elderly and very stooped black man, came shuffling down the corridor to the entrance of my cellblock. He peered through the small opening in the metal door and whispered something to the nearest prisoner. It was to the effect that Tommy and Abe were locked up in the first floor cellblocks, opposite one another. Then he turned around and shuffled back down the corridor and returned to his quarters downstairs.

I must have sat for an hour without moving a muscle. The men around me had, hesitantly, made attempts to resume their card games. There was little talk, however, because of an ominous quiet that had settled down on the whole group of black prisoners. Anytime there was the slightest sign of any noise from the outside, or sounds coming up from downstairs, everyone, including me, would freeze in his tracks, realizing whatever was going to happen would only be a matter of time.

Eventually, I got up and began pacing up and down the floor. I was too keyed up to sit down or stand still any longer. Somehow I felt like I should have been still running, not back to my home in that lonely part of Marion, but away from white folks–as far away as I could get from them! My hands remained wet with perspiration no matter how many times I wiped them on my shirt and overalls. My throat felt desert dry. No amount of water from the spigot of the sink eased my thirst.

The call to lunch sounded. Only a few of the men had any appetite. Most of the food was returned to the kitchen on the dumb waiter. Time became an excruciating drag on human endurance. There was a large void. I returned to my cell and laid down across my bunk.

About three o'clock that afternoon, one of the black prisoners came back to my cell and told me someone was at the door wanted to talk with me. I just knew it was my mother. She had finally found a way to see me! Now I could fall down on my knees and ask her to forgive me for adding more gray hairs on top of her head. I would tell her how sorry and miserable I felt and how, if I had my life to live over, things would be very different.

Like a little boy at Christmas time in Toyland, I bounded up the corridor of my cellblock to the door. I was not at all prepared for who was waiting for me at the door. Immediately I recognized Mayor Jack Edwards. He was a slightly built white man in his late twenties or early thirties with graying temples and rather effeminate mannerisms.[68] His thin pinched nose seemed to be forever sniffing something unpleasant. He was nattily dressed in a blue palm beach suit and held a white Panama straw hat in his hands.

As I approached the door, I saw another white man standing behind the mayor. He was a slender young fellow with flaming red hair. A white handkerchief covered the lower half of his flushed face. I stiffened.

I studied the masked man's face, his eyes, cold, blue, and steely, staring at me! I got the message that he meant to kill me by just looking at me! No matter how long I live, I will never forget that look and the man who directed it to me. I have never in my life seen a clearer example of raw racial hatred as I look back on this scene.

Jack Edwards spoke first. "Your name James Cameron?"

---

[68] Mayor Edwards was indeed just twenty-seven years old when he was elected in 1929. According to Dr. James Madison, who interviewed him much later in life, the mayor enjoyed the amenities of the Roaring Twenties, such as jazz, speakeasies, and drinking. Despite the laws of Prohibition, the easygoing mayor allowed gambling and the sales of bootleg liquor, so long as the Chicago mobs were not involved. He supported these as local businesses, estimating that there were about fifteen to twenty speakeasies in his city.

Mayor Edwards was also one of several white members of the local branch of the NAACP, the National Association for the Advancement of Colored People (Madison, 2001, 36).

"Yes, sir."

"How old are you?"

"Sixteen, sir."

"Have you ever been in trouble before?"

"No, sir."

"Have you any brothers and sisters?"

"I've got two sisters and no brothers."

The masked man spoke up then. His voice was husky and expressionless. "Have you got a Mother?"

"Yes, sir."

"What does she do for a living?"

"She washes and irons clothes for white folks."

"Have you got a father?"

"No, sir. I have a step-father, though."

"What's his name?"

When he had asked me those few questions, he pulled the mayor over to one side and whispered impatiently to him. The only words I caught were "Come on. Let's get the hell out of here!"

They turned and left me standing there. They walked down the wide corridor outside my cellblock toward the stairway without another word. I stared after them, wondering, remembering the masked man's hands as they gripped the bars on the huge steel door leading into my cellblock, his knuckles as white as the handkerchief he wore as a mask. Why had the mayor brought that man up to the jail to see me?[69] Why was his face masked? Why didn't the mayor mask his face, too?

When Jack Edwards was running for mayor of Marion a few months ago, I recalled he had seemed like such a nice and gentle man, friendly. I remember having gone one night with my mother to hear him speak to a political gathering. He had bragged about his many friends and supporters all over town, blacks as well as whites.

I thought of the many times Edwards had come into the interurban station where I worked as a bootblack to get his shoes shined. He was one of the most generous tippers I knew. And sometimes I would joke with him while I shined his expensive shoes, which were shining like new when he took a seat on the stand. Surely Edwards must

---

[69] He may have been a newspaper reporter. Many reporters had descended on Marion that day in anticipation of the lynching.

have realized that I recognized him. Everybody in Marion knew him by sight. Was he working with the Ku Klux Klan? Had he brought that masked man up to my cellblock so he could find out which one of us to take out and hang?

Yes, that must be it, I reasoned. It had to be that way, otherwise it didn't make any sense. I felt a sinking and twisting sensation in the pit of my stomach, an aching hollowness. I didn't want to believe that people could be so false and deceitful. Yet all my young life I had heard tales about how the white man always wanted everything for himself; how he is in the habit of using just such fraud and deceit, violence and force, to have his way in anything. That was how he had gained control of the land from the rightful owners, the American Indians, and had stolen and enslaved black people to work that land for him.

I was still standing there glued to the door when the old black trustee, stooped and shuffling as bad as before, came back upstairs again. He told me that my mother had tried to see me on three different occasions, but the sheriff had turned down her requests. "He's got a standing order dat no visitors is gwine to see ya!" Then he shuffled back downstairs.

The black men in the bullpen and cellblock began murmuring again. Their faces were masks of acute apprehension. Perhaps, some of them had seen this sort of thing happen before in their lives.

"Dat's jist whut dey is plannin on doin," one of them said. "Ah jist knows it! Ah kin feel it in mah bones!"

All of the black prisoners knew what he was talking about. No one argued with him. If there had been any doubt among them, any hope at all, it was dispelled by the visit of the mayor and that masked man! Something evil and vicious was in the air. They sensed it. In their hearts and minds, as well as in the hearts and minds of millions of black men, women, and children in America, ugly scars from the past were deeply etched. The ugly shadow of death under which they had lived all their lives, and under which I was born, was rapidly becoming a real and terrible force. And perhaps they felt less secure in their own lives as they realized, under the circumstances, that three of their very own racial group were about to be sacrificed to the demon god of white supremacy. Every degree of the ritual would be milked dry of its essentials. The terrible cost of being a black man in America reinforced itself in the minds of those prisoners in the Grant County jail with me.

CHAPTER EIGHT

Demonic Terror

Evening began settling down over the city of Marion. The newly installed streetlights blazed away with the brightness of daylight in the gathering twilight. The crowds around the jailhouse grew larger, busier, but strangely hushed. The bullpen inside my cellblock was a picture of a grotesque tableau as black prisoners huddled silently in groups of three and four, smoking tasteless cigarettes and pipes, chewing tobacco that had lost its tang. They were cocking their heads to one side and then another at each suggestion of sound. Their breathing had become heavy and rapid. The pain of living, of vegetating, was excruciating.

Earlier in the day, I later learned, the only black physician in Marion, Dr. Bailey, had received word from his white friends in the town that three black youths in the Grant County jail would be lynched that night. They would be taken from the jail and lynched by a Ku Klux Klan mob. His white friends told him of the general plot that had been planned with the precision of a military coup. His white friends were not in sympathy with the intention of the mob. Dr. Bailey tried to call Governor Leslie on the telephone all that day to request troops to guard the city against race rioting and looting, and to protect Tommy and Abe and me. Those calls were never completed.[70]

---

[70] Actually it was Dr. Bailey's wife, Flossie, who worked the phones all day. Mrs. Dr. Bailey, as she was formally called, was the head of the local branch of the NAACP. She tried to reach Marion's Mayor Edwards, who, according to his secretary, had left town that afternoon for Indianapolis. She also called the office of Indiana's Governor Leslie, who was fishing in Canada, according to his assistant–who hung up on her (Madison, 2001, and Carr, 2006).

Figure 28. Katherine "Flossie" Bailey was the head of the Marion branch of the NAACP. She tried to get Marion's mayor and Indiana's governor to stop the impending lynching. *Barbara J. Stevenson*

News of the impending lynching in Marion was broadcast over the radio stations in the state and heard throughout the Midwest. Front pages of newspapers were alive with rumors of a lynch mob gathering around the jail in Marion. Many whites as well as black people tried to call the governor, only 68 miles away[71]. None of them were able to reach him. For some reason, the lines to the statehouse and the governor's mansion were blocked.

Most of the town's black men had, earlier in the day, moved their families out to Weaver, Indiana, an all-black community about seven or eight miles from Marion, for safekeeping. The men planned to return to Marion with arms and ammunition to combat the tactics of the mobsters. Only a handful of them stayed in Weaver, singing hymns and praying to God to save them from the wrath of white folks. During the days of slavery, Weaver had become famous as an important station on the route of the Underground Railroad.[72]

About five-thirty, after the evening meal had been brought up by the dumb waiter and sent back down by most of the prisoners, three burly uniformed law enforcement officers came upstairs and got me out of my cellblock. They escorted me downstairs to Sheriff Campbell's office. There, a reporter for the Marion Chronicle was waiting to interview me. The man was a short, pale-looking fellow with a robust round body that looked as if it had been stuffed into the wrinkled, rust-colored suit he wore. There was no doubt about it, the man had a cheap expense account. His name was Drysdale

---

[71] In Indiana's capital city of Indianapolis.

[72] The Underground Railroad consisted of white and free black abolitionists who helped slaves trying to escape slavery in the South by providing secret "stations" where they could rest, be fed, and meet their "conductor" to the next station on their way to freedom in Canada.

Brannon.[73] He stood beside the sheriff, who was seated behind his desk smoking a black cigar.

The cheesy-looking reporter studied me for several long seconds after I had been ordered to take a seat on the bench in front of the desk. Then he started questioning me. I told the man the same truth, the whole truth, although I understood by that time that the truth was no longer important. It simply didn't matter at all. I went through the same motions, answering the same questions for the hundredth time.

"Ask the girl. She can tell you I had nothing to do with any rape or shooting anybody," I told the reporter near the end of the interview.

"You'll never get out of this. You know that, don't you?" he crowed at me.

I had no answer for him. He seemed extremely pleased with himself and my predicament.

Sheriff Campbell interrupted him for the first time. He asked Brannon if it was true the wounded man was really near death.

"Yes, he's going to die–if he hasn't already. He's shot all to hell, just full of holes," he answered.

The sheriff wanted to know if he was through with me. "Yeah, take him away," he told the sheriff.

The same three officers who had brought me downstairs led me back to my cellblock on the second floor. They had been waiting outside the sheriff's office while the interview was being conducted. As the big steel doors clanged shut behind me, the rest of the prisoners crowded around loaded with questions.

"Whut did dey wan dis time?" somebody asked.

"Oh, they had a news reporter down there from one of the local newspapers. He asked me a lot of questions, but I think he just came to see me to gloat over telling me that I am really in for one hell of a time, that the white man somebody shot is going to die. He acted like he was real mad at me, and I have never seen the man before in my life."

"Aw, hell!" someone groaned.

"Wus de udder boys down dere, too?"

"No. At least, I didn't see them."

The men engulfed the path of silence and drifted away, back to their eternal card games. Others resumed their restless pacing backward and forward in the bullpen,

---

[73] Brannon, like Mayor Edwards, was a white member of the NAACP's Marion Branch.

stopping religiously to look out the windows at the crowd in the streets below. Some of them retired to the semi-privacy of their cells and sat on their bunks with bowed heads.

The crowd of whites on the streets had reached a staggering count by this time. There were thousands of them.[74] They all sifted about restlessly. All the card games in my cellblock broke up.

I did not know it at the time, but the wounded man had died. Certain members of the Marion Police Department had taken the victim's bloody, white shirt and hung it on the flagpole that extended from the roof at police headquarters for the whole town to see. It was like waving a red flag in front of a raging bull!

Mayor Jack Edwards had left town "on business."

The only black uniformed officer on the force, Officer Harley Burden, had his service revolver taken away from him by superior officers and was ordered to direct traffic—at an intersection three miles away from the county jail.

An evening newspaper reported:

> Marion.....Claude Deeter, 23, of Fairmount, who was shot by three Negroes last night on a road near here, died in the Marion General Hospital this afternoon. Three men are held who, police said, have confessed that they shot Deeter in an attempted holdup and also attacked Miss Mary Ball, 19, his companion. Harley Hardin, county prosecutor, said he would endeavor to obtain the death penalty for these men. Abe Smith, 19, is the one who is said to have admitted to assaulting the young woman. Thomas Shipp, 18, and James Cameron, 16, are the others under arrest. Each accused the other of firing the fatal shots.

About eight o'clock that night, restless and unbearably tired, nerves worn to a frazzle, my thoughts returned to my mother. Surely her heart must have broken into a million pieces since my arrest. I could not help shedding more tears for the trouble I knew in my heart I had caused her. Then I imagined how she would take it if the mob treated me like some of their victims I had read about and heard about—dragged alive behind a fast moving automobile through the black community of the town until the flesh was scraped off their bones. Or drenched with gasoline coal oil and set afire, a human torch! Some of the victims were nailed to trees and crude surgery was performed on them—ripping out their genitals, and then the body was used for target practice.

---

[74] The next day, newspapers would put the size of the lynching crowd at 10,000 people. Mayor Edwards put it at 15,000.

These were warnings to other blacks that the white man is the boss. Oh, there were a lot of ways a man could die–especially a black man! The mob out in the streets below my window probably knew them all well and more. Victims had been lynched, burned at the stake, used for target practice, drowned–or they simply disappeared.[75]

Like a man in a stupor, I trudged back to my cell and sat on the edge of my bunk with my head in my hands, bowed, praying to God for some sort of deliverance, any kind, from this Valley of Death. Exhausted beyond words, I fell into a catnap. As soon as my eyelids closed, I was startled by the crashing and tinkling sound of broken glass. Several black prisoners rushed back to my cell, grabbed ahold of me, and shook me wide awake. They were so afraid that their blackness had turned a grayish-ashen color. Somehow I felt that this night had been set aside for me to face the gauntlet of death. The trumpet was sounding. The bells were tolling for me!

"Dey're chunkin rocks thru de windows!" Somebody shouted at me. "Get UP, get up, dey're trying to break into de jail!"

I sprang up from my bunk as if charged with electricity, ran as fast as I could up the corridor inside my cellblock, past rows of cells and out into the bullpen. All around me prisoners were rushing out of their cells into the corridor, scrambling, trying to look out the windows while dodging flying glass. I stopped at the very first window I came to and stole a look into the streets below. The crowd had grown out of proportion. The scene made me feel as if my whole body had turned to stone and the blood had stopped flowing in my veins.

A mob, huge, angry, stretching as far as I could see into the night in all directions greeted my sight. I had never seen so many white folks in my life. There were thousands of them. It was something I had not been able to picture in my mind's eye while guessing what it would really be like. This herd stretched out before me was no figment of my imagination. This was the real thing!

The white people of the town had gathered outside the county jail in anticipation of doing their thing. They were demanding from the sheriff those "three niggers" and from the tone of their voices, it was clear they were not going to be denied. They had gathered from all over the state of Indiana, from as far away as the northern and southern parts, to centrally located Marion. There were at least ten to fifteen thousand of them against three. The odds were fitting for the mentality of the crowd.

---

[75] Cameron does not exaggerate here. Newspapers of the times documented the brutality of lynchings, as did photographers (Allen et al., 2000).

Yells became louder. They stomped their feet. They cursed. They threw rocks at the windows as fast as they could draw back their arms. Some carried pistols, shotguns, high-powered rifles, sticks and stones. Others held torches, ropes, bats, clubs, pick handles, ax handles, crowbars, and anything else they could get their hands on to inflict their type of barbaric pain and torture. The whole town was, seemingly, driven by a reign of lawlessness and stark terror–and the law enforcement officers did not object to any of this.

I recognized a few faces from homes near my own neighborhood. I saw customers whose shoes I had shined many times. Boys and girls I had gone to school with were among them. People I had watched buying tickets regularly at the interurban station ticket window. People who had sold me foodstuffs in stores, and neighbors whose lawns I had mowed and whose cars I had washed and polished. These people populated the crowd around the jail.

"Burn the god-damn jail down!" they screamed.

"Open up, sheriff, or we'll tear your jail to pieces."

"Turn those black bastards, those animals over to us. Turn them loose!"

"We know how to treat black-assed niggers!"

"Them nigger sons-of-bitches!"

"Get those goddamn niggers out here!"

I found it hard to believe. It was terribly frightening. They were my neighbors. There were many people there whom I liked and (I thought) liked me, too. Had they changed? Or had I? Had the whole world gone stark, raving mad?

A thought entered my mind that the sheriff and policemen would come out of the jail and break up the crowd and send them back to their homes. Many in the crowd wore the headdress of the Ku Klux Klan, but without the patented white robes and a mask to hide their identity. Their faces were bare. Many of the Klan members could be seen acting as monitors in the crowd.[76] They had on their full regalia but their faces were bare, too. The whole event was a wide-open deal. There was a manner of gaiety

[76] The Klan had a strong presence in Marion during the early 1920s but went into decline after the Stephenson scandal in 1925 (p. 40). Newspapers of the day did not report a Klan presence at this lynching. Nonetheless, it is very likely that some of the lynch mob and spectators had been or still were members. Cynthia Carr (2006), a journalist who grew up visiting her grandparents in Marion, discovered that her grandfather had been a member and was present at the lynching. She went to Marion in 1994 to research his involvement and publish that story.

among the people in the crowd, a carnival atmosphere. The only things that seemed to be missing were vendors hawking peanuts, popcorn, and cracker jacks!

Presently, there came to my ears a loud roar, something like a cheer, as Sheriff Jacob Campbell emerged from the front door of the jail with his two pearl-handled revolvers strapped around his waist. He held up his hands for silence. The noise gradually subsided. "These are my prisoners," he said loudly. "Go home!"

Perhaps I imagined it, but I could not detect a note of sincerity in his voice.

The mob thundered its disapproval:

"We want those niggers–now!"

"We know they are in there!"

"Get the bastards out here!"

"We're going to hang every goddamn one of them!"

I stood frozen at the window. The sheriff looked awfully small and helpless against that huge, defiant crowd. Apparently he felt the same way because he quickly disappeared back inside the jail, slamming the door behind him.

Very shortly, four men in shirtsleeves left the front part of the jail and ran around to the rear, in the alley. A crowd followed after them. They carried five-gallon cans, which I suspected contained gasoline.

Panic-stricken all over again, I ran around the bullpen to the alley side of the jail, to another window, and looked down into the alley below. Fumes from the cans rose ominously. It was gasoline all right! The men were dousing the side of the jail with it, trying to set the building on fire!

Matches flared. Flames leaped along the wall of the jail, lighting up the demonic white faces. Within moments the flames sputtered out and the drenching began all over again. Matches flared again, and the gasoline burned brightly and fiercely, but the stone and brick building did not catch on fire. The men did not give up, though, until they had tried to burn the jail down four times and had run out of gas.

I prayed a prayer of thanks to God.

The group of devils in the alley returned to the front of the jail where the main body of the mob was increasing their demands for "them niggers."

I went back to the front window on the street side of the jail. My clothes were dripping wet with perspiration. Many of the other black prisoners were having sweating fits too. Most of them were looking out from other windows on the front side.

About fifty men had advanced to the front door of the jail. Most of them were armed with handguns and rifles, besides other "tools." Behind the locked doors, Sheriff

Campbell and a few of his deputies, along with a score or more of policemen from other cities, stood looking at the crowd. I found this out through the jail grapevine or scuttlebutt who informed the men in the cellblocks not to worry, that enforcement officials from Muncie, Kokomo, Anderson, Fort Wayne, Logansport, and Alexandria were standing guard.

I noticed a lot of uniformed policemen in the crowd, perhaps fifty of them! They were laughing and talking with members of the mob, acting like interested spectators. The bolder members of the mob were arguing with the officers inside, giving them hell, demanding Tommy, Abe, and me. "Go home," one of the out-of-town officers shouted from the inside, "or we'll shoot to kill!"

That's when Sheriff Campbell immediately swung into action. "No, no, no! Don't shoot! There's women and children out there! Don't shoot!" he ordered.

I did notice that most of those in the front lines were women and children, while the men seemed to lag behind. When the mob leaders heard the sheriff order the other officers not to shoot into the crowd, that was all the information they needed. It was as if they were acting on cue. "Get a sledge hammer!" one of the ringleaders ordered. The old tried and proven dodge had worked again for the white supremacists, as they surrounded themselves with their women and children to serve as a protective bulwark.[77]

A sledgehammer was produced as if by magic. A husky man in bib overalls and a battered felt hat began hammering on the brickwork around the front steel door. Each time the hammer came down and banged against the bricks and stone, the crowd roared its approval.

The door was strong. The man in the overalls was strong too. But after awhile he spent himself out and turned the hammer over to another large man, and the banging continued uninterrupted. The policemen inside the jail corridors with the sheriff were strangely quiet. The large number of uniformed policemen mingling with the crowd watched, said nothing and did nothing. The banging on the casement continued. The cheering went on louder and louder. As far as I could see, white faces with open

---

[77] It was common for women and children to attend lynchings and even actively participate. For two famous photographic examples, see the little girls in their Sunday best at the lynching of Rubin Stacy (in the Introduction to this book) and the little boys, one in a tie, beneath the dangling feet of Lige Daniels (Allen et al., 2000).

mouths screaming for blood, black blood, were whooping it up—yelling for *my* blood. A victory spirit was in the air.

In my cellblock, both white and black prisoners began offering words of encouragement to me. One of the black men standing at my elbow, pointed to a squad car parked on the jailhouse lawn. It was surrounded by members of the mob. My eyes followed a pointing finger—and I was shocked once more. Sitting astride the hood of the car and holding onto the radiator cap much like a cowboy sitting in the saddle, was Patrolman Neeley, whom everybody in town knew. My friends and I had been kidded by him many times whenever he saw us uptown. He was one of the friendliest cops on the force. Now he was still being friendly, swinging his feet, laughing and talking with members of the mob nearest him. I got the impression he was having one hell of a good time.

Suddenly, the mournful wail of sirens split the air. Four or five local fire trucks roared upon the scene and came to a skidding halt. Some of the crowd refused to move out of the way. Several of the trucks got close enough to hook their hoses to water plugs. "Watch out!" Somebody yelled. "They're gonna try and knock us down with water sprays!"

One of the firemen suggested that, if the hoses were cut, nobody could get sprayed. Members of the crowd clambered atop the trucks and in minutes every hose had been cut and sliced with pocketknives.

The huge men taking turns swinging the sledge hammer at the front of the jail, struck the door and its casing with massive John Henry blows. Racial hatred supplied them with the strength of a hundred Samsons. The mob behind them chanted impatiently, spurring the leaders on. The inevitable happened. For nearly an hour the door had stood up under the heavy and constant pounding. Now the bricks around it began to crumble into red dust and the limestone to ashes. They laid aside the sledgehammer and began yanking out the bricks and stones with their bare hands, hands which were bleeding from busted water blisters caused by the continuous gripping of the hammer handle. Four strong men grabbed ahold of the exposed edges of the door and actually ripped it out of its facing![78]

---

[78] In the 1940s, while Cameron was living in the neighboring town of Anderson, Indiana, he returned to Marion and interviewed two hundred witnesses to that night. Most of them had believed the rumor that he was dead, but were happy to see him alive. They undoubtedly provided some of the details that Cameron himself could not have seen from his cell.

The jubilant roar of the crowd all but shattered my ear drums. Angrily, the frenzied horde swarmed through the jagged opening, as irresistible as stampeding bulls. The Grant County jail in Marion, Indiana, was theirs! It was their prize to do with as they pleased! The mighty siege was over! To the victors belonged the spoils!

Inside the jail, in the wide corridors, the mobsters saw police officers armed with sub-machine guns, revolvers, shotguns, repeating rifles, and tear gas. Not one piece of this equipment was used to thwart the aim of the mobsters. Sheriff Campbell had not rescinded his order. No officer did anything.

The maddening throng stormed past the officers and rushed directly to the west wing of the first floor. There, they gathered around the door leading into the cellblock. Miraculously, one of the leaders produced a ring of keys. One of them would fit the steel-covered barred door leading into that wing. The sound of a voice came through the locked door. "Thomas Shipp," a voice from hell commanded above the roar of the crowd. "Get over here!"

None of the prisoners inside the cellblock moved. The mob shut off its roar abruptly. Long seconds seemed to pass. One of the prisoners coughed. Was it Tommy? Keys could be heard jangling ominously in the deathly silence. One of the men searching for the right key seemed confused. But they knew what they wanted. One of the men, in apparent disgust, came forward and showed which key was to be used to unlock the door. The door swung open in a creaky sound.

The leaders paused, momentarily, studying the frightened, ashen faces of six black prisoners in the cellblock. There were nine white prisoners incarcerated in the wing with them. The leaders' movements had become precise, deliberate. Some of them must have killed in this fashion before. They savored the moment before the kill. To them it was just a matter of time for Tommy. Forty or fifty men walked into the cellblock slowly, jamming the corridor in front of the row of cells, forming a column of death. The men behind the bars, in their respective cells, stared blankly at the procession. The mobsters asked for Tommy again. Still, nobody answered.

This was all a part of the game of superiority they were playing, however. They had already visited Tommy's cellblock as they had, no doubt, visited Abe's and mine. They knew who Tommy was and where he was. Finally, they walked back to the cell where Tommy stood. No questions were asked. They reached in and grabbed ahold of him with violent and merciless hands. He was beaten and kicked unmercifully. When he reeled and sagged to the floor, senseless, they dragged his limp body out of the cellblock.

From the second floor, I could see the bloodthirsty crowd come to life the moment Tommy's body was dragged into view. It seemed to me as if all of those thousands of people were trying to hit him at once. They surged forward, like trees swaying in a violent storm. In a matter of seconds, Tommy was a bloody mass and bore no resemblance to any human being. The mob kept beating on him just the same. Even after the long, thick rope had been placed around his neck, fists, clubs, sticks and stones continued to pummel his body. It was at once terrifying and sickening to watch. Yet, I couldn't turn my eyes away. Some irrepressible force held my gaze to the scenes being enacted in the streets below me. I was glad when they dragged Tommy's body around to the side of the jail, where the mob hung him from the window bars of the cellblock where Abe was locked up.

I was told that despite all of that inhuman beating, Tommy had regained consciousness just before they hung him from the window. He had actually returned from the dead. In that brief instance, the instinct of life flickered like a hurricane wind. He fought the mob, savagely, for a few seconds, only to be knocked out for good. The rope, looped through the bars of the window, did the rest.

The crowd cheered wildly, jumping up and down in an insane and intense excitement at Tommy's feeble writhings at the end of the rope. For all of twenty minutes, they pushed and shoved among themselves to get a closer look at the "dead nigger!" The spectacle whetted their murderous appetite. They began chanting for "another nigger!"

Again, the police officers in the corridor of the jail stood by, helplessly, as the mobsters stalked back inside the jail. They went directly to Abe's wing of the jail. It housed the cellblock where he was confined with twelve white men and an elderly black man. There was no reply. The same heavy silence that had settled over Tommy's cellblock engulfed Abe's.

"Aw right, Smith!" the leaders of the mob shouted. "You're next!"

The specter of death was everywhere. The grim reaper was in the form of many persons, young and old, men and women, ready, willing, and able to kill for their vaunted ideals.

"We want Abe Smith!" a voice from the crowd inside the jail called out.

"Ain't nobody heah by that name," one of the white prisoners lied.

Abe and the old man had hidden as best they could under the bunks in one of the rear cells. It was a poor hiding place. They were found at once. The old man was grabbed and yanked and dragged to his feet.

"Is your name Abe Smith, nigger?" one of the mobsters wanted to know. He was grinning when he asked the question as if he derived the most insatiable thrill out of being judge, jury and executioner.

"Naw, suh, boss," the old man whined, pitifully. "Not po' ole Henry!"

Just then, a tall, blond haired, lanky mobster edged his way forward through the mass of Klansmen. "Hell, no," he said. "This ain't Smith. This is old man Henry, and he's a good old nigger too!" Old man Henry smiled a faint smile of gratitude.

"Here he is!" someone called out, excitedly. Abe started fighting the mob right away. He knew what to expect having seen the mob desecrate and mutilate the body of Tommy before his very eyes as they hung him from the cellblock window. The mob pounced on Abe and beat him severely until he sagged into unconsciousness. Again, they dragged the body of another victim, his body torn and bleeding, onto the street.

The crowd came to life as it had done earlier, only more so. These who were not close enough to hit him threw rocks and bricks at him. Somebody rammed a crowbar through his chest several times.

I watched from my window upstairs knowing that Abe was dead before they hung him[79] on a tree in the courthouse square. He was hanged one block from the jail. Then the mobsters returned to the barred window where Tommy was hanging amid a bunch of souvenir hunters who had ripped off all the clothes from the lower part of his body. They tore his body down, covered it with one of the sheets that was worn by a full-dressed kluxer[80]. They dragged him by the rope around his neck, like a dead horse, through the street, to the same tree and hung him alongside Abe.

---

[79] Abe fought back under the lynching tree, according to Charlotte Vickery, an eyewitness interviewed by the British Broadcasting Corporation (BBC) in the documentary film *Unforgiven: Legacy of a Lynching* (Paul Sapin, 1995). She says that Abe tried to keep the ascending noose from tightening around his neck, so the lynchers had to let him down and break his arms before being able to hang him successfully. A video clip of her testimony can be viewed online (Kaplan, *An Iconic Lynching in the North*).

[80] As is common with eyewitness accounts, there are conflicting details. James Madison (2001) believes the white cloth was a torn feed sack, and the body it covered was that of Abram Smith. When Cynthia Carr (2006) asked Abe's brother Walter to identify him in the lynching photograph, his identification agreed with Cameron's.

The cheering began anew. It sounded much louder this time, more refreshed, more hilarious in tone. The people howled and milled around the lifeless bodies, their voices a mumble jumble of insane screams and giggles. As other members took pictures of the spectacle, they vied with one another to have their pictures taken alongside the tree showing the bodies of Abe and Tommy swaying in the breeze. After about fifteen minutes of celebrating, the mobsters started back toward the jail.

I knew I was the clean-up target!

CHAPTER NINE

The Miraculous Intervention

I could hear the tread of the mobsters tramping up the stairs to the second floor. In another moment they would be at the door of my cellblock. They would open the door, walk inside, and all hell would break out. Time was running out for me. Outside the door was a jamming bunch of violent, ruthless, black-hating white men. The men carried ropes, shotguns, knives, clubs, swords, and rifles. One of the men held a sub-machine gun in the cradle of his arm. He acted like he knew how to use it too. He was a big, husky, bushy-haired man with cold-looking eyes, glassy-looking, like he was on some kind of a "fix."

The men gathered around the door of my cellblock. They were the elite group of intimidators. Their act now was to complete the path of death, destruction, and tyranny. While they were deciding on their anticipated kill, I closed my eyes for a moment to will my disappearance. I opened them again when I heard the eerie jangling of keys on the key ring. I was still in the cellblock. There was no time to hide. There was no place to hide. Events happened so fast there was not even time to pray.

At the sight of the mobsters, the black prisoners began jumping around, apparently searching for cover in their miserable mental agony. Even the three white prisoners were nervous. All of the prisoners were just plain scared!

I was caught in a part of the cellblock with seven or eight other black prisoners. Big John was among them. Somehow I felt a small measure of safety with them so near. I believed with all my heart, perhaps because I wanted to believe it, that they would have fought the mob to their death had they anything with which to fight.

The man with the sub-machine gun entered the cellblock first. Oddly, a young white girl, very pretty, still in her teens, followed closely behind him. Her eyes were wide, like a frightened and startled doe. They seemed to be full of question marks and uncertainty. While the machine gunner held us in our tracks, several other men dressed in the headgear of the Ku Klux Klan flooded the cellblock with the others.

The corridor inside the cellblock was jammed tight with mobsters. They stood there, peering at the cowering knots of us prisoners.

Sheriff Campbell shouldered his way through the crowd. One of his service revolvers was dangling limply from his right hand. He was breathing hard and perspiring profusely. He paused, uncertain of his next move. There was a harried look about him.

Meanwhile, two men with drawn pistols had separated Charles (the other sixteen year-old boy) and me from the rest of the men. "What's your name?" Charles was asked.

"Charles Haynes" he answered shakily.

"Mine's Henry Burton," I blurted out without being asked what my name was. I was not about to give them my real name.

Sheriff Campbell made his way over to the small group of mobsters surrounding me and Charles. "Come on!" he said to the men, impatiently. "Let's get the hell out of here! These are nothing but boys. Cameron isn't in here, anyway. You've already hung two of them. That should satisfy you!" He then turned around and moved out of the cellblock.

The mobsters moved and shuffled about restlessly. They paced up and down in the cellblock, pondering their next move. Every reference they made to me was prefaced with an angry epithet: "That black-assed son-of-a-bitch! He thinks he's a smart nigger. We'll find him!"

Reluctantly, they withdrew from my cellblock and returned to the gay crowd down in the streets. I began to hope for the first time. Now, I had time to say a few prayers. I prayed for deliverance from my enemies.

One of the first mobsters to reach the crowd in the streets shouted out: "Cameron ain't in there!"

"That's a damn lie," came the angry response from the crowd. "He's in there and we aim to get him! We want him!"

The whole multitude seemed to yell its approval. They stomped their feet. They began chanting the way crowds do at a football game for their favorite action hero:

"We want Cameron!"

"We want Cameron!"

"We want Cameron!"

I thought I would die during that religious chant of the Ku Klux Klan. To think they wanted me that bad! I could have sworn my heart stopped beating with every chant. Again I prayed, wondering if any kind of a prayer would do any good. I wondered if Tommy and Abe believed in prayers and had they prayed to God, too, before their terrible deaths.

The noise being made in the streets by the crowd made it clearly understood that they were not going to accept anything less than the three of us: Tommy, Abe–and me! Repeated shouts, chants, demanding that I be dragged out of the jail, fell upon the ears of the leaders of the mob. I was the one person they wanted more than anything else in the world.

The ringleaders huddled together and talked briefly among themselves. They then turned around and re-entered the jail. The crowd thundered its approval. A point had been made and agreed upon. The cheers were wild with enthusiasm. I was it again!

The mobsters marched back upstairs to my cellblock. Again the machine gunner led the way inside. No one dared to breathe.

Inside the cellblock the machine gunner barked out an order, a command in a deadly tone of voice. "Aw right, all you niggers get over to this side of the cellblock." He pointed the barrel of his infernal gun to where he meant for us to line up.

We moved slowly, painfully, and formed a nervous, ragged, broken line of humanity along the wall of the wing. I tried to hold back the tears but they kept rolling down my cheeks. My own whimperings, though, were lost in a jungle of pitiful bleats from the black prisoners all around me. The mob might take one of them–or all of them! Who was there to stop them? Who was going to stop them? Law and order for the black people of America was nothing but a national farce, a complete mockery. It had always been that way. When would things ever change? Black people were not equals. The white people, the mob, made its own law and regulated its own order.

"James Cameron is in here and we mean to git him! NOW WHERE IN THE HELL IS HE?" members of the mob wanted to know.

An old black man in a tattered plaid shirt and baggy pants dropped to his knees. He held out his hands in supplication as if in prayer to God.

"Please, Mister White Folks," he sobbed. "Dat boy ain't in heah, honest he ain't!"

The mobsters didn't believe him. One of the mobsters kicked the old man in the face. The toe of the kluxer's shoe went into the old man's mouth, knocking him back against the steel bars of the cells. The old man spit out seven or eight bloody, rotten teeth. His face immediately took on a swelling, resembling a grotesque mask created by some make-up artist in some way-out horror movie.

"Don't you black-assed sons-of-bitches lie to us," one of the leaders shouted. "If you don't tell us which one of you is Cameron, we'll hang every goddamn one of you niggers in this jail."

I waited, afraid to move a muscle. Now the chips were down, really down. Now was the time to present myself as a living sacrifice. But nobody in the line moved. Heavy, labored breathing was the only sound. Impulsively, I acted like I was going to give myself up when Big John and another black man grabbed ahold of me and held me back. I got their message.

And outside the jail, the crowd had become very impatient. They took up their chant again: "We want Cameron! We want Cameron! We want Cameron!"

Human tension was racing to a climax. Human endurance was speedily approaching its capacity. Seven or eight of the black men glared their defiance at the mobsters. They had become too angry to remember their own fear—if they had any. But they were helpless and powerless to offer any kind of resistance to the mob. They stood with me.

One of the mobsters stepped forward and slugged one of the defiant men across the mouth with his fist, knocking him to his knees. Then all but the black prisoners standing with me broke ranks and fell down on their hands and knees. They began to crawl and grovel to members of the mob nearest them, like dogs welcoming their masters back from a trip.

One of the black prisoners standing nearby sprayed one of the groveling men with vomit. The latter ignored it and kept right on begging for mercy. The standee kept right on puking on him.

"Tell us where Cameron is or we are going to hang every goddamn one of you niggers!" the mobsters repeated their threat.

Still, nobody pointed me out. The crawlers renewed their sobs and pleas with increased fervor. They made every kind of obeisance to those representatives of the god of white supremacy. They hugged the mobsters' knees, kissed their hands, and begged them to spare their lives. Several of the men were bawling like little children lost in a frightening world. They begged with tongues thickened with stark terror. Tears rolled down their cheeks and into their gaping mouths.

"Lawdy, Mister Bossman, we ain't nothing but jist a bunch of po ol' niggers in heah for train riding. We ain't done nuttin."

"Lawd, ham mercy!"

"Please don't hurt us, Mister White folks!"

It was a sickening and unbelieving sight. I am sure I would not have believed it had it been told to me by someone. But I was there. I heard the words. I saw the scene. I felt all the anguish and anxiety the pleaders were going through.

"Please, don't hang us, Mister White Folks!"

"Aw right," a man with a shotgun called out. "Let's take all of these black bastards out and string up every goddamn one of them."

"No! no! no!" came a scream from one of the crawlers. It came from Charles' father. "Please! Please! Please! Don't hang us, Mister Bossman!" He hugged the man's knees and tried to kiss his hands, to caress him, to plead with him. A huge fist crashed down on the man's head, knocking him flat on the floor.

"God damn it, nigger! Tell us where Cameron is! This is your last chance, you damn fool!" the mobster shouted at the man in a fit of racial anger.

Still whimpering and pleading, Charles' father looked up at the mobsters around him. He looked at his son standing near me. He was a completely broken man in mind, body, spirit, soul, and heart. He lowered his head for a moment, as if in prayer. Then, slowly, painfully, it seemed, he turned eyes full of fear and anguish and surrender to the spot where I stood. His voice quavered. His whole body shook with the emotion of naked terror. Uncontrolled tears ran from his bruised and bloodshot eyes. The index finger on his gnarled hand was unsteady, shaking like a leaf in a windstorm, as he pointed to me!

"Dere he is!" he said finally, and slumped to the floor.

The other black men down on the floor on their hands and knees, now that the ice had been broken, sobbed out their agreement with Charles' father:

"Dat's him! Mister White Folks! Dat's him! It ain't none ob us! Dat's him!" All of them seemed to be babbling at once as I was being singled out for the mob.

For a brief second no one moved. But every eye in the cellblock was on me. Then the mobsters came in and took hold of me. The nightmare I had often heard about happening to other victims of a mob now became my reality. Brutally and dehumanizingly faced with death, I understood fully what it meant to be a black person in the United States of America.

They surged forward in one great lunge, knocking and trampling the black prisoners around me. Some of them got their hands on me, right away, three on each side, and then the merciless beating began. I tried to break out of their grasp, but there were too many of them. They beat and kicked me in the corner of my cellblock for several minutes before dragging me out of that part of the jail. Their grips were like bands of steel. They knew now how to hold a captive, because they had just lynched Tommy and Abe, my two buddies. I was in the clutches of the same murdering hands that had lynched them on a tree on the courthouse lawn.

All the way down the corridor outside my cellblock, all the way down the steel stairway, the angry pounding continued. So many clubs and hands were aimed and swung at me, they got in each other's way. Now and again, one of the men holding me would cry out in pain, but they never released their holds on me.

Somehow, not because I wanted to, I remained dimly conscious. Through a maze, a thick haze mixed with my own blood, I saw the crowd come to life as we emerged from the jail.

"Here he comes!" they shouted.

"It's him!"

"They got Cameron!"

"We got him!"

"We got him!"

"We got him!"

The crowd pushed and shoved for a chance to get close enough to hit me. Only a few were successful, it seemed. I was too weak to fight back anymore. The cruel hands that held me were like vises. I sagged and reeled lifelessly, but I still did not completely pass out. More fists, more clubs, more bricks and rocks found their mark on my body. Only the strongest and the biggest were able to get in close enough to inflict inhuman pain. The weaker ones had to be content with spitting on me and throwing things at me. Some of those holding me caught spit in their faces as much as I did. Little boys and girls, not yet in their teens, but being taught by their peers and neighbors how to treat black people, somehow managed to work their way in close enough to bite and scratch me on the legs.

And over the thunderous din rose the shout: "Nigger, nigger, nigger!" Again and again the word rang out until it seemed as if that was the only word in the English language that held any meaning in their lives. A crowbar thumped against my chest. A pick handle crashed down against the side of my head.

"I haven't done anything to deserve this," I heard myself mumbling, weakly. My voice was barely audible coming through bruised and swollen lips. I barely heard myself. No one else could hear me. I was too numb by that time to feel the pain anymore. The cruel and merciless blows that continued to fall no longer held any meaning. Once or twice, I thought I saw a kind face in the press around me. To each of them I called out for some kind of help while, at the same time I gave to others a pitiful look, imploring mutely for mercy at their hands. But nothing happened. The mob mauled me all the way up to the courthouse square. Not once did they stop pounding on me.

Many uniformed policemen of the Marion Police Department helped the mob to clear a path through the swarming thousands of people so that they could get me all the way up to the tree where Tommy and Abe were hanging in shredded clothing.

"Where's the rope?" somebody called out the question.

I felt my stomach shrinking. My whole body felt as if it was encased in ice packs. I was shocked into something approaching full consciousness. What a way to go!

I screamed as loud as I could above the din and the roar of the crowd that I had raped no woman. I had killed nobody!

Rough hands grabbed my head and stuffed it into a large noose. The rope was handled so roughly until it caused a rope burn on my neck. For a moment I blacked out. I recovered in a moment, though, as they began shoving and knocking me closer to the tree and under the limbs weighed down with the half-stripped bodies of Tommy and Abe.

Now was my Judgment Day! All my days and nights seemed to flash before me in my mind's eye. I remembered what my mother had told us about sinners facing death, about the thief on the cross with Christ: "The Lord will forgive and have mercy on their souls if only the sinners will call on Him!"

I knew I had nothing to lose and everything to gain. "Lord," I mumbled through puffed lips, "forgive me my sins! Have mercy on me!" I stopped thinking then. In my own mind's eye I was already dead and was glad to be leaving a world filled with so many false and deceitful people.

One end of the rope snaked out, sailed up out of the mob and fell across the limb of the tree. But before the crowd could hang me, it happened! A voice rang out above the deafening roar of the mob. It was an echo-like voice that seemed to come from some place far, far away. It was a feminine voice, sweet, clear, but unlike any voice, any sound, I had ever heard. It was sharp and crisp, like bells ringing out on a clear, cold, winter day.

"Take this boy back. He had nothing to do with any raping or killing!"

That was all the voice said!

Abruptly, impossibly, a deadening, deafening quiet settled down over the mob as if they had been struck dumb. No one moved or spoke a word. I stood there in the midst of thousands of people and as I looked at the press around me, I thought I was in a room where a photographer had strips of film negatives hanging from the walls to dry out. I couldn't tell whether the images on the film were white or black, there were just images of the mobsters on filmstrips that surrounded me everywhere I looked. Time stood still for that one instance. The maddening fury of that mob had been quelled in the twinkling of an eye. A young eternity passed as I stood there like one hypnotized.

Then the room full of negatives disappeared, and I found myself looking into the faces of what had been, moment ago, images. And hands that had already committed cold-blooded murder became soft and tender, kind and helpful. I could feel the hands that had beaten me unmercifully removing the rope from around my neck! Now they were caressing hands! The angry press of men, women, and children around me melted instantly, miraculously! I suddenly found myself standing alone, under the death tree–mystified!

The mob had drawn back as if I had some sort of a plague. Many heads were bowed. A path had opened from the tree on the courthouse lawn where I stood to the steps of the county jail. Slowly, painfully, I started limping back toward the jail, dragging myself as best I could. Each step was a prayer and each prayer was a "thank you, Jesus!"

No one touched me on the way. No one called out any angry racial epithets. I looked into the faces as I limped along. They were tired, serious faces now, with shame staring out of their eyes. Their gazes invariably dropped when their eyes met mine.

I do not pretend to understand the why of this event. For even though the voice had sounded so clearly in my own ears, no one else in the mob heard it! Yet all obeyed its command at that instance. I later interviewed hundreds of men, women and children who said they had been in the crowd that night. Not one of them said they heard that voice! Their explanation was, "You were just lucky!" [81]

But there is no doubt in my mind that I heard it. I DID HEAR THAT VOICE! It called out strained and sincere, with a definite note of command in its tone. I can still

---

[81] Madison (2001) reports some eyewitnesses saying that Sol Ball (the uncle of the woman allegedly raped) stood on top of a car and shouted the words that saved Cameron. Some others claimed it was Rex George, head of the local American Legion. Carr's research points to Marion Police Captain Charles Truex as the savior (2006). She also cites the NAACP's field secretary, Walter White, who investigated the lynching just days after it occurred. White credited the rescue to Truex, as well as to pleas from Jimmie and two white friends (boys aged fourteen and sixteen).

hear it sometimes. Thousands of times I have asked myself why did I only hear that voice? I am convinced that I did not imagine it, that no person in the mob spoke those words. No mere mortal could have commanded such obedience and submission from that angry ten to fifteen thousand white supremacists. For that voice had spoken only once and the raging fury of that mob was instantly kind and gentle and understanding. The mobsters rendered full obedience to the command of that voice. Perhaps, I have told myself, they had tired of wanton and malicious killings. Maybe it had been because I looked so much younger than Tommy and Abe. I can give no explanation. But in my own mind I believed and still believe that God answers prayers. Praise His name!

When I reached the steps of the front of the county jail, Sheriff Campbell took me by the arm and supported my sagging body. He led me downstairs to a basement complex.

I was still sagging and reeling, groggy and wobbly. All of my clothes had been torn to shreds. I was black and blue with bruises and ugly swelling marks on my body. I could barely stand and walk. A tiredness weighed heavily on me as though I could have laid down and closed my eyes and slept forever. I could not understand why I had remained in some kind of a conscious state throughout the terrible beating I had received. Silently, I gave thanks to God for my deliverance.

When Sheriff Campbell and I reached the bottom of the basement stairs in the county jail, he told me "The militia is arriving in town, boy, and we're going to try and get you out of here."

Of course, it was too late for that. He had had all day long to get the three of us out of the jail to a place of safekeeping but had chosen to keep us there in the jail at Marion under his so-called protection.

We made several turns in a maze of dimly lit passageways before the sheriff led me up to a solid steel door. He opened it, stepped outside and peered into the darkness. At last he beckoned me to him. He seemed as frightened and uncertain as I was. He couldn't have been pretending.[82] The awesome spirit coming from the sheriff communicated itself to me. I approached the door, cautiously, and stepped outside, about three feet from the door. I stood there with the sheriff.

---

[82] Sheriff Campbell may have been scared of the repercussions for him, because, at that time, an Indiana law provided stiff penalties for a sheriff who allowed a mob to remove prisoners from his jail.

National guardsmen in regular army khaki uniforms and battle helmets were beginning to surround the jail.[83] The sight of them infuriated the mob into a hysterical mass. The soldiers got them under control in a hurry. They began pushing and shoving and clubbing those nearest them. The belligerents among the hanging mob put forth a last ditch stand. Skulls were cracked, right and left, by army rifles. The solders kicked the people out of the way as fast as they could get to them. "Get the hell off the streets, you bastards!" the troops told the crowd. They were a teed-off bunch of young fellows. "Move back, you sons-of-bitches, and be quick about it," they swore at the members of the crowd.

I could see army trucks with soldiers at attention behind 50-caliber machine guns mounted on the trucks as they jockeyed for position around the jail. Bayonets were affixed to rifles the soldiers held in their hands. They forced the mob away from the jail, knocking them down as fast as they could get to the stubborn ones, shoving them back any way they could get ahold of them, swearing at them every inch of the way. They never asked the same member of the crowd to do something twice.

The sheriff and I stepped back inside the jail and closed the door. He just stood there with a frightened look in his eyes. Perspiration ran from the top of his head as if someone had opened a water spigot on it. He opened the door a little when the diminishing roar of the crowd told him that that side of the jail had been cleared. In a few moments he closed the door and looked at me. He was breathing hard, as if having difficulty. He was nervous and fidgety, and tried to look apologetic, like a drunk person trying to look sober. Guilt was written all over his face. I studied him, wondering what was on his mind. "See that car parked at the curb out there?" he asked me.

I stuck my head out of the door and saw a black sedan that had been placed at the curb. "Yes, sir." I told him.

---

[83] What Cameron saw were the police officers and sheriff's deputies from nearby cities and counties that arrived to surround the jail about an hour after the lynching. According to several area newspapers, Sheriff Campbell had called his colleagues for reinforcement. The National Guard would not arrive for another two days.

On August 8th, the morning after the lynching, the NAACP led by Flossie Bailey met with Mayor Edwards. Edwards called the governor's assistant, L.O. Chasey, and asked him to send troops. He, too, was rebuffed. Later that day, however, Sheriff Campbell called and told Chasey that he feared violent retaliation from Marion's black community. The National Guard arrived early the next morning and stayed for three days, until Smith and Shipp were buried.

"My deputy and three out-of-town policemen are going to try and get you out of here for safekeeping."

When he had finished telling me this bit of news, I heard the sound of footsteps behind me. I glanced over my shoulder. A giant of a man in shirtsleeves approached me and the sheriff. The man stood over six feet and six inches tall and looked like a mountain of solid muscle. His face was ruddy and damp, and he was hatless, an egghead. A large pistol hung from a scabbard at his hip. He stared at me with mixed emotions until the sheriff pulled him aside and gave him his orders. Whether he would obey them or not would be another matter.

When the briefing was over, the man turned to me and said "You wait here!" He emphasized what he meant and where he meant by pointing his forefinger at the spot where I was standing. He then opened the steel door and walked down the concrete ramp to the sidewalk where the black car was parked at the curb. Sneakingly, like a thief, he glanced around then quickly slid into the car behind the steering wheel. He looked over his shoulder and gave the sheriff a signal.

"Get into that car as fast as you can, son," the sheriff ordered me.

I looked out the door instinctively. No one was in sight. The national guardsmen had cleared that side of the jail all right, but I could still hear the crowd yelling and swearing back at the soldiers on the front side of the jail, as the troops forced them still farther away.

I bolted down the ramp and jumped into the rear of the sedan. It was a big, black, shiny new Studebaker, a free wheeler. I sat alone on the backseat. On my right side I noticed two high-powered rifles and an automatic shotgun resting against the door.

About a minute went past. Then three plainclothesmen in shirtsleeves sauntered up to the sedan and got inside, one up front with the driver and two in the backseat with me.

"Get your black ass down on the floor!" one of the men ordered me.

I didn't know it then, but I was in for a round of brutal insults.

I slid down to the floor of the car. They covered me with the floor mat. The motor came to life with a roar, and the car leaped forward in its pick-up, tires squealing loudly as if to give the escape a public notice. Swiftly, silently, the car whisked through the dark, turbulent night. Where? I had no idea. I didn't know where they were taking me. I feared the worst. For all I knew, my so-called saviors might have something in store for me, carefully planned, that would make whatever actions the mob could have done to me seem minor.

I hugged the floor and listened to the crude conversation flowing between the front seat and back seat. "They really beat the shit out of that Smith nigger. He had holes in him like a sieve!"

"Yeah, and they beat the hell out of that other black-assed nigger too, before they broke his neck!"

Just then a foot kicked the mat under which I was covered and a voice asked, "Were you scared, nigger?" The officers seemed to relish the act of calling me a nigger. I fumed. I thought if I had been disrespectful to them and had called them obnoxious names, I would have no legitimate complaints when they insulted me. But there I was, not wishing to bother anyone, and all they could think of was to ask me a damn stupid question.

Hell, yes, I was scared! I wanted to tell them not to call me white folk's names like that. Instead I answered "Yes, sir."

"They really beat the shit out of your black ass, didn't they?"

I nodded my head. There they go again, I thought, always trying to dehumanize people who were different from them.

One of the detectives in the backseat chuckled loudly and deeply. "This nigger back here is as white as a sheet!" he chortled.

All of them had a good laugh over that remark.

There was a period of silence. The quietness was broken by the sound of a question being asked. "Is this the way?" the driver wanted to know.

"Yes. Turn off here, to your right, and go over to the main street," came the answer.

I shifted my cramped position under the floor mat covering me and peeped out through an opening my fingers had discovered at the bottom of the window on my left. The men in the back seat seemed relaxed. My eyes roved up to the top of the car and then out of the window. I saw a large silo with a sign on it that read: HUNTINGTON FOOD STORE.

"Oh! we're in Huntington!" I blurted out like a damn fool.

"How in the hell do you know you're in Huntington? You must have been here before. We had a couple of niggers who came over here last month and they stole a slew of chickens, some Rhode Island Reds, Plymouth Rocks, and White Leghorns, and I'll bet you're one of those damn niggers," one of the officers said.

"No, sir, not me," I hastened to assure him. "I've never been here before."

"You're a damn black-assed liar! How did you know you were in Huntington?"

"I just saw that sign that read Huntington Food Store, and I guessed that's where we are."

By this time, the sedan had made several sharp turns and finally came to a halt in front of a small red brick building. The detectives got out of the car. "Aw right, nigger," one of them said to me. "Let's get inside!"

I could tell it was a jail as soon as I saw the bars covering the windows. A deep weariness had come over me. I was so tired of the ride underneath the floor mat of the car, of the racial insults, the horrible beating I had received at the hands of the mob. I got out of the car stiffly, and was led up the front steps of the building. The jailer turned on the lights and recognized the detectives before opening the door. He had been sleeping. He swore angrily about the urgent knockings that had awakened him.

"What in the hell is coming off here?" he wanted to know. "Is this one of them damn niggers from that mess over in Marion?" He was sure that I was one of the boys.

"Yes. The mob hung two of the niggers and beat the hell out of this one before they turned him loose. They even had a rope around his neck and wouldn't lynch him! We had orders to bring him here for safekeeping–just in case the mob changes their minds about him," the officers told the turnkey, winking their eyes as if enjoying some joke.

One of the men grabbed my head and bent it over so the jailer could see the rope burn made by the mob when they snuffed my head inside the noose.

"Hell! I don't want him in here," the jailer snorted at my rescuers. He was a small, wiry, wrinkled man with bluish-gray hair and a cantankerous air, which somehow made him seem likeable. "They might find out he's here and come over here and tear my jail down!" He was raising hell in a humorous sort of way. The detectives got a big laugh out of him.

They locked me up in a cigar box type cell. The jail was much smaller than the one in Marion. It had only six cells, three on each side with a hallway in between. The middle cell was unoccupied.

There was a young white girl in one of the cells across the aisle. She seemed to be crazy, sitting there wringing her hands with a look of grievous suffering. She stared in space with vacant eyes in an agitated state of mind. She didn't say a word. She didn't even know I was there.

The other cell was occupied by an elderly white man. The man's head was covered with a short white hair. His face was withered and thin, very wrinkled. Every look at him showed evidence of many years of living. His eyes were at once wise and sad. They were the eyes of a saint. This old man had a few words to say:

"Son, I am sorry for what happened over in Marion to you and your folks," he began as soon as we were alone. "I couldn't help overhearing the police who brought you here talking about the lynchings to the turnkey. People here in Huntington knew a lynching had been planned for Marion since early this morning. My son and I had a fight, because I tried to reason with him, tried to make him understand why he should stay out of Marion and not run off to see people killed like that. For all I know, he might have been one of the actual participants in the mob. He might have been the one who put that rope around your neck and caused that rope burn. He had me arrested and put in jail. Told everybody I was crazy. I am sorry, son, sorry to my heart."

"I know I never taught my son to act like that," he went on sadly. "And God is my judge. Maybe someday people will grow up and stop hating other groups of people as much as they do. Please believe me when I say I am sorry, son, when I say I am really sorry!"[84]

He was the sorriest man I had ever met. I could think of nothing to say to the gentleman. The old man said it all. I stood there staring at him, hoping in a way that he knew I understood what he was talking about. Finally I turned away from him and began pacing the floor of my cell. I walked back and forth till daybreak began creeping in. Every time a car passed by I would jump to the window to look at the occupants. Each flashing beam of headlights made me wonder if it was a car from Marion with mobsters searching for me.

---

[84] There have always been white people who opposed the tradition of lynching, including in Marion, as we have seen. It can be hard for individuals to resist peer pressure and oppose practices that are strongly upheld by their community. This old man paid a price for protesting the lynching to his son.

CHAPTER TEN

Safe at Last?

At daybreak, the detectives came for me. They were the same insulting characters who had brought me to Huntington. I was led from my tiny cell to the rear seat of the same automobile that brought me there. They covered me with the same floor mat. As the car began to roll one of the men said "We're going back to Marion, nigger!"

This news sounded strange and frightening to me. I was even more afraid to ask them why they were taking me back to Marion. Instinctively I braced myself for another round of insults, however the trip back to Marion proved uneventful. Maybe the officers had their fill ridiculing me the night before. At any rate, we rode on in silence. I wondered about the silence and what they could be thinking. I wondered if the mess I was in would ever be straightened out.

When the car reached the city limits of Marion, it stopped. My nerves grew taut. The men in the car checked their revolvers. Those in the rear seat with me had their guns pointed downward, toward the floor mat that covered me, as they checked their artillery. Then they placed handguns in their laps. Would they shoot anybody who tried to take me away from them? Or, would they, too, fear the lawless men in the crowd. Maybe they would just say "Here he is, come and get him!"

"Well, here we are back in Marion again," one of the men said later.

I was already chilled to the bone from the brisk morning air and that statement made my body temperature drop even lower. Marion was the last place in the world I wanted to be, but it was the best place in the world I could think of to be from.

"Drive around the courthouse square," the driver was directed.

I could hear the newsboys hawking and selling extras:

"READ ALL ABOUT IT! MOB LYNCHES TWO NEGROES HERE LAST NIGHT! READ ALL ABOUT IT! EXTRA! EXTRA! EXTRA!"

Figure 29. The imposing Grant County Courthouse, its dome topped by a statue of Lady Liberty, on the square at the heart of Marion's downtown, circa 1900. By 1930 the small maple trees surrounding it had grown large enough to hold the lynched bodies of Abe and Tommy. *Marion Public Library Museum*

I hugged the floor of the car a little tighter.

"Hey paper boy," one of the detectives called out as the car rolled to a halt. "Bring me a paper!" After the man got the paper, he pulled back the mat covering me and told me to take a look at the news. I raised my head and looked. On the front page was a picture of Tommy and Abe, with ropes around their necks, swinging from limbs of the tree. Below them were many upturned faces, pointing and laughing at the spectacle. The picture and the words in the paper blurred as anger swelled inside me. I shoved the paper aside in disgust, hating every white man in the world. I was sick with rage, a killing rage, and silently swore my revenge. Someday, when the prejudice of the world turned against the white man, I hoped to be around.

The driver drove around the courthouse square. "Those niggers are still hanging on the tree," he remarked in a matter-of-fact tone of voice.

"Yeah, and look how their necks have stretched," came a comment from one of the men in the car.

I raised myself off the floor to see Tommy and Abe. I was sorry I did. It was a gruesome sight. I felt like vomiting. I couldn't control my tears.[85]

At that precise moment, one of the detectives grabbed me by the top of my head and shoved me down, roughly, like ramming rags in an already filled bag. He swore hotly at me: "You god-damn son-of-a-bitch! You keep your black ass down on that floor before this mob sees you! I ain't gonna get hurt protecting a damn nigger like you!"

"I tell you what we ought to do," another detective suggested. "Let's get a twenty-foot rope and put it around this nigger's neck and turn him loose! Then if he can get through the mob, we'll let him go free!"

All the occupants of the car exploded in wild laughter. What a wonderful suggestion! They kicked the mat under which I was covered and asked me whether I would like such an arrangement. I didn't answer them. My cup was running over. I was too angry to speak a word. Every foul epithet I had ever heard in my life was pressing hard against my teeth, ready to explode. Had I been crazy enough to allow them to pass my lips, I felt they would have been more than enough for my immediate death at their hands, right there in that car. I bit my lips until they bled. I held my hands tightly. I was a one-man mob inside my gut. I wanted to kill a white man! Any white man would do!

I heard one of the men say that the National Guard had come all the way to Marion from Fort Benjamin Harrison in Indianapolis, sixty-eight miles away, in forty-eight minutes.

We left Marion and drove on down through Alexandria, then Anderson, and, finally, to the State Reformatory at Pendleton. This was on a Friday morning. The sedan pulled up in front of the administration building, an imposing red brick structure, which rose

---

[85] The bodies of Tommy and Abe were left hanging until around 5:30 a.m. the next day. Some young people tried to light fires under the bodies, but they were hung so high that the fires just scorched them, according to one newspaper. Throughout the night, spectators came and went. Some took pictures with their personal cameras, photographs that apparently have been hidden away in Marion attics. Many took pieces of clothing and body parts as souvenirs. One man took Abe's shoe to exhibit in his shop window. Another took a toe. Many took small pieces of the hanging ropes. When nothing else was left, people stripped pieces of bark and whole limbs from the hanging tree (Carr, 2006).

No Marion undertaker would handle the bodies, so a black mortician from nearby Muncie came to care for them.

four stories high. [86] Two of the detectives got out of the car and disappeared inside the building. A few minutes went past. Then one of the men came out, got me and marched me through the swinging thick glass entrance doors. Our noisy footsteps echoed noisily on the terrazzo floor. We stopped at the nearest window in the wide corridor. The word CLERK was printed in bold black letters against a white background over the top of the window. A thick-jowled man in steel-rimmed spectacles peered out at me. He was an old man.

Figure 30. The entrance to the Indiana Reformatory. (Baird, *History of Clark County, 1909*)

"What's your name?" he wanted to know in a rasping voice.

"James Cameron."

"Age?"

"Sixteen."

"Address?"

"31st and Popular Streets, Marion, Indiana."

---

[86] The Indiana Reformatory lies some fifty miles south of Marion. It was built in 1923 on thirty-one acres of land using inmate labor. The prison housed about 1600 maximum- and 200 minimum-security prisoners. Now called the Pendleton Correctional Facility, it remains in use today. Inmates today work for private industries, making clothing and doing laundry, just as Jimmie would eventually do.

By this time at least twenty guards of the institution had gathered in that part of the building, which I later learned was the guards' hall. They began to crowd around me. They wore dark blue, policeman-like uniforms. It was at a time in the morning when they changed guards. Some of them were laughing at the way my clothes had been ripped off, shredded as if they had gone through a sauerkraut machine, and at the way they heard I had been beaten by the mob. A couple of them wanted to know how it felt to have a rope around my neck. Others commented at the unnatural ashen whiteness of my complexion. Still others wanted to see my rope burn.

While this bunch of men were enjoying themselves at my expense, another bunch of guards had entered the scene. They were altogether a different group. They failed to see any humor in my predicament. The difference between them and the bunch ridiculing me was as great as day is from night. They were the ones I noticed most of all. They were human beings who simply stared at me from a distance. And the more they stared at me, the more the tears trickled down their cheeks from sorrowful eyes. They were tears they could not control. They were tears they could not hide. They were tears they were not ashamed to shed. They were tears shed for me!

That old white gentleman back there in the jail at Huntington and those white guards standing there crying over my misfortune were the first white people I had seen in a long time who really seemed to care. Somehow, all my life it seemed to me to be the most important incident in my life: for me to remember those tears and who shed them for me. They are etched in my memory, stamped upon my heart. It is something that happened in my life that offers a special source of moral strength for my soul during trying times. I can't erase those pictures from my brain.

After answering the clerk's questions, I was turned over to one of the guards who had poked fun at me. The man escorted me to a huge steel-barred cage only a few feet away from the window. A big barrel-chested, red-faced and balding young man was on duty in the cage. I heard the guards call him "Baldy." Baldy pulled a lever and turned a large wheel resembling a steering wheel on an automobile. I could hear the gears on the unit meshing noisily at the top and bottom of the massive steel gate as it slid open on a track rail. The big gate banged shut as if a huge trap had been sprung. Baldy seemed to get a great kick out of seeing it close like that. There, inside the cage, he searched me and my guard. Then he returned to his control panel. The other side of the cage slid open and the guard led me through the Guard Hall, out through the prison yard, and on down to the guardhouse.

In the guardhouse I was taken to a shower room in the front of the building. When I had finished taking a refreshing bath, another guard doused my head with kerosene and handed me a glob of Blue Ointment to rub on various parts of my body that might have become infected with vermin. While I was being deloused, several white inmates in gray dungarees were busy placing a hospital bed, mattress and chair in one of the narrow cells nearby. This was a part of the prison known as the "Hole." One of its punishment quarters was to be my safekeeping cell.

A pair of freshly laundered coveralls were handed to me. After putting them on, I was led to my cell. With the bed and chair on one side of the room and a toilet commode on the other, my floor space amounted to something like one by four feet. Most of the time I was compelled to lay across the bed. There was more room there than on the floor. There was a small opening, about as large as an eight by ten picture frame, high up near the ceiling, which served as a window. I had to stand on a chair or on top of my bedstead to look out of the opening. It was higher than any window I had ever seen.

I noticed my drinking cup was a can originally made for some other purpose, probably an oiler, or for the placing of flowers on some grave. It was cone-shaped and stood about ten inches high, like a giant ice cream cone. It was all rusted inside. I called for the guard and asked him for another cup and something to eat. But my request wasn't necessary. The guard had already made such arrangements. He replaced my rusted container with a brand new, shiny tin cup, which inmates had made in the tin shop. Presently a steaming hot meal of dried hash, gravy and milk was brought to me by the guard. It was much better than the food that had been offered in the jail at Marion. At least I could eat it. That was the first time in about fifty hours that I had been able to eat and rest. I slept like a dead man.

The relief man had to wake me for lunch. I had large chunks of stewed beef, potatoes, gravy, syrup, milk and bread. I did not leave a crumb on my plate. I felt like a new man when I had finished. But I was still hungry when the guard came to pick up the plates.

My body was reacting to the sustained nervous strain I had undergone. I was slowly quieting down inside, but very, very slowly. I examined myself all over. My body was one huge sore lump, with black and blue marks all over it. No bones had been broken, and, surprisingly, there were only a few lacerations. Yet I felt that something was seriously wrong with me. I thought I knew what it was but couldn't put my finger on it.

Then it dawned on me–my head was aching! That's what it was! It had been aching all along, a dull but persistent pounding ache.

I had been brought to the Reformatory on a Friday morning. The next day after a deep sleep, I woke up early. A dream of a mob storming the Reformatory walls had disturbed me. I awoke restless, nervous, and on the verge of screaming my head off. The veins in my body acted as if they wanted to push through my skin. I got out of the bed, walked to the door of my cell, and rapped on the bars with my tin cup. The guard came back to see what was the matter. I figured if I had something to read it might take my mind off the present for a little while. I asked the guard for some literature to read.

Very shortly, he returned from the prison library and handed me an assortment of books and magazines. Among them were the Holy Bible, *Up From Slavery*, and *Pilgrim's Progress*. Immediately after breakfast I commenced reading Booker T. Washington's autobiography.[87]

I was still nervous and tired. Lying there on my bed reading, I became drowsy. It was an effort to keep my eyes open. I had just blinked my eyes, it seemed, when all of a sudden, I bolted upright in my bed. I listened, motionless, afraid to even breathe. Sure enough, I heard it again and again and again! There was no doubt about it. There was only one other place in the world where I had heard an uproar like that before–in the jail back in Marion, when the maddening crowd had screamed for my blood. The shouting grew louder and louder.

Frantically I jumped out of bed with a prayer on my lips. I grabbed my chair and placed it against the rear of my cell under the little window. I had to turn my head sideways to get even a partial view of the prison yard. I couldn't see anything or

---

[87] In *Up From Slavery: An Autobiography* (1901), Booker T. Washington recounts his life as a slave child during the Civil War, his struggle to get a college education, and his establishment of Tuskegee Institute (a college and vocational training school that aimed to help the newly emancipated black population pull themselves up by their bootstraps). The school Washington founded is now Tuskegee University. *Up From Slavery* was named the third of the one hundred best nonfiction books of the 20th century by Modern Library. Cameron kept a copy in his personal library until the day he died.

Pilgrim's Progress by John Bunyan was published in 1678 in England. It is an allegorical tale about a man named Christian and his companions who experience various trials and temptations on their way to the Celestial City (heaven). Since the 17th century, it has been a classic on how to live a Christian life and one of the most widely read books in the English language.

anybody. There was no life in the courtyard. Maybe the mob hadn't battered down the three-feet thick, thirty-five feet high walls yet!

Reaching for my cup, I rapped on the cell door again. The guard came back immediately and opened the door. My frightened eyes bore into his, searching for sincerity, truthfulness, decency and the milk of human kindness.

"What's all that yelling about? Where is that shouting coming from?"

He, too, had defined the look in my eyes, a look bordering on the edge of insanity. His voice was calm, deadly serious, reassuring, as he put me at ease. "It's only a ballgame, sonny. It's not a mob. We have a ballgame in here every Saturday. That sound you keep hearing are the visitors and the prisoners whooping it up, letting themselves go."

I was relieved to hear that bit of news but my whole day was ruined. I could not get my mind back on my books. I kept thinking of Tommy and Abe hanging on that tree back in Marion, and but for the grace of God, I could have been hanging there with them.

Several days passed. I lost track of time. But of one thing I felt certain, time had ended for me under that tree on the courthouse lawn in Marion, Indiana.

CHAPTER ELEVEN

Big Emotions

One evening the guard came back to my cell and took me out for a walk, up and down outside the guardhouse, on the south side. It was on one of those walks three days later that I learned I had company in the guardhouse. He was a white man named Bill Williams. Bill had been in safekeeping for quite some time.

He was a 28 year-old rugged six-footer with close-cropped blond hair. He had a scowl on his face that seemed permanent. He had been a policeman on the force in Indianapolis. The badge he had worn had been used as a shield for burglaries and, finally, murder. The law enforcement officials in Naptown had placed him in the Reformatory to await trial. They were afraid some of his many friends on the police force might try to help him escape at the county jail.

I would play catch with Bill. We used a softball loaned to us by the guard during these outings. When the guard wasn't paying much attention, we were able to sneak snatches of conversation. That's how I found out about Bill's adventures as a burglar and a thief. He told me when he'd get off duty late at night, he often slipped back to his beat and broke into buildings he had been casing while guarding them earlier on duty. He bragged to me that the police department in Indianapolis was baffled for over a year by his escapades. However one night another policeman, an honest and dedicated one, caught him in the act of burglarizing a store. There was a shoot-out and he killed the other policeman!

Bill figured he had little chance of escaping the electric chair. Desperation was in his every glance and gesture. If there was any way to break out of the Indiana State Reformatory, I felt sure he would find it. His actions and talk made me nervous and scared.

The fresh air helped me a lot, but my head kept aching for a long time. I was afraid my eyes were going to pop out of their sockets. Why didn't that pain go away? Why did my head have to hurt all the time? I wondered if I was going crazy.

More days inched along with me not knowing from one day to the next just what was being done in my case. I did a lot of thinking. There was nothing to do but read, think, and remember.

I remembered a class play in which I had appeared in school. It was the story of a youth who, after graduating from high school, decided that he had enough education. He was not going any further in school. He was going to get a job and make some money right away. After the graduation exercises he knew his classmates frowned on his intentions. They were startled by his revelation. All of them wanted him to continue in school because the class planned a reunion in twenty years.

But he had made up his mind and was going to stick to his decision to drop out of school. He went home and retired early that day, but for some strange reason sleep would not come to him. He tossed and squirmed in his bed until from sheer exhaustion he dozed off. It was a troubled sleep that engulfed him.

What a dream he had that night! He dreamed of the class reunion twenty years into the future. Most of the class were present. John, Bertha, Susie, and Henry were all deceased. But Walter was a very successful real estate broker; George was famous as a chemist; Grace was a registered nurse; Louis was a partner in a prosperous law firm; David was a noted brain surgeon; Charles was a general manager of a large industrial plant in a Midwestern city; James was a successful writer with several of his works having been made into movies; Bill was a captain of detectives; Bart was a vice-president of a large banking house, and Norman owned three drugstores.

Everybody except him had achieved a certain degree of success. He had nothing to show his classmates. Immediately after his graduation he had taken one job after another but was never satisfied with what he was doing. The years flew past. He was a common laborer, earning only enough money to live from payday to payday. By the time he was a full-grown man, he realized he had suffered much because of his lack of knowledge and proper training. He had encountered many good positions along the way, but lacked qualifications to fill them. He had quit school too soon.

In his dream he felt ashamed of meeting his old classmates at the reunion. When he awoke, he realized what a lucky break it was for him, that it had only been a dream, a bad dream, a dream that shocked his sensibilities. He decided to stay in school. Then twenty years later his life would amount to something more rewarding than a series of unsatisfied tasks.

I also remembered that Tommy was in a class play once, and that his class made plans to have a reunion twenty years later. Now there would be no reunion for him.

I wondered if there would be one for me. I had already started out by making one hell of a mess out of my life at an early age. I was convinced that people make their own luck, good or bad. It's all according to their conduct.

An item in a smuggled newspaper read: "Marion...Prosecutor Hardin yesterday received two letters from Indianapolis and Gary, threatening his life if his efforts to determine prosecution of any members of the lynching mob continued. The prosecutor will turn the letters over to federal authorities."

Figure 31. Tommy Shipp at about age 16, just two years before he was murdered by lynching. This picture is from a group photo taken at the D.A. Payne School, where he and Jimmie were friends. *Cameron Family*

Two weeks after the double lynching, the officer in charge of the guardhouse opened the door of my dungeon cell and called out to me, "Come along, boy. There's a visitor in the office to see you."

He led me to the office of the Assistant Superintendent, Mr. Dowd, in the front of the guardhouse. The guard escorted me through Dowd's office to an adjacent room, which was the Captain's office. My mother was in that office waiting for me. It was the first time since my arrest that she had been allowed to visit me. Big emotions are expressionless, deep as heaven is far from the earth, and just as wide. The joy I felt at the sight of my mother amounted to my being born again.

When she saw me, she jumped up from her chair and ran to me, hugging and kissing me all at once as if I were a five-year-old child. She kept crying, "My son, my son, my son!"

I tried very hard to be a man, but the tears came anyway. I couldn't hold them back. I didn't want to hold them back. It was really a bit of heaven to see her again after the hellish nightmare I had undergone. She would understand. All mothers whose hearts are overflowing with love for their children understand these things.

The interview guard pulled a handkerchief from his pocket to blow his nose and still the tears that had suddenly clouded his vision.

"Son, they just let me know where they had taken you only last night. I came down here right away. I tried to visit you in the jail at Marion, but that mean old sheriff wouldn't let me," she told me. "Some old black man told me they had taken you over to Fort Wayne, then down to Indianapolis. He told me one of your eyes had been knocked out! He told me one of your arms and both of your legs had been broken!"

I could see the relief, pain, sorrow, worry, and countless questions crowding into her tear-filled eyes all at once. "That old man was lying to you, mom. I'm all right. I don't know why people go around saying things like that about people that aren't true."

She looked me over, probing my body with her tender and loving hands, touches that spoke with eloquence all their own in sympathy, compassion, and forgiveness. Her arms went out and around me. She hugged me again and again and again, still crying. I was crying, too. The strength of her hugs sent new strength coursing throughout my tired body.

After a while we both calmed down. She told me that most of the well-to-do and freedom-loving whites in Marion were clamoring for an investigation of the lynchings by the state attorney general's office. Money was being collected by the local chapter of the National Association for the Advancement of Colored People to be used in my defense.[88] Also Walter White, Executive Secretary of the NAACP, had arrived in town the very next day after the lynchings to personally investigate the incident.[89]

---

[88] The Marion branch of the NAACP, led by Mrs. Dr. Bailey, collected funds for Cameron's defense. By four days post-lynching, Bailey had secured Attorneys Brokenburr and Bailey (no relation), two high-profile black lawyers from Indianapolis. They would take the case and also file damage suits for the families of the two dead boys–at whatever fee the Association could manage. The NAACP national office decided soon afterwards that they could not defend Cameron, because he had signed a confession during his interrogation.

[89] Walter White actually arrived a week later and worked in Marion for two days. White, who headed the NAACP for almost a quarter century, investigated lynchings around the country. A blonde, blue-eyed black man, he often intentionally "passed" as white and as a journalist. This enabled him to interview spectators and officials–access that would have been denied a black investigator.

Then she told me about my stepfather, Hezikiah Burden. He had been away somewhere, for several weeks, one week before my arrest and one week after. When he returned home and found out what had happened to Abe, Tommy and me, he almost had a stroke. At any rate he went completely out of his mind and started swearing and cursing at every white person in the world. He swore he was going to "kill every white son-of-a-bitch on the Marion police force." There had been nothing Mother could do to stop him. There was no reasoning left in him.

He had pushed her out of his way and went to his gun cabinet, opened the doors, got out all of his firearms, checked them, and loaded them. He had a .22 caliber rifle, a 38-56 lever action Winchester rifle, three shotguns: a 12-gauge, a 16-gauge, and a 20-gauge. He also had a 410-gauge combined with an over and under barrel plus two .38 caliber revolvers.

Satisfied his arsenal was in good working condition, he asked my mother to help him kill some "white folks." She told him no. She tried to tell him that she had enough trouble worrying about me without starting any more. Pleading, she tried to talk him out of it, but she was talking to a stone wall. He had made up his mind; the lynchings and the terrible whipping I had undergone made him crazy. He kept talking and mumbling something about white people always breaking treaties with the Indians, taking all the best land away from his folks, placing them on scorched-earth reservations, and then when oil and gold was discovered on the God-forsaken soil, the white man had hatched up further charges against the Indians and stole the land back again! He told Mother that white folks were always picking on Indians and black people. He ranted and raved like a madman. He just had to shoot some white people or die in the attempt.

"I've stood all I can stand," he told my mother. "If you don't come along with me, I'll kill you, too! This is as much your fight as it is mine. It's more yours than mine!

Flossie Bailey had sent telegrams to the NAACP requesting assistance before and immediately after the lynching. However, those telegrams were "passed on to the authorities" and "repeated all day on the street." Bailey asked that White correspond with her "by special letter," so their communications could not be intercepted by the authorities.

In a letter to Mrs. Bailey on August 11th, White asks, "Would it be advisable for me...to stop at one of the hotels or with colored people?" She counseled him to "keep your racial identity a secret as the hotels do not keep colored people." He came as a white man (Archives of the Anderson, Indiana, branch of the NAACP).

Somebody's got to show those goddamned peckerwoods they can't take the law into their own hands and get away with it. They have got to be made to stop somewhere along the road. It's all right for them to break the law anytime they feel like it, but they want us to abide by the law. They can go straight to hell as far as I am concerned!"

His logic was a flaming, searing, human emotion with more truth than hysterics. It had been brought about by factors more dynamic and dominating than the double lynching and mistreatment of me, his stepson. It went back, in nearly every instance, to the Indian Wars[90] and the Emancipation Proclamation.[91] There had been too many false hopes, fears, frustrations and unkept promises. There was too much confusion, fraud and deceit. All of these injustices deeply etched in his mind rushed to the fore.

Because my mother would not help him shoot up the Marion Police Department, he leveled one of his revolvers at her. He had turned into a madman gone berserk!

My sister Marie broke for the back door of the house, screaming for help at the top of her voice. Hezikiah snapped off a shot at her. The slug hit the casing of the door first,

---

[90] "Indian Wars" is one term for many conflicts over three hundred years, beginning with the first European colonial settlements in 1622 until the early 1900s. The Indian Wars are a very complicated subject, one poorly explored in most American history classes—and far too complex to fully explain here. Here is a very rough sketch: The settlers from Europe fought the Native American nations for their lands and resources. The Indian nations resisted forcefully, but were pushed ever westward. (During the 1800s, many of these battles took place in Indiana.) William Henry Harrison, governor of the Indiana Territory, conducted a major land grab, under orders from President Jefferson. The Shawnee leader Tecumseh organized an alliance of tribes that fought the U.S. expansion for years, but ultimately he was killed and his army defeated in 1812. As white farmers, gold miners, and businessmen moved west of the Mississippi, the battles continued. Finally, many Indian nations were forced onto reservations and into poverty.

[91] The Emancipation Proclamation, an executive order issued by President Lincoln on January 1, 1863, declared all enslaved black people free in the ten southern states still in rebellion against the Union during the Civil War. As each Confederate state was conquered by the Union, the slaves there were freed.

While the Proclamation did not free every slave, it did make the end of slavery a goal in the war. That goal was finally realized when the Thirteenth Amendment to the Constitution was ratified in December 1865. The Reconstruction period that followed the Civil War promised much to the newly emancipated people, such as access to education and the vote. Sadly, it lasted only a dozen years. The Jim Crow period that followed—the period in which Cameron's story takes place—was a time of segregation, lynching, race riots, and broken dreams for African Americans, including Hezekiah Burden.

then ricocheted into her arm above the elbow, and came out at the top of her shoulder. The impact of the bullet knocked her down, but not out. Blood spurted from the wound. Mother kept hollering at her to get up and keep running. With a superhuman effort Marie struggled to her feet and started running again, calling out for help.

Hezikiah then turned on my mother with his fists. He knocked her down and shoved one of his revolvers deep into her stomach. He pulled the trigger. The gun misfired. She screamed and broke away from him. For some strange reason, he did not follow after her. She ran outside screaming at the top of her voice for help.

Very shortly, the police arrived at the house, but Hezikiah was not there. He had slipped across the road and was lying in a culvert. As the police approached the house cautiously, Hezikiah opened fire on them. He was using one of his rifles. Two of the officers went down. The remaining four officers ran for cover. Presently reinforcements arrived and a pitched gun battle began. Hezikiah was forced to leave the culvert when a spray of bullets began to find the range. The police were closing in on him. He came out of the ditch like a wild man, firing one of his rifles like a machine gun. Another policeman went down. Hezikiah was still unhurt. He zigzagged into a cornfield about twenty feet away from the drain crossing and hid among the eight-feet high stalks. Again another policeman went down as they closed in on him. Before he disappeared, another policeman hit the dirt with one of Hezikiah's bullets in him. It kept up like that for about two hours, with Hezikiah retreating when he had to. He always managed to find another hiding place just in the nick of time.

As darkness fell, the police lit torches and surrounded the large cornfield. They stopped all traffic moving in the immediate vicinity of Western Avenue. They set up an all-night watch. Not one of them dared to enter the cornfield. Not only did they not know which part of the field Hezikiah was in, they wondered why so many policemen were necessary to put down a one-man army. The watch was held because they were sure of Hezikiah's aim. From time to time, however, whenever anything in the field appeared to move, the officers fired high-powered rifles and sub-machine guns into the field. The torches and strong searchlights could not penetrate into the corners and thickness of the field.

Hezikiah could have escaped during the night. Police thought he had. Some of them hoped he had. Angrily, they were surprised the next morning when, at the crack of dawn, shots rang out from inside the cornfield again. Two more policemen went down.

An airplane dispatched from the state police barracks at Pendleton arrived and began a low circling of the cornfield. Rifle fire from the rear cockpit of the plane hit the ground around Hezikiah. One of the bullets found its mark and fractured his right hip and leg. But he kept right on firing at the police on the ground and at the plane flying overhead. Laboriously, he began crawling out of the cornfield. As he emerged from the field he shot two more policemen. Then he collapsed, unconscious. The police approached his inert form cautiously, a dozen guns trained on him. When they reached him, he had begun to return to a state of semi-consciousness. He couldn't move a muscle. The officers loaded him into an ambulance with some of the policemen he had shot. Regaining consciousness and some strength on the way to the hospital, Hezikiah managed to reach over and tried to choke one of the wounded officers to death with his bare hands! Prevented from carrying out this design, he contented himself by spitting in their faces! Police had to gag him and use restraints on him.

Mother also informed me that Hezikiah had been patched up by the doctors and had been hospitalized for two months. It was thought for a while that his right leg would have to be amputated. But he wouldn't agree to such an operation and won his choice. None of the policemen victims died from gunshot wounds inflicted upon them by Hezikiah. Five of them had to be retired early on disability because they had suffered near fatal wounds.

At Hezikiah's trial, his white attorneys proved that he was temporarily insane at the time of the shootings. Whoever heard of a non-white raising that much hell with white folks unless he was out of his mind! His attorneys asked the jury: "What would you have done if the police stood by and permitted a bunch of black people to storm the jail and harm your boy? You would have done the same thing if you had a streak of man-hood in you!"

Hezikiah's lawyers raised so much hell in the courtroom until the presiding judge jailed them for contempt. Two hours later, after thinking the situation over, the judge released them from jail. In the end, Hezikiah received a sentence of from one to ten years in the state prison at Michigan City, Indiana, in the northern part of the state. In a year's time he was paroled and returned back to Marion, a highly respected ex-convict![92]

---

[92] Some readers might be tempted to question this story, but it was reported in both Marion daily newspapers. The papers called it a simple domestic quarrel. The police believed Burden planned to shoot his wife Vera, then commit suicide. Burden had called Marion's undertaker saying he'd be giving him some business within the hour. The white reporters were probably not told about Burden's threat to retaliate for the lynching by killing white people, so assumed he was referring to the bodies of Vera and himself.

While my mother was busy telling me these things about Hezikiah, I thought of the times recently when I felt like he did.

The interview limit was over. It had lasted for an hour. With a great effort Mother tore herself away from me after a prolonged hug and advice to be a "good boy." I found a sort of humor in this remark because what other kind of a boy could I be behind the three-feet thick walls of the Indiana State Reformatory!

The guard escorted me back to my cell in the main part of the guardhouse. Alone again, I cried as long as tears would come. I kept thinking about how much I had hurt my mother, the one person in the world I should not have hurt at all. I was wishing I could have gone back home with her, but not to Marion. I thought of the rough years she had endured trying to raise three children to decent maturity, working with all her might, struggling day in and day out to make ends meet, to keep her little family together.

Maternal doctrine had impressed upon me that all humans have a rendezvous with destiny. Whatever the outcome, man had it within himself to reason and contribute or detract from the progress of civilization and Christianity, thereby determining, to a large degree, his ultimate fate. The gloom of utter despair clouded in on my every thought and mental image. That mob should have killed me back there in Marion, I thought.

As soon as his wounds were dressed, Burden was rushed to the State Reformatory in Michigan City, Indiana, "to prevent a repetition of the mob spirit which resulted in the lynching of two colored youths on the night of August 7." There was a hearing but no trial, because Burden pled guilty "in a clear voice." Lawyers represented Burden at his hearing (*Marion Chronicle*, December 18, 1930).

The newspapers made no mention of Hezikiah's relationship to the third youth almost murdered in that lynching. They reported only one officer seriously wounded and another with a shot to the hand. They may have minimized the impact of the cornfield standoff so as not to arouse the white public. On the other hand, Cameron (or his mother) may have somewhat exaggerated the number of wounded policemen. Both newspaper and eyewitness accounts can be influenced by emotion, so are not always accurate. What does seem clear is Cameron's pride in his stepfather's righteous anger, courage, and marksmanship–and that Hezekiah stood up for him. Apparently the black community, too, respected him for challenging the white authorities complicit in the lynchings.

The very next day my mother came to see me again. She had obtained a special permit from the office of the superintendent of the institution. She had only just begun to tell me all the things that had happened in Marion since the lynchings.

I asked her how Tommy and Abe's mothers were getting along. [93]

"Abe's Mother went stone blind in her grief," she told me. "The day after the

lynchings, the mob drove up and down in front of her house and in front of Tommy's mother's house. Members of the mob shouted out to the mothers, 'Yes, we hung your son-of-a-bitching son! You can't do anything about it, either!' 'We just hung a couple of old black-assed niggers, and one of them was your son! Ha! Ha! Ha!' 'As soon as the soldiers leave, we're going to run all of you black-ass bastards out of

Figure 32. Grace and William Deeter, parents of Claude, the young man who was shot during the robbery that led up to the lynching. The Deeters, devout Christians, had opposed the lynching and forgave their son's killers as he lay dying. The Deeters are seen here on their farm, dressed in their Sunday best, with their daughter Faith. *Deeter Family*

[93] Apparently Cameron's mother did not know—or did not tell Jimmie—about the visits that Grace Deeter, Claude's mother, made to the homes of the lynched boys the day after. The Deeters were very devout, and their church opposed capital punishment. As Claude lay dying in the hospital, his mother asked him to forgive his murderers. Claude did so. According to her grandson Carl Deeter, Jr., Mrs. Deeter went to mourn with the grieving parents. She told them that Claude and his family forgave their sons and had publicly opposed the lynching. For more on this story, including a video about the Deeters' forgiveness and a newspaper article of the day about their opposition to the lynching, see the *Freedom's Heroes* exhibit in America's Black Holocaust Museum online.

town!' 'We're going to declare a nigger holiday and you're going to be the main fare!'"

All day long the tirades of racial hatred continued against black people. In downtown Marion, the mobsters dared anyone to take the bodies down from the tree. Abe and Tommy had hung there until late in the afternoon. When the state attorney general arrived from Indianapolis, he defied the threats of the remaining crowd and amid curses, stepped up to the tree. He positioned a stepladder under the limbs of the tree and cut the ropes suspending the bodies with a small pocketknife. He eased the bodies down to the ground. His face was as white as snow. He was not frightened, just angry and ashamed that he was white!

A black funeral home in Muncie, Indiana, sent a hearse to pick up the bodies. When the hearse arrived on the scene, the attorney general was still there, standing guard over the bodies, keeping the people from mutilating them any further.

The sight of the hearse inflamed quite a few of the people standing around watching the activities. "Let the buzzards pick their bones clean!" they shouted. A detachment of the National Guard moved in quickly and began to get rough with the crowd.

The driver of the hearse was a real dark black man. The crowd began taunting him, calling him everything but a child of God. He was too frightened to be antagonized. He kept his mouth shut and went about his business quickly and quietly.

"We're gonna tear your goddamn hearse to pieces," the mob reproached him. "We're gonna let these damn niggers rot out here!"

The bodies were finally loaded. The driver prepared to leave. He overheard someone in the crowd say that the bomb would explode the moment the ignition of the engine was turned on. He got out of the hearse and looked all over the motor. Then he checked the undercarriage. There were no bombs. The state police escorted the hearse and bodies into Muncie.

People from all over Central Indiana wanted to view the bodies. The sheriff in Muncie told the undertaker to go ahead with his plans for a public view of the bodies on the enclosed porch of the funeral home. Then he sent a messenger to the Ku Klux Klan in Marion who had threatened his life for being impartial in upholding the law. He told them: "If you ever try a stunt on me like you did on the people in Marion, I'll take great pleasure in killing every damn one of you. Nothing like that will ever happen in Muncie, Indiana, as long as I am the sheriff!"

His name was Pat Garret, the same as another famous sheriff of the Old West. People from all over the Midwest knew the sheriff's reputation as a fearless lawman. He wasn't afraid of the devil himself. The mobsters in Marion knew he meant business in every word he had sent to them. All of America had just heard and finished reading about him in the newspapers, how he, almost single-handedly, captured the FBI's most wanted criminal, its Public Enemy Number One, Gerald Chapman[94], as he alighted from a train in Muncie while every law enforcement officer in the country was searching for him. He had been caught with a suitcase full of nitroglycerin, a highly explosive compound which he used to rob banks. Yes, the Kluxers knew the sheriff's courage and the principles by which he lived. There was no room for doubt or argument in the word of Pat Garret.

The very next day, Tommy's body was brought back to Marion. He was buried in Weaver, Indiana, about seven or eight miles away. Abe was buried in Muncie.

My mother wanted to know if the Reformatory officials had beaten or molested me in any way to force me to say something about my troubles.

"No, ma' am. I am getting along as best as can be expected."

Then I told her how nice the guards in the guardhouse were to me, how they took me out in the afternoons for exercise and brought me books and magazines from the library.

"How do you feel, son?" she wanted to know.

I told her how I was feeling. I spared no details in telling my mother how the crowd had come to life as we emerged from the jail. I told my mother all about the awful beating I had received from the police, of their threats and insults, the disrespectfulness of the detectives who had spirited me away from Marion for safe-keeping. When I had finished reliving this ordeal, I was wringing wet with perspiration.

My mother was crying again. She just sat there and looked at me with all the patience, tolerance, understanding and comfort a mother could show during times of great stress.

"Now you know what I meant by your running around and staying out late at night, don't you?" she reminded me quietly and pointedly. "If you'd only listened to me, this never would have happened."

"Yes, ma'am," was all I could say. I bowed my head in shame.

---

[94] Chapman led a Prohibition-era gang during the 1920s and was known as the "Gentleman Bandit for his interest in music and literature." He was romanticized by the public as a prison escape artist, like Jesse James before him, and was the first criminal to be called "Public Enemy Number 1" by the press.

If only I had stayed my mind on the principles of right. Mine had been the choice. My conscience had battled with me to do the right thing. But being easily persuaded, I had doomed my fate by yielding to temptation instead of to the decent seeds of manhood that had been so generously planted in my soul by my mother. Now was my long, long hour of degradation. Sorrow was an infinitesimally [small] word to describe the crushing shame that engulfed me like a straitjacket.

CHAPTER TWELVE

Inside the Walls–in Body and Mind

In taking stock of my surroundings, I found the Reformatory was a city set apart from the rest of the world. The gray engulfing walls measured 35-feet high and three-feet thick, laced with high-tensioned steel. The walls covered an area of one hundred acres. It was squared off like a prizefighting ring, surrounding every inch of the inside prison area. It was a spot of ground, another world, where men stood still, many of them whose lives had been shattered forever–beyond any kind of rehabilitation.

A first-class hospital looked after the health of the inmates. It was manned by a civilian physician and a dentist. [They used] assistants and aides, [prisoners] who had been interns and practicing physicians and surgeons on the outside. But crime had turned them into just another number, a vital statistic of the state penal system.

All the modern buildings came as a surprise to me. One was a barbershop where only white prisoners learned the trade. A shoe shop, laundry, and pressing shop were all integrated and combined in a spotlessly clean building. The prison's pastries and other baked goods were baked in the cook room by whites only, under the supervision of a civilian worker. All food was steam cooked.

Each of the two huge cell houses contained three stories of cellblocks with seven hundred prisoners in each house. Strict segregation was the order of the day. Two large dorms contained over three hundred beds each, one for blacks and one for whites.

The print shop afforded white men the opportunity to learn the trade. White prisoners published a weekly prison newssheet. The shirt shop, tailor shop and BVD[95] factory were all [racially] integrated. The convict labor in those buildings produced

---

[95] The BVD Company, then as now, made men's underwear.

merchandise for public sale.[96] In the foundry and engine house, integrated prisoners were taught the skills of core making and boiler firing methods. The library and school formed a convenient combination and were open to all inmates on an integrated basis, as were the symphony orchestra, the jazz ensemble, and the military band.

Ninety-nine inmates out of a hundred would swear that their interracial baseball team was the best in the state. Major league scouts often attended games behind the walls in search of talent. Sometimes a prisoner would show phenomenal ability, and big league scouts would offer contracts on the spot. Such lucky breaks enabled fortunate men to secure favorable consideration from the parole board or the governor's commission on clemency.

On Sunday mornings the prisoners filed into a beautiful white chapel for religious services. The building also served as a movie house for the showing of the latest films and stage plays. This was especially true on field recreation days when inclement weather would not permit baseball or other forms of outdoor activities.

Twelve hundred inmates could eat in the spacious mess hall at one time. It took seven minutes to fill up, fifteen minutes to eat, and another seven minutes to empty. An early mess and a late mess were served three times a day.

After being confined for two months in my narrow cell in the guardhouse, the lack of really proper exercise began to take its toll on my health. I was listless and had become frail and weak–consumptive in appearance. There just had to be something wrong with me. The prison doctor, Dr. Williams, [a white man and former] mayor of Anderson, Indiana, had been giving me some white powder in an envelope for medication, but my head seemed to hurt more and more and ache for hours at a time. I was completely rundown, morose, spiritless.

---

[96] During Jim Crow, blacks were jailed for such offenses as hanging out together on street corners or failing to show sufficient "respect" to whites. Southern states instituted formal "Black Codes," laws against such offenses as "vagrancy," that applied to blacks only. Northern states did not adopt such formal laws, but as more black migrants moved North, an informal system of customs developed. The North, for instance, did not make laws requiring residential segregation of the races, but hundreds of "sundown towns" sprang up, towns and cities where blacks were not allowed after sundown.

As we can see in Cameron's account, convict leasing (that is, prisoners working for corporations and/or the government for little or no pay) existed then–as it does now–in both North and South. For more information about racial inequities in the U.S. justice system, see Alexander (2012), Blackmon (2008), and Loewen (2005).

I had reached that mental stage where sometimes I'd sit on the edge of my bed and say to myself "Fly over to that corner!" and I would point to the corner I meant to fly to. Sure enough, I could actually feel myself floating through the air obeying this command. It would be a dreamy, lackadaisical floating through the air. Then I would laugh and think that feat very funny and laugh out loud. It was real funny to me!

All the time my mother kept visiting me every two weeks. I told her that my head had stopped hurting me but she could tell by the painful look in my eyes and my general appearance that I was not well. She did not look good to me, either. I could tell that she had lost a lot of weight. As I studied her, pangs of regret wracked my heaving bosom as I wondered if God would ever forgive me for having done this terrible thing to her.

On one of those visits she informed me that she had engaged two prominent black attorneys from Indianapolis to defend me. They were Bailey and Brokenburr.[97] Already they had succeeded in having my trial switched from Marion to Anderson. Along with this change of venue, she told me, I would shortly be transferred to the Madison county jail in Anderson to await trial. Then she could come and see me every day instead of once every two weeks.

Figure 33. Attorney Robert Brokenburr was known for his work in civil rights cases and was the first black Indiana state senator. *Indiana Historical Society*

I should have known that my mother did not believe me when I told her I was feeling great. She sent a black physician down to see me from Anderson, to give me a complete physical examination. He arrived one day while I was in the midst of flying all around inside my cell. I had become addicted to this sort of game as I tried, desperately,

---

[97] Flossie Bailey had continued to press the NAACP national office to help Jimmie. Earlier they had refused, because he had confessed to the crime. This time the NAACP agreed and engaged these two excellent lawyers to represent him at trial. Making sure the trial would be held in Anderson instead of Marion was key to preserving Cameron's life and sanity. African American attorneys like Bailey and Brokenburr were frontline activists in the 20th century civil rights movement.

to escape the dull, persistent pounding aches behind my eyes. I was the original Superman! After the doctor examined me, he refused to tell me what was wrong, if anything.

The very next day, my Mother came down to visit me and told me the doctor's diagnosis: "He said you are suffering from a severe brain concussion. He said you're young and will outgrow it in time and be well again."

Then she told me not to worry, be a good boy, trust in God to right all wrongs, and to pray constantly. That was my dear mother.

I did pray at times. But hate had been growing in me so much that it seemed all I could do was hate. That hatred was for white people in general. No doubt, that poison in my system added to the aches and pains in my head. I imagined myself out of prison paying back white people for every crime they had committed against me and other black people. I wanted to kill the white bastards for using force, violence, fraud and deceit; for channeling black people's lives into narrow choices, deliberately creating a way of life outside the pale of American society; for not regarding black people as human beings or an integral part of the community group as they did other ethnic groups. I was nurturing an urge to kill and keep on killing white people.

I recalled a story my Grandmother India told me about something that had happened during her childhood. The incident had happened shortly after the Civil War in America. She and her playmate, another little black girl, had been playing in a vacant field. Her little playmate had run into a nearby cornfield to hide. When she went in a white man followed after her, and no one knows what became of the little girl. My grandmother never saw her playmate again.

I also remember when I was nine years old. We were still living in Birmingham, Alabama. I had sauntered uptown one day to watch the fruit peddlers purchase their fruits and vegetables directly from the cold storage boxcars that were parked on the 16th Street sidings. I had played hooky from school that day. A white man grabbed ahold of me and held on to me. At first, I thought the man was a truant officer. I had been caught once before by Charley Geetchee, a black truant officer. But this man was a large, mean-looking white man in tan and tattered work clothes. He was a burley-type, tobacco-chewing, red-faced fellow.

The man half-led and half-dragged me to the courthouse square, several blocks away. It was actually the county jailhouse yard. A large crowd of white people were milling around a hangman's scaffold that had been erected on the grounds. It was a scene where a public hanging was about ready to be performed, legally, by the high sheriff! My abductor stopped right in front of the scaffold with me squirming in his grasp. He spoke for the first time.

"I want you to see how niggers die!" he told me. Was that an omen?

I was scared stiff. I begged people around me to make the man turn me loose so I could leave. No one heeded my pleas. My plight seemed very amusing to all of them. The big man seemed to hold me tighter. Presently a sad-looking black man was led up the thirteen steps to the floor of the scaffold and hanged amid a great flurry and ceremony of laughter. I will never forget the sight of that poor man's body plunging through the trapdoor with that rope around his neck. I had never before seen a man killed in such a brutal fashion in a carnival atmosphere.[98]

A few minutes later, the big white man, his face flushed with pleasure as if he had just received a relaxing sedative, turned me loose. Once out of his filthy grip, I ran from that monster man, as fast as I could, wiping away my tears. I ran all the way home. When my mother came home from work that day, I told her all about what had happened to me. I never played hooky again. (Several years later the state of Alabama prohibited public hangings.)

Another time I had helped one of the fruit peddlers sell a whole wagonload of apples up in the Highlands on a Saturday. The peddler gave me a whole dollar bill for my efforts. It was the most money I had ever seen at one time that I could call my own. On my way back home, I sat down on a street curb and pulled the bill out of my pocket just to see if it was really true—that I had a dollar bill! I would take it home and give it to my mother. She would know what to do with it.

While I sat there turning the bill over and over in my hands, a white hand suddenly reached down, like the dart of a snake's feeler, and snatched that dollar right out of my hands! Full of apprehension, I looked up to see what was happening. When I did, I heard a voice say, "That's my dollar! I just lost it!" I hung onto the man's arm, trying to get my dollar bill out of his hand. I was crying for my money back. The man shoved me

---

[98] This may or may not have been a legal hanging, that is, capital punishment carried out following a proper trial and sentencing by a judge. The presence of a built scaffold seems to suggest this. Nonetheless, it could have been a lynching, an illegal hanging in which the mob, acting as judge, jury, and executioner, took the law into their own hands. Many lynchings were conducted with the cooperation or outright participation of law enforcement officials. Just because the "high sheriff" was present does not prove the execution was legal.

roughly and walked on down the street with my dollar bill! There had been nothing I could do about it.

I knew lots of stories like that. They fed my hatred of white people. They commanded my attention when I had no idea of paying any attention to them. So did the following stories from one of the Anderson newspapers:

> Marion…The jury in its final report declared Jacob Campbell, Grant County sheriff, from whose jail two Negroes were taken and hanged, handled the situation on the night of the lynchings in a prudent manner. The report exonerated him of any blame of criticism in connection with the death of the Negroes.
>
> The Grand Jury in its report said the testimony taken in connection with the lynching showed Sheriff Campbell had conducted himself and directed those acting under him in a prudent manner and had he acted differently it is more than probable that a race riot would have ensued and several innocent persons would have been killed or injured.

Another news item stated:

> Marion…The Grand Jury indicted James Cameron, Negro, who was in company when Deeter was killed, on charges of first-degree murder, first-degree rape, and with being an accessory after the fact.
>
> Members of the mob were not indicted.
>
> The Grand Jury, which investigated the lynchings of two Negroes on the courthouse lawn here, was dismissed today without returning any indictments against members of the mob.

In Indianapolis, Indiana:

> An investigator, whose name was withheld, today submitted to State Attorney General Blain W. Ogden, a detailed report of his findings in connection with an investigation of the lynchings of two Negroes in Marion.
>
> The report mentioned about a half dozen names of persons alleged to have participated in the lynching of Abe Smith and Thomas Shipp, who had been arrested for murder of Claude Deeter, 23, of Fairmount, and assaulting Miss Mary Ball, nineteen, of Marion.
>
> The investigator said that on the morning following the hanging of the Marion Negroes in the courthouse yard, he talked to a young man who said he saw members of the mob take the Negroes from the jail.

The young man, the report added, pointed out a stab wound in the body of one of the Negroes and told the investigator he had seen it done.

Sheriff Campbell, the investigator said, was told about the young man, but the sheriff made no effort to learn his identity. The investigator said that a day or two later he was riding with the sheriff and pointed out the informer, but that Sheriff Campbell did not attempt to question him.

The report stated a ringleader of the mob is under indictment of a statutory charge of rape and that prosecutor Hardin knows the man.

A man paroled from the state Reformatory, the report set forth, is understood to have wielded the sledgehammer which was used to batter down the jail door. The man who tied a rope around the neck of one of the victims to drag him from the jail has been identified by the man's son, the investigator revealed.

In conclusion, the investigator expressed the opinion that there was 'plenty of time to have taken those men out of the jail to a place of safety.'

My mother showed me this news clipping during an interview:

Marion...The death penalty will be asked for James Cameron, age sixteen, third member of the trio taking part in the shooting of Claude Deeter and the attack on his eighteen-year-old companion, Hardin announced.

The car was parked on a road near the Mississincus River in the vicinity of the old Evans-McBeth Glass Company. Prosecutor Hardin promised a rigid probe of the facts.

Prosecutor Hardin announced that he would summon the County Grand Jury to investigate the lynchings. The mob had acted in the belief that. "If we don't do something, they'll just let them go free!

CHAPTER THIRTEEN

The Milk Of Human Kindness

Days passed. I began looking outside myself again. In the evenings when Bill and I were outside the guardhouse in the prison yard for our daily exercise, I noticed the grass appeared much greener to me, much more so than it had ever seemed before. The whole yard seemed to me to be one giant blanket of velvety green. And for the first time in my young life, I began to notice the flowers. They seemed to beckon to me, demanding my attention. They bloomed in rich profusion all over the prison yard, pale, fragile, exquisite creations of nature, full of life, fresh, invigorating, exalting my soul.

While walking among the flowers I experienced emotions unlike anything I ever felt before. Perhaps this awakening was a part of my growing up. I could actually feel a strange sort of quietness taking over in my troubled bosom, my mixed-up mind. I wondered if this was a crystallization of my destiny. Could the beauty of all those flowers descend upon me in such a fashion as to open my eyes and heart and soul to the handiwork of God and the goodness in all creation? I knew—even though it came to me through the muck and mire of my own tribulations—that something sweet and wonderful was beginning to happen to me, to haunt me, to stir up inside me in a strange, mysterious and healing way. It was all very puzzling to me. The multi-colored lilacs, exquisitely shadowed with a beauty all their own, the delicate posies, the sturdy leaves of lilies, the high majestic ferns, were reaching upward toward the sky, as if in prayer. Many other flowers whose names I did not know blended their fragrances and scented the air with a soul-pleasing aroma. Their delicate and fragile-like beauty conveyed a message of comfort and serenity to me.

Many times I would hold a rose, a red rose, cup it in my hands, and stare at it as if in a trance, letting its mysterious powers soothe and strengthen me. Theirs was a majesty and strength I had never dreamed of. It mattered not that the revelation came to me behind prison walls.

I wondered, too, why I had never noticed the beauty of the flowers my mother always kept around our house. And the grass that was just as green that I had to mow in disgust. Within the narrow confines of my dungeon cell, I had plenty of time to delve beneath the surface of things, of people, of places. Everything seemed quite different now.

The day finally dawned when I was transferred from the Reformatory safekeeping cell to the county jail in Anderson, Indiana. I was glad to get out of that narrow confinement. I had become very frail during my four months confinement there. The transfer took place about a week before the New Year (1931) at which time the newly-elected county sheriff, Bernard Bradley, would be sworn into office at midnight.

Word reached Anderson that a mob of Marion die-hard Klansmen numbering about five hundred strong, were coming over to Anderson to storm the Madison County Jail, drag me out and lynch me. The mob sent word that they were going to break in the new sheriff as an obedient servant of the Ku Klux Klan.

Of course that news disturbed me greatly. I was already in poor health. The brain concussion was still nagging me, still haunting my every glance. A bag of bones covered with tight, ashen yellow-colored skin best described my physical appearance. In my great fear upon learning this bit of electrifying news, I requested an immediate interview with the new sheriff.

Sheriff Bernard Bradley stood about six feet and three inches tall. He weighed about one hundred and ninety pounds. He was a lean and hard-built man. He carried his shoulders squarely in a manner that commanded respect. There was a look about his rugged features and sky-blue eyes that showed his wisdom and strength. His hair was sandy-colored. His nose was finely chiseled, his lips thin, and he had a square jaw. He was about 39 years old.

I couldn't remember all the things I had planned to say to him. As he opened the door to my cellblock and walked down the corridor to where I was sitting on my bunk, I blurted out:

"Please, don't let them hang me, sheriff, please, please!"

I could see the sheriff's eyes dancing and yet there was a seriousness in their look at me. Perhaps he could detect a tinge of humor in the situation, but sensed that I was serious and did not let himself go into a fit of laughter.

"Listen, Jimmie," he told me. "Nothing is going to happen to you while you are in my care. I promise you that. As long as I am sheriff of Madison County, every one of my prisoners will have their day in court.

"I hope those kluxers won't be crazy enough to come over here. If they do, I'll have my buddies on guard here at the jail and scattered all over town. They'll have orders to shoot to kill. So, don't worry about anything like that. Nobody's going to take any of my prisoners away from me."

He convinced me that he meant every word he had spoken to me. Still, lynchings had happened before. They could happen again. I couldn't help but worry about the situation.

There were ten white prisoners and five blacks upstairs in the cellblock with me in the old "Riverside Hotel" as the jail was called, because it was on the bank of the White River. One of the whites was serving an 11-day jail sentence. He had five more days to go. This seemed like a lifetime to him. Time was passing too slowly; he griped and bellyached all over the cellblock.

Figure 34. Bernard Bradley was born in the small sundown town of Elwood. When he was elected sheriff for Madison County, he moved to Anderson, where he would live for the rest of his life. Bradley was active in Democratic politics and served three terms as sheriff. Sadly, his compassion for and protection of Jimmie and other inmates may have cost him. He would die at the young age of fifty-two from bleeding ulcers. April 30, 1946, *Elwood Call Leader*

"I don't know if I can do five more days," he moaned over and over again, pacing up and down in the cellblock and walking in and out of the bullpen. "I don't think I can make it!"

One of the white prisoners in for bank robbery got fed up with the man. He walked over and confronted the groaner with a baleful look that was mean enough to kill the man by itself.

"If you don't shut your goddamn mouth up and keep quiet," he spat out, "I'll pick up something and knock your goddamn brains out! I'll kick the shit right out of you!"

Most of the prisoners in the cellblock thought that was what the man was going to do right then and there. He was furious at the crybaby.

"The idea of you bellyaching, squawking and yelling your damn head off about a lousy little eleven days!" the angry prisoner continued. "The rest of us in here are facing ten, twenty, thirty years, and even life for some of the things we have been accused of doing."

Then he looked up at me standing nearby. "And some of us might even get the electric chair!"

Things were awful quiet in our cellblock for the next five days.

That very same night a black man was locked up in the cellblock with us. He had been traveling through the town when nightfall caught him.[99] Rather than be out in the streets in the event a crime was committed and he just might be accused of committing it, he would always choose the older American custom of travelers and ask the county sheriff in whatever town he might happen to be passing through to put him up for the night. When the turnkey went back downstairs, the man asked us about the busy activities he had noticed downstairs.

"What's going on down there?" he wanted to know. "There's a dozen or more men down there armed with rifles, shotguns, sub-machine guns, revolvers, and everything else. I just came in here to spend the night. I am a stranger passing through."

---

[99] In the early 1930s, black travellers learned which towns were "sundown towns" in two ways: by seeing a sign at the town's entrance stating a version of "Nigger, don't let the sun set on you here," or by word of mouth from other black folk. Many sundown towns did not then—and do not now—have such signs posted, so the black traveller in this case took preventive action when the sun began to set.

In 1936 a black postal worker named Green published the "The Negro Motorist's Green Book," with the help of his contacts in the Postal Workers Union around the country. It was updated yearly until the late 1970s. The guide told black travellers about the towns, restaurants, beauty parlors, hotels, and nightclubs where they would be welcomed.

I felt much better when I heard this bit of news. The new sheriff seemed all right. The rest of the prisoners explained to the freeloader why things were out of hand.

"Goodness gracious! So that's where they hung those two boys! Great day in the morning!" the lodger exclaimed. "I was out on the west coast when I read about the lynchings in this state. It happened about three or four months ago, didn't it? To think I had planned to go on to Marion and spend the night in that jail! I am glad I was too tired to keep going tonight."

The next morning, after breakfast at taxpayers' expense, he took off in the opposite direction from Marion.

Marion is only 29 miles from Anderson. Two hundred officers, heavily armed, patrolled the grounds around the Madison County jailhouse, and all the streets leading to it. This force was augmented by countless white citizens, most of them American Legionaries of the Fortieth and Eighth Division and pals of Sheriff Bernard Bradley.

In the black neighborhood known as Hazelwood, it was a fact that many of the inhabitants had been heavily armed with handguns and rifles and were ready for the mob. The local police did not interfere. They welcomed all the posse and help they could get.[100] Rumors were persistent that Sheriff Bradley had armed many of the black people to help him protect me. When word of these developments reached the Klan leaders in Marion, my proposed lynching was called off.

Many blacks and whites came to visit me in succeeding days. Many of the whites had come just to apologize with tears in their eyes. Nearly all of them expressed sorrow at being members of the white race. They had tears in their eyes. This fact caused me to undergo all sorts of emotions. Quite a few of them gave me money to aid in my defense.

---

[100] At that time, county sheriffs and city police chiefs had small staffs. These officers were generally not much better trained than civilians. Often they had to use their own personal vehicles. When a need for more staff arose, a posse was assembled. The posse was made of civilians using their own weapons and cars. Such a posse accompanied the Marion police when they rounded up Abe, Tommy, and Jimmie.

Law enforcement units still use posses today. Now such volunteers are called "reserve police officers" or "reserve deputy sheriffs." A recent example: On April 2015, a deputized volunteer, seventy-three-year-old Robert Bates, killed an unarmed black man, Eric Harris, in Tulsa, Oklahoma. Bates, an insurance company CEO, had donated money, cars, and equipment to the sheriff's department and participated in over 100 operations of the violent crimes task force. A Tulsa police officer reported that the agency had 130 such reserve deputies.

Many of the blacks told me that carloads of them had tried to reach Marion on the night of the lynchings. They had all been turned back by the state police. Marion was closed to all in-coming traffic. Some of the blacks had been so angry they had crawled through muddy cornfields and desolate wooded areas on their stomachs, like snakes, to avoid the police and roadblocks. But there had not been enough of them to combat the mob and the police.

"If we'd made it," one bricklayer told me, "we'd killed every white son-of-a-bitch we could lay hands on. Then, we'd tore up that god-damn chicken-shit town and burned it to the ground!"

I had been in the "Riverside Hotel" for several weeks when the other prisoners began commenting on my general rundown physical condition. They were thinking that I might have some kind of a disease and that it might be contagious. I had lost a lot of weight, had no appetite, and the skin on my legs looked like fish scales. During the weeks, my mother came to visit me almost every day. When she couldn't get there, my sisters Marie and Della would come.

She sent another doctor to examine me one day. He reported that if I didn't get out of jail and get some proper exercise and sunshine, I was almost certain to contract tuberculosis. The life sounds in my body were very low.

Sheriff Bradley heard about my chronic condition and sent upstairs for me. The turnkey escorted me downstairs to his office where he offered me a chair.

"Jimmie, I want you to give me your word that you won't run away," Sheriff Bradley began his talk to me. "You're a very sick boy and I want to help you. You need plenty of fresh air and sunshine." He leaned forward in his chair and smiled at me. "You need someone to help you out of a difficult situation. I've been thinking a lot about you, lately. Now I've made up my mind about you. I know what I want to do. I know what I am going to do. I want you to treat me like a father and I'll treat you like a loving son." He paused to allow his words to sink in.

I had no idea what the man was driving at and just sat there and looked at him. I was beginning to feel a strangeness, though, a something that was building up inside my bosom. It was a great expectation, an apprehension, a something tangible. I could feel its tentacles tightening up on me. I studied the sheriff's face, looked into his eyes, watched the movements of his hands, and noticed how the movements of his body blended in with every word he spoke. And I wondered. I wondered because no white man had ever spoken to me like that before. My concentration, my search could detect no deceit or falsity in the words that tumbled out of the mouth of Sheriff Bernard Bradley.

He kept on talking. "Jimmie, I am going to make a turnkey trustee out of you. I want you to do nothing but keep the jail yard nice and clean and stay out in the fresh air and sunshine as long as you can. Above everything else, don't overwork yourself. There are some dumbbells out in the garage and you can try and build up your body with them.

I want you to go to the store for the rest of the prisoners whenever they want candy, tobacco, and cigarettes, to be their errand boy. Will you do that for me? Will you let me help you? Will you let me be your buddy?"

I was stunned, speechless! What kind of a man was this sheriff? All the time he had been talking to me I had looked him straight in the eyes. I could feel the human warmth, the milk of human kindness, the passion of understanding and tolerance and brotherly love, yes, brotherly love, the deep concern for the plight of another human being, the sincerity of his every word as he spoke to me.

Didn't Sheriff Bradley know that the state of Indiana had thrown the whole of the statute book at me, that I had a first-degree murder rap hanging over me, plus armed robbery, auto-banditry, bad associates, and rape to boot? For a fleeting moment, I was tempted to think the man was just playing with me. But he sounded so real! No! He wasn't playing with me! He had meant every word he had spoken to me!

"I'll be good to you, sheriff. I'll be true and honest and trustworthy," I managed to say as I felt myself, suddenly, begin to choke up inside. "I'll be your buddy if you want me to. I'll never do anything to make you sorry. I'll do anything you want me to do," I told him.

Then, suddenly, I could not hold back the tears. Flood time was mine. It seemed as if a giant beam of light was flooding my whole body with soothing rays of happiness. I was so filled with joy I felt like one who had lost his mind–just floating away. I couldn't contain myself. My tears were wild and uncontrollable. They came in torrents, like spasms. Every movement of my body spoke eloquently of thanks to God and to Sheriff Bernard Bradley, for their goodness to me.

How could I let the sheriff be any nicer to me than I could be to him? I felt I would rather die than betray a man who was willing to trust me in order to help me.

I felt my back being patted and then the voice of Sheriff Bradley came through the sunbeam, "That's a good boy, Jimmie, I knew I could trust you. We're going to get along just fine. Just you wait and see!" Gee Whiz! Holy Smokes! His patting me felt so good! No white man had ever patted my back like that before–or since.

"Thank you, Sheriff Bradley, thank you so much!" was all I could think to say. As I spoke those words to one white man, I could feel the sickening hatred in my heart for all white people leaving my body replaced with tears that didn't seem to want to stop flowing.

Water, the greatest purifier of all elements, now condensed to tears, was ridding my body and mind of cancerous bitterness and prejudice toward my fellowmen. They were isms that have no place in human society. I was glad to see and feel this deadly sickness go out from me. It had been killing me by degrees. Now my world would seem just a little bit brighter, my cares a little bit lighter. Such hatred and wasting away were especially difficult to carry for a sixteen-year-old boy, in poor health, and in jail! Its weight had been a staggering load for me to bear.

Somehow, I seemed to understand all at once how it is between blacks and whites. A lot of them were irresponsible, mean, dishonest, and cruel, but not all of them. There were good people and some bad people all over the world.

Some of the irresponsible ones didn't like Sheriff Bradley's treatment toward me. They abused him verbally. The most popular label was "nigger lover." The sheriff would laugh it off most of the time when people scandalized his name. Sometimes, however, he would curse them out. But just the same, every morning at 7 a. m., the door to my cellblock would open, and I would step out into a world of limited freedom feeling like a sparrow in flight.

As I look back on Sheriff Bradley's approach to race relations I realize he was a weird sort of white person. When I say weird I mean that his behavior was mysterious and outside the natural law. I see his kindness and love to me as the intervention of a supernatural influence. His nature made him belong to another world. I say this because every day when the sheriff was at the jail, if he wasn't busy delivering prisoners to some institution or picking up some to bring back to Anderson, or out of town on official business, or in court, he could be heard, all over the jailhouse singing his favorite church song. It was the one written by George Bernard and known to all churchgoers as "The Old Rugged Cross." All I have to do is think about Sheriff Bradley (which is every day of my life) and I can hear him singing:

"On a hill far away stood an old rugged Cross,

The emblem of suffering and shame;

And I love that old Cross where the dearest and best

For a world of lost sinners was slain.

So I'll cherish the old rugged Cross,

Till my trophies at last I lay down;
I will cling to the old rugged Cross,
And exchange it some day for a crown."[101]

If we didn't hear that song in the mornings, we would hear it at noon or later in the evening. I am sure he has obtained his crown bestowed upon him by a gracious God for his goodness to me. When he died a part of me died, too.[102]

But I have found in cherishing Sheriff Bradley's memory, that the events that took place with him grow brighter with each passing year. I know now that he was nothing but the Spirit of God walking around with a badge on his shirt! God rest his soul!

I must mention one more fact concerning Sheriff Bradley. He lived in Elwood, Indiana, about 10 or 12 miles from Anderson, but in the same county. Even at that time, when he was elected sheriff of Madison County, the huge sign that greeted black people

---

[101] Ironically, this song was also a favorite of the Ku Klux Klan. The KKK was a self-styled Christian Protestant organization. As U.S. Supreme Court Justice Sandra Day O'Connor noted, "Typically, a cross burning would start with a prayer by the "Klavern" minister, followed by the singing of *Onward Christian Soldiers*. The Klan would then light the cross on fire, as the members raised their left arm toward the burning cross and sang The Old Rugged Cross" (*Virginia v. Black*, 538 U.S. 343, 2003).

Another interesting note: Sheriff Bradley was a devout Roman Catholic. The Old Rugged Cross is a Protestant hymn and not likely to have been a part of Mass at his church. It was an unusual choice to be a Catholic's favorite song.

Sheriff Bradley was born and raised in Elwood, Indiana, which was a sundown town where the Ku Klux Klan had a very large following and influence. At that time, the KKK not only demeaned and violated blacks, but also Catholics and Jews. Therefore, Bradley grew up as a part of a denigrated minority. This may have played a role in his ability to empathize with Jimmie.

[102] Sheriff Bradley died in 1946 following surgery for stomach ulcers. According to his daughter, Margaret Bradley, Cameron and Bradley had kept in contact. They both lived in Anderson at the time (interview by the editor in Anderson, Indiana, in October 2006).

working in the town or passing through as a motorist read in bold relief: NIGGER, DON'T LET THE SUN GO DOWN ON YOU HERE!"[103]

When Wendell Willkie, a Democrat turned Republican, was nominated for President of the United States and ran against Franklin Delano Roosevelt in 1940, the "nigger" sign was removed temporarily to avoid embarrassment to Willkie, a Hoosier and resident of Elwood. After the election the sign was put back in its usual place for highway traffic to see. As far as I know, that very sign might still be there to this very day.

In my remembrance of Sheriff Bernard Bradley, I have to point out to the world that this Rose of Sharon, this Lily of the Valley, this Bright and Morning Star was privileged to grow up in such a mud puddle as was Elwood, Indiana. I know now that America has many roses of the caliber of Sheriff Bradley growing in "mud puddles" all over the land!

As a trustee, first I would go downstairs to the basement and visit Nick, the affable Greek cook. To Nick, all the prisoners white and black, were "my boys." "You my boy," Nick would say to me in his inimitable way. "I fix you something nice, eh?" It was tough to hate anyone around Nick.

He was a thin, swarthy-faced man in his sixties. He was completely bald, not a strand of hair anywhere on his head. His eyes were as limpid as a cow's, and his face knew only two expressions, cheerfulness or apology. He was alone in the world, having no known relatives, so adopted prisoners were the only family he knew. There was nothing he would not do for us short of aiding in our escape, and there was nothing we would not do for him.

After breakfast in the kitchen with Nick, I usually went upstairs to the sheriff's office where another trustee, Pat Mitchum, an elderly black man, waited for me. Pat was a town character, one of those lovable southern types. He wasn't sure of his age. He knew everybody in town and everybody knew him. He had grown children and

---

[103] "Sundown towns," cities and suburbs where African Americans (and sometimes other minority groups) were not allowed after dark, were established around the country, but predominantly in the North, from the 1890's through the 1960's. These all-white enclaves used legal technicalities, police patrols (harassing and arresting blacks for no offense other than DWB, "Driving While Black"), race riots and other forms of white-on-black violence to maintain their racial "purity." These practices resulted in forcing blacks into urban ghettos. Some of these practices are still employed today (Loewen, 2006).

grandchildren scattered all over Anderson, in the white neighborhoods as well as the black. He could talk glibly from sun-up to sundown and never repeat himself. A head full of coal-black hair topped his very wrinkled and very dark face from which protruded two of the merriest-looking eyes anyone could ever wish to see. They were black piercing orbits that gave notice to the world that he, indeed, knew what life was all about. The skin on his face had been scarred with pockmarks left by smallpox when he was a child. Average build, he suffered from corns on all ten toes, plus calluses and bunions all over his feet. He had one of the most careless shuffles imaginable.

Pat and I would leave the jail, and he would take me around to meet some of his friends in the black section of Anderson. His friends accepted me readily. I began to feel a lot better about life. A person just can't live without other people in his life–all kinds of people: black, white, red, brown, and yellow.

There were three or four houses Pat and I visited every day. At each house Pat would talk the lady of the house out of food or some home brew[104] or something for the both of us. It was screaming fun to sit back and listen and watch that old man in action. He really had a line with women. He was Aesop and Uncle Remus, rolled into one. I never had time to think of my troubles with Pat around. When I did have time, I was too busy thinking of the things Pat had pulled off that caused me to crack up with laughter.

Sometimes I would go to Sheriff Bradley's living quarters in the front of the jail and baby-sit with his three small children while Mrs. Bradley went shopping or to visit friends. They had one boy and two girls. The eldest was around five years old. I would take them out in the jail yard and pull them around in their little red coaster wagon. I taught them to ride their tricycles, and gave them piggyback rides. If there was any racial hatred in me, it was drowned out by the laughter and innocence of Sheriff Bradley's children.[105]

Ironically, I could not tell anyone except my mother how I had come to feel about white people. She looked at me compassionately and said, "Son, if it wasn't for the really good white folks who believe in freedom for everybody, we black folks would be in far worse shape than we are. You just keep on having faith in God. You just keep

---

[104] Homemade liquor.

[105] In her 2006 interview with Dr. Kaplan, Margaret Bradley fondly recalled Cameron pulling her in the wagon when she was small.

your hand on the throttle and your eyes on the rail. You just keep on praying. There are plenty of good white folks in this old cruel world of ours!"

The many black visitors I had, as well as the ones I visited with Pat, often talked to me of hatred and revenge. I had my first lessons in the loyalties and counter loyalties, emotions that tie people into unknotted relations, one way or another, most of their lives. The beginning for me was to admit that some white people were fine and decent and good.

One day, while Pat and I were making our rounds in Hazelwood, we stopped at one of our favorite kitchens: Mrs. Darrow's. While Pat was in the kitchen talking her out of some home brew, I stood in the front room looking out the window at the street traffic passing by. I could tell by the squeals and delightful screams and giggles coming from the kitchen that it wouldn't be long before Pat would win his case.

Then I saw a white man, about 35 years old, riding a bicycle up and down Forkner Street. He had a small, blond-haired girl sitting on the handlebars as they rode backward and forward from 14th Street to 15th Street. His little passenger was having the time of her life.

I noticed the man casually at first. Suddenly, my gaze froze. I recognized the man as one of the mobsters who had grabbed hold of me in the jail at Marion, one of the men who had helped to drag me out of the jail and into the hands of the infuriated crowd in the streets.

A shadow of the old intense hatred rose in my bosom. Even that didn't last long, though. It was difficult for me to believe that that happy-go-lucky man with that equally happy child had been capable of doing the things I knew he had done.

I called Pat and Mrs. Darrow to point out to them my discovery. The three of us stood framed in the large bay window for several minutes until the bicycle rider finally disappeared. It was difficult for them to believe, too. Still, I was positive. That man had held on to my arms during that awful beating I had received from the mob!

It was then that Pat told me some of the stories he had heard concerning the lynchers. Many members of the mob had met violent deaths on the highways after the lynchings. Rumors had it that their deaths were attributed to the ghosts of Tommy and Abe. One man's car had been hit by a train. Just before he died, he told his friends he had seen a vision of what he had helped the mob to do. The scene was the last thing he could remember before the accident. Another man, about to die after an accident, said he had been driving down the highway when the image of one of the mob's victims grabbed the steering wheel of his vehicle, causing it to turn over three or four times.

One of the known mobsters had shot and killed his whole family–his wife and two children–before committing suicide. Many of the members of the mob had lost their minds and were confined in mental institutions. The rumors, intertwined with facts, were endless.[106]

In about five months time, thanks to Sheriff Bradley, the grace of God working through him, and some awful tasting medicine my mother kept bringing me from a drugstore basement warehouse, I regained my health. I had developed a wolfish appetite and was gaining weight rapidly.

I usually went to see Johnny Mack Brown, Buck Jones, Bob Steele, or Charles Starrett in one of their hard-shooting western movies after running chores for the prisoners. One day, while walking around uptown wondering whether to go to the movies, I came face to face with Judge Carl Morrow. He was the jurist that newspaper accounts said would preside over my case in the Madison County Circuit Court system. The judge was a pale gaunt man with a pair of stooped shoulders. He had thin, wispy, white hair. He was dressed all in black with a bow tie dangling from an antiseptic white collar. He looked more like an undertaker than a judge. The judge and I stopped a few feet apart and stared at each other. He was dumbfounded. He was the first to find his voice. It was even and serious. "Hello there, boy!"

"Hello, judge," was all I could think to say. We nodded to each other and passed on.

Later on that evening when I returned to the jail, Sheriff Bradley asked me whether I'd seen the judge uptown.

"Yes, sir, I saw him. I ran right into the dude."

"He called me on the telephone and told me I ought to keep you locked up," Sheriff Bradley told me. "I told him to run his courtroom and let me run my jail!"

The sheriff laughed heartily and slapped his thighs. It was a delight for him to have a chance, as a Democrat, to tell the judge, a Republican, just what he could do and where he could go after he got through doing it.

Thereafter, for the sake of peace in the divided official family in Anderson, I tried to stay out of the judge's pathway. But, as luck would have it, I bumped into him almost every day. We'd always greet each other evenly. The judge would stop and stare at me, shake his head in a bewildering and disbelieving fashion, and walk on. At any rate, he never bothered Sheriff Bradley about me being an honorary citizen of Anderson.

---

[106] For her book, Cynthia Carr (2006) researched and wrote about the many myths and mysteries surrounding the lynching and its aftermath.

While awaiting trial, I was surprised at the number of friends I had. I was even more surprised to find that most of them were not the same people I had considered my friends. Some of my relatives had stated, very bluntly, that they would have nothing at all to do with me, with a jailbird relative! One of them, thirty-five years later, actually killed another man over what he thought was too much attention being paid by a black to his white girlfriend he was shacking up with! It seemed to me that most of my playmates shared this feeling about me, about jailbirds! What happened to some of them is another story. That's why I never pass judgment on people, because I never know what might happen to me before being called home to God.

But the boys and girls, black and white, whom I had thought of as mere acquaintances were the people who came to see me regularly. They always had something cheerful and comforting to say. Of course there was disturbing news too.

One visitor from Marion told me that Tommy's family was having a hard time making ends meet; that no one wanted to give them employment.

After my mother moved from Marion to Anderson to be nearer me and to be able to visit me more often, she baked me a large goose. I thought it the prettiest bird in the whole world. Mother baked it to a golden brown, and it was richly spiced. Much maternal love had gone into the preparation as a special treat for me. There was a tantalizing aroma all around it, which meant plenty of good eating.

I had done quite a bit of running that day and was tired. So I ate only a small portion of the fowl before going to bed. I was determined that more attention would be given that bird the first thing in the morning. Drawing a chair up close to the bunk in my cell, I laid the goose on it. I then crawled into the bunk and stuck my hand out from beneath the covers to clutch the delicacy. Upon awakening in the morning, I was shocked! My hand held a mere skeleton! Every ounce of meat had been purloined from my goose!

Out of control, I ran out of my cell and up and down the cellblock screaming, "Who stole my goose? Who stole my goose?"

Every prisoner in the cellblock began quacking like a duck and honking like a goose. Most of them waddled up and down the corridors in imitation of a goose. They wiped their mouths with their hands and patted their stomachs, laughing. Tears were running out of their eyes. I cursed and yelled. They laughed all the harder. Finally, I laughed, too.

CHAPTER FOURTEEN

Judgment

The Cameron murder trial began eleven months after the lynchings. My old sidewalk nemesis, Judge Morrow, was on the bench. He had already granted my attorneys, Bailey and Brokenburr, three postponements of the trial. They had wanted the public to have a chance to forget about me. Each time they obtained a postponement, they succeeded in having one of the many charges against me quashed.[107] Now I was, finally, going to trial for being an accessory *before* the fact to first-degree murder. The penalty could be as much as death in the electric chair or life imprisonment.

Accompanied by Sheriff Bradley, I entered the courtroom that first day wearing a gray flannel suit my mother managed to buy for me. My face was expressionless, as my attorneys had commanded me to show no emotions. But, deep down inside, I was scared, really scared. I thought if I did escape the electric chair, I was not at all sure that no new mob might try to carry out its own brand of justice! What if I were set free? A mob or even one angry white man might kill me on the streets in broad daylight with hundreds of witnesses standing by. There would be nothing done to bring the killer or killers to justice. No white jury would turn in a verdict of guilty against a white man for killing a black man! In my mind's eye I saw myself being killed on my way to a movie by the man I had seen riding his little girl on the handlebars of his bicycle.[108]

---

[107] Rejected by the court.

[108] Jimmie's fears were well founded. Very few lynchers have ever been brought to trial, much less convicted. Even in our day, whites who kill blacks often escape punishment. (One well-known recent example: the trial and acquittal of George Zimmerman, a white and Hispanic man who admitted killing Trayvon Martin, a black teenager, in 2012.)

The courtroom was jammed with people.[109] Black and white faces lined the walls and filled every seat. The spectators were about evenly divided. They looked like the keys on a piano, or salt and pepper in the same shaker.

The first day entailed selecting a jury. Twenty-seven jurors in a row asked to be excused because, as they put it, they were prejudiced against black people. Finally, my jury was selected. It was made up of twelve white people, ten men and two women.[110]

I found myself being very alert throughout the whole day. I watched every expression, every glance, every movement of the jurors' eyes as they were being examined by my attorneys. I was listening for what I call enemies and friends. Mostly, though, I was listening for the sounds of impartiality.

I remember one time when my lawyers were questioning a man as a prospective juror, the fellow seemed to be overly condescending. He was really trying to sell himself to my attorneys. Sheriff Bradley came over to our table and whispered a few words into the ears of my lawyers about some of the things he knew about the man being questioned. Whatever it was Sheriff Bradley told them, it worked because my attorneys got rid of that fellow in a hurry. He wasn't going to be allowed to have any part in the Cameron murder trial.

My mother sat at the defense counsel table with me. She looked worn and haggard, and watched the questioning of the jurors as closely as I did. At times, she bowed her head and talked to the Man upstairs.

The second day Judge Morrow gave the jury their instructions. They were not to read any newspapers during the trial. They were to be guarded day and night and kept together until the case had been decided.

The two prosecutors also briefed the jury. They said the state would prove, beyond the shadow of a doubt, that the defendant, James Cameron, did, in the presence of witnesses and with malice aforethought, plan, abet, assist, encourage, aid, order and participate in the premeditated murder of one Claude Deeter; that the defendant had

---

[109] The courtroom was also stifling, with temperatures reaching 100 degrees.

[110] In spite of the citizenship provided to blacks by the 14th Amendment to the U.S. Constitution, the U.S. Supreme Court ruled in 1880 (*Virginia v. Rives*) that seating an all white jury did not violate black defendants' civil rights. One hundred years later, the U.S. Supreme Court ruled that putting a black defendant on trial with a jury purposely selected to be all white denied that black person equal protection under the law (*Batson v. Kentucky*, 1985). Despite that, racially motivated jury selection still goes on.

done all in his power to bring about the death of the hold-up victim who had been shot to death in cold-blood; that the defendant did hold the hands of the victim's lady companion while the rest of his buddies took turns criminally assaulting her!

My attorney objected strongly to the state's opening remarks. I was not being tried for rape, my attorneys pointed out, but for being an accessory before the fact to first-degree murder. Judge Morrow ordered the prosecution to keep their remarks strictly on the charge "for which the defendant is being tried."

Having two prosecutors on my case came about as a result of my case being changed from one county to another. The prosecutor in the original county, Grant (Marion), retained jurisdiction of the case, but the prosecutor from the second county, Madison (Anderson), also assumed jurisdiction because of my change of venue.

Prosecutor Hardin was a large man, standing nearly six feet and six inches tall, and weighing around two hundred and fifty pounds. He looked every inch the harangued politician he was. His horn-rimmed and thick spectacles looked like two magnifying glasses covering his eyes. They gave his eyes a piggish appearance when viewed from the front. His hair was rumpled and tangled and jet-black with streaks of gray beginning to show through and around the temples. He was clean-shaven.

"Speaking as the prosecutor from Marion and Grant County, I have heard it said that this defendant is not going to get a fair trial. That's a blatant lie! I want you to know that our fair state does not expect you to allow prejudice and discrimination to influence in any way your decision in this case. It must be a just and deserving one. We want you to judge this boy as if he were a white boy on trial for his life."

At that precise moment, his courtroom manner was being grossly exaggerated. Politics was making its bid in my trial. I listened to him in utter disgust, hoping he would drop dead for standing up there and lying to the jury like that.

"The state in which we live is not going to ask for the life of the defendant in the electric chair," he droned on. "We had thought it best at the beginning to do so and so stated. We do not think that that is punishment enough for the hideous crime he has committed.

We will ask, instead, that he be sent to prison and there remain for the rest of his natural life, never again to enjoy the company and privileges of free and upright people.

Judge fairly without prejudice in your hearts. We don't want it said that our state is any worse on black people than in any other state."

After making those few remarks, the prosecutor from Anderson and Madison County spoke along the same lines.

Bailey, the senior partner of the two lawyers defending me, addressed the jury.

"Ladies and gentlemen of the jury," he began, "after such an arduous task of picking a fair and impartial jury, we want you to know that we are completely satisfied and confident as to the outcome of this trial. We will prove, beyond the shadow of a doubt, that the defendant was not actually involved in any murder, as the prosecutors for the state would have you believe without any reservations.

The defense will prove that the defendant, James Cameron, was at least a mile away from the scene of the crime at the time of its commission. We will also prove that force was used to get a confession from the defendant and that this confession is in error in every detail. We will prove that the defendant is an average American boy and was, and is well thought of in his neighborhood. That he is a youngster devoted to his hard working mother, that he was not himself on the night of the commission of the crime for which he stands accused. His innocence will be proven to you. After hearing the evidence on both sides, we feel confident you will return a verdict of acquittal. I thank you."[111]

The courtroom was buzzing with excitement. The defense attorneys were going to shoot for an acquittal! My mother allowed herself a faint smile as Bailey concluded his remarks. He was a portly, moon-faced man with light brown skin. He had won my mother's confidence, and she seemed to relax a little.

Court was adjourned until one o'clock that afternoon. I was taken back to the jail by Sheriff Bradley. He told me not to worry because everything was going to turn out all right.

That afternoon when court reconvened, a parade of witnesses for the state began. I wondered how in the world all of those people could possibly know me. I had never seen any of them before in my life. I sat at the defense table with my mother and attorneys. A local newspaper was on the table. It had a long story on the front page about me. The story said that the state militia saved my life in Marion. The headline across the top of the page screamed:

CAMERON FACES ANOTHER BATTLE FOR LIFE.

It had not been the militia, though, that saved me. I could never forget that. It had been that *voice*. If that mysterious voice had not spoken when it did and quieted the murderous fury of that mob, the militia's arrival would have been too late. Because that

---

[111] Jimmie's attorneys based part of their case on the claim that their client was immature for his age, a claim backed up by the testimony of his mother and younger sister Della.

night, after I had been allowed to walk back to the County Jail in Marion, about twenty minutes, more or less, had elapsed before the first contingent of soldiers arrived in the town. That was time enough to stretch many black necks.

The first witness for the state was the attending physician of the victim, Claude Deeter, of the Marion General Hospital. He had treated the wounds of the hold-up victim. There had been three punctures, one through the upper chest, one through the right hand, and another one in the left forearm. The wounds were caused by some sharp instrument, narrow, possibly a revolver bullet, or a poker, something on that order. He said they had all the appearance of gunshot wounds. He had not found any bullets in the body. The victim died a few hours after being rushed to the hospital by police ambulance.

Next came a farmer to the stand. He said he had heard shots ring out that night and immediately grabbed his shotgun and ran to the edge of his farm. He looked down into the valley below from where the sound of the shots came. He thought he saw two or three black boys by illumination of the moon. They got into a car and drove away from the valley. This pattern quickly followed the firing of the shots. He yelled at the occupants of the car to halt. When they failed to obey his command, he fired his shotgun loaded with #14 slugs at them. He heard a young lady screaming and crying. He remembered that the charge of his shotgun blast had possibly hit the rear of the get-a-way car.

Hurrying down into the valley below, he found a white man, badly wounded, who had crawled out of a cornfield through a pool of blood, and onto the road where he lay unconscious. He notified the police at once.

There was no doubt in his mind but that he could positively identify the boys if he ever saw them again. The moon was shining that night almost as bright as the noonday sun.

I felt what was coming next. I could feel it in the air. I sat there at the defense table looking at the farmer, my body cold, taut, wondering if the witness was going to tell a damn lie and say I was one of those boys. I felt I would spring out at the man if he said I was one of the boys in the car that made a get-a-way.

From the behavior pattern of the Marion Police Department, there was nothing in the world I would not put past them. Since the members of the department could lie faster than a dog could trot (my grandmother told me that a dog can trot all day long and never get tired), the police could have told the farmer to testify that I was one of the boys.

"Is this one of the boys?" The Marion prosecutor threw out the question as he pointed his finger at me.

I was ordered to stand up and face the witness. All the time the prosecutor kept his finger on me.

The farmer took his own good time in looking me over. The scrutiny he gave me was as if I were prize stock, and he wanted to make sure he was getting his money's worth if he bought it, that the deal was going to be to his complete satisfaction. There was an ominous hush as everybody in the courtroom watched the witness look me over. They waited, breathlessly, for his answer. Finally, it came.

"Nope. It weren't him," the witness said.

Something snapped inside me. I felt spent and relieved at the same time.

A heavily-built, double-chinned white woman, about forty-five years old, was called to the stand. She stated that she had been out riding that night and turned off the bridge road into the area where the victim had been shot. She was positive there were three boys in the car that pulled over to the side of the road to let her pass.

The boys had been in a '26 or '27 Ford convertible. The car was bearing toward the bridge road, out of Lover's Lane, as she was heading into it. The boy at the defense table was not one of the boys she had seen in the car that night.

The arresting officers were called to the stand. One of them said he was a motorcycle patrolman at the time of my arrest. He said he was a personal friend of the victim, Claude Deeter. He had joined in the search for a convertible with possible buckshot pellets dents in the rear of the car. Eventually such a vehicle was found. It belonged to Thomas Shipp. Shipp had been arrested. He confessed to the crime, naming Abram Smith and James Cameron as his accomplices. Shipp had revealed that Cameron was the ringleader, and that the gang planned to terrorize the whole state of Indiana with bank robberies, murders, and rapes!

The officer positively identified a .38 caliber revolver exhibited by the state as murder evidence in the case. It was a gun, he said, which he found in Shipp's possession. He had also aided other officers in arresting Cameron at his home. Cameron had been asleep in bed.

"What did Cameron do when you awakened him?" the Marion prosecutor wanted to know.

"Well, the court wouldn't allow me to say that because there are ladies present," came the answer.

The courtroom exploded with rocking laughter.

During the cross-examination of that officer whose name was Roy Cox, he snapped his answers to the defense attorneys. It was evident he didn't like the idea of black men questioning his motives and actions. My black attorneys poured it on him good. They seemed to know just what kind of questions to ask him that infuriated him more and more.

He had been on duty at the time of the double lynching. There had been nothing he could have done without orders from his superiors. Those orders did not come. Even if he had received such orders, it was doubtful he would have carried them out. He described the lynchings as "poetic justice." He concluded, "It's too bad they didn't hang Cameron right along with the whole damn shooting match!"

When he was excused, Attorney Brokenburr whispered to me that such belligerency and apparent racial hatred from a witness had been in my favor. "That kind of testimony always backfires."

Nevertheless, I failed to see his point. I was frightened of the way Cox had testified, the hateful looks he threw at me from the witness stand. My heart pounded furiously. There was a tightening of the chest muscles that made my breathing difficult. I would not have been surprised to see the officer grab his service revolver out of his holster and commence firing at me in a murderous rage, so ingrained was Cox's display of hatred toward me. His mode of conduct and behavior puzzled me.

The next officer was Patrolman Burden, the black policeman who had questioned me at home and in the squad car on the night of my arrest. He was the first officer to testify the next day.

He knew all three of the boys, Abe Smith, Thomas Shipp, and James Cameron. All of them had talked freely to him about the crime they committed that night. They admitted holding up the man and his lady friend, of shooting the man and raping the woman. There had been no coercion whatsoever in obtaining a confession from all three of the boys.

During cross-examination, my attorneys asked him if it was true that he had made a statement to both of them at the time of their investigation in Marion that Cameron had been forced to sign a confession. Also that he had been in the room when Cameron had been brutally knocked down and severely beaten by the police, and that the police were holding Cameron for purely political reasons.

"That was not true," Officer Burden said. He never in his life made that kind of a statement to anybody. It was a weak denial. He kept casting nervous glances at his superiors in the courtroom.

My attorneys then asked permission of the court to testify against the witness. After a legal tussle, which my attorneys won, permission was granted. The state prosecutors squirmed and whispered excitedly among themselves at this maneuver. Their vehement objections had all been overruled.

Bailey and Brokenburr took turns questioning one another concerning the statements that Officer Burden was alleged to have made to them in Marion. They corroborated one another's testimony. Cross-examination was useless. The facts stood out too clearly.

Officer Burden was placed back on the witness stand and his cross examination continued. He was perspiring profusely, anxiously watching his superiors as if in search of a cue. He had not made the statements attributed to him. He hadn't known that there was going to be a bloody shirt hung out on the flagpole at police headquarters; he knew nothing about it. Although Burden stuck to his story, he was such a confused and nervous man when my attorneys got through with him, he practically called himself a liar.

Sheriff Jacob Campbell then took the stand. He said that the defendant had been brought to his office at police headquarters and, of his own accord, signed a confession admitting that Smith raped the girl and Shipp shot the man.

"I really wanted to help Cameron all I could because he is nothing but a boy," he testified. "No one laid hands on him and neither did any of my deputies. The mob overpowered me and my deputies, but I did manage to save Cameron and spirited him away to safety. I did the best I could, under the circumstances."

A merciless cross-examination followed. The mob had overpowered him and his deputies. He had hesitated to shoot into the crowd because of the women and children present. He didn't think he had been negligent in the performance of his duty. There was nothing he could have done any different.[112]

As soon as the mob returned Cameron to the jail, he had spirited him out of town as quickly as possible. He had tried to reason with the crowd but they just wouldn't listen. He sent for reinforcements from nearby towns. There simply was not enough officers to cope with the mob.

---

[112] At that time, Indiana could legally prosecute a sheriff for allowing a prisoner to be taken from his jail. Campbell was not prosecuted. Instead, he was *commended* by the Grant County Grand Jury for preventing a race riot. This same Grand Jury indicted James Cameron for first-degree murder, rape, and armed robbery. They did not, however, indict anyone for the lynching.

He hadn't seen any of the mob carrying weapons. No, he was not a member of the Ku Klux Klan. He recognized no one in the crowd as being from Marion. On the whole, he thought, the people in Marion were typical law-abiding citizens. Every member of the mob had been an outsider; he had never seen any of them before that night.

For the first time I saw Mr. and Mrs. Deeter, the parents of the victim. Mrs. Deeter was a full-bosomed woman in steel-rimmed spectacles. Both of them reminded me of the Salvation Army missionary workers I had seen and heard singing hymns and preaching on the streets of Marion. I wondered if they thought, if they believed, that I had killed their boy.[113]

Their faces were pale and drawn. There was a look about them of deep mourning. Their thoughts seemed not focused on

Figure 35. William and Grace Deeter had six sons and a daughter. Claude, who would die in the hold-up, is the tallest boy, in the center. He was the Deeters' firstborn. *Deeter Family*

my trial but on some other days, years ago, questioning this and questioning that–why, what, when, where, who? Looking at them I wanted to cry. Tears of compassion rushed to my eyes but they did not overflow. Sorrow shot an arrow into my heart. A feeling of weakness and helplessness overcame me. I wished that Tommy and Abe could have guessed at the grief they would cause by killing Claude Deeter, as all the evidence indicated. It might have made all the difference in the world.

Mr. Deeter was asked to take the stand. He spoke quietly without a trace of bitterness in his voice. He told the court that he and his wife were not there to seek revenge. "Whatever is God's will," he said, "let it be done. We loved our boy and we

---

[113] Carl Deeter, Jr., the grandson of Mr. and Mrs. Deeter and nephew of Claude, said the Deeter family believes to this day that Cameron was the shooter. Nevertheless, they forgave him. Carl felt that Cameron had redeemed himself by his good works since the incident (editor's interview with Carl Deeter, Jr., in Marion, Indiana, October 2006).

miss him. But maybe it was God's will. He knows what is best for all of us. His will be done."

Court was adjourned.

The next day, Miss Mary Ball, the victim's lady companion, took the stand. She stated she had a dinner date with Claude Deeter, that they had driven out to Lover's Lane afterwards. They were sitting in the back seat of the car, talking marriage plans at the time of the hold-up. She was certain she could recognize the boys if she ever saw them again. No, the defendant, James Cameron, had not been one of the boys who committed the crime. She did not remember seeing him there at all. She had seen pictures in the newspapers of the two black youths who had been lynched on a tree in the courtyard in Marion. She went to view the bodies while they were still hanging on the tree–the very next day. They were the two men who had committed the crime.

No one held her hands. She had not been raped. No attempt had been made to rape her. After her companion was shot, the two youths left the scene immediately.

"This is one of the most ghastly and flagrant cases of introducing a signed confession into such an asinine trial that I have ever presided over. The Marion Police Department and the Sheriff's Department of Grant County should be reprimanded for doing this awful thing," said Judge Carl Morrow who was plainly disgusted. Without any motion from the defense attorneys, he threw out my signed confession.

My attorneys wanted him to declare a mistrial but the judge wouldn't go along with that plea.

I was placed on the witness stand for four hours. I told and retold my story. The prosecutors finally gave up trying to trip me up as if they thought I was lying about the whole thing. I told them the same story over and over again and again. Every piece fitted with the next, like a giant jigsaw puzzle. The whole picture was clear to everyone.

Several witnesses came forward as character references, including Sheriff Bernard Bradley. When they finished extolling my virtues, I felt pretty good. Of course no mortal could have been as good as the boy they described. After the pastor of my church and my mother Vera testified, both sides rested their case.

In their summation to the jury, the prosecutors called me a natural sneak and a born coward. They said that when the fear of being recognized dawned on me, I dropped my tail between my legs like a thieving dog caught stealing chickens, and ran away from the scene of the crime, a crime that I had willfully concocted and initiated. Life imprisonment was too good for me, but because of my age they hesitated to ask the death penalty.

"As long as boys like this criminal are allowed to run around and set off a chain reaction like this in killing people, and can sit here so calm and cool, thinking, no doubt, that he is going to walk out of this courtroom a free man, no one will be safe in our world. He is rotten and cunning clear through. He said he was scared. That was his reason for holding up the victim, and wantonly, fiendishly, and cold-bloodedly murdering him. A man whom he himself admits was overly nice to him, a man who wouldn't let anyone else shine his shoes but the defendant. Yet, the reward for such brotherhood affection was death at the hands of the very boy he thought the world of."

The state law was read to the jury. It pointed out that I was as guilty as if I had actually pulled the trigger of the gun that sent those death-dealing bullets into the body of the victim. Prosecutor Hardin ranted and raved for two solid hours. After he had finished, the Anderson prosecutor tried to surpass him in emotional appeal to the jury. He broke down and cried genuine tears of grief as he addressed the box.

"In many years, all the years I have practiced law," he sobbed, "never, never, have I seen a crime so shocking, so bereft of human decency, and as repulsive as the one you are being called upon to render a verdict. Send this boy away. Send him so far away he'll never see daylight again!"

Attorney Bailey spoke quietly in summing up for the defense. He began by thanking the jurors for their patience through five hot and humid days, listening attentively and courteously to both sides. Of course, he added, there was no doubt as to the defendant's innocence.

"The state has called this boy many vile names," he continued, "but this boy is no coward or sneak thief. He's just a plain boy, like any American boy, black or white. The state contended that the defendant held the hands of the girl while she was being raped. You heard the testimony of the young lady herself repudiate that very accusation. She stated, under oath and as the state's star witness, that she had not been raped. Now, if the state is mistaken, has misrepresented the facts in this sore contention that no attempt had been made to molest her, how many more false and deceitful and malicious charges have been leveled at the defendant?

We know that a crime has been committed and, as a result of that crime, three human beings are dead. Many lives have been shattered as an aftermath, many hearts have been broken, many dreams have been smashed asunder. Two of the human beings died at the hands of a mob when law enforcement officials stood by and allowed a Ku Klux Klan-aroused mob to take over the whole city, a mob whose ringleaders are known to authorities, yet they have gone unpunished for the crime of murder in its worst context. The other death came about at the hands of God knows who.

Surely such an intelligent-looking jury as the faces I see before me at this moment could not be tricked into believing that this boy, James Cameron, is guilty of committing murder. His confession has been repudiated. You heard the awful evidence of how it had been obtained from him under terrible physical duress. You know now how it was falsified with what the police assumed happened. You know the charges against him have not been proven. The only evidence the prosecutor can, truthfully, use is the testimony of the defendant himself. You heard the defendant tell his story. Can you not help but feel deep down in your hearts that he was telling the truth, and nothing but the truth, that he told everything just as it happened as far as he knows?

The defendant has suffered greatly for the minor role he was forced to play in this combination of circumstances, in the commission of this crime for which he stands accused. His year in jail awaiting trial resulted in poor health for him. His treatment at the hands of the mob was more than sufficient punishment for his misdemeanor, his thoughtlessness."

Bailey went on for an hour. Then Attorney Brokenburr, a tall, dark-skinned, suave, debonair, highly-polished, distinguished-looking man, continued for another hour.

In his charge to the jury, Judge Morrow instructed: "You have heard the evidence in this case. Now judge impartially. If you think the defendant is innocent, bring in a verdict of acquittal, not guilty. You will have five verdicts to choose from. Namely: guilty of being an accessory before the fact to first-degree murder, to second-degree murder, to involuntary manslaughter, to voluntary manslaughter, or an acquittal. If you think the defendant is guilty and cannot arrive at what degree of guilt you wish to place upon him, he should be given the benefit of the doubt and you should vote for the least penalty."

Each verdict and its meaning was exhaustively explained to the jury. When the judge had finished, they filed out of the jury box to the jury room to deliberate upon the merits of my case.

I was led back to the jail by Sheriff Bradley.[114]

Two hours and forty-five minutes later we were on our way back to the courtroom. The jury had reached a verdict. The foreman of the jury handed a slip of paper to the

---

[114] Jimmie and his attorneys needed to be protected by Sheriff Bradley and his deputies at all times, because they were in constant danger (Madison, 2001, 108).

clerk of the court who in turn handed it to Judge Morrow. The judge glanced at it, then handed it back to the clerk to read aloud in the courtroom.

"We, the jury, find the defendant, James Cameron, guilty of being an accessory before the fact to voluntary manslaughter!"

Then I remembered what Sheriff Bradley had whispered in my ear that second day of my trial. I smiled. Sheriff Bradley sure knew what he was talking about. What a man!

Cheers and shouts exploded in the courtroom. Joy appeared on most of the faces. Even the jury was smiling! Bailey and Brokenburr were jubilant. Black and white faces wrinkled in smiles, came forward and congratulated them: "A brilliant victory!" "A real victory over the forces of evil!" "You gentlemen were simply wonderful!"

Before long an Anderson newspaper hit the streets in an EXTRA. The headline read: CAMERON WINS AGAIN!

Judge Morrow finally restored order and indicated that he was ready to pronounce sentence on me. I was led before the bar by my attorneys, standing on each side of me. Judge Morrow cleared his throat, adjusted his glasses, and gazed down at me.

"Have you anything you wish to say before sentence is passed upon you?" he wanted to know.

"No, sir." I answered.

"Then, according to the findings of the jury and of the power vested in me by the State of Indiana, I do hereby sentence you, James Cameron, to be imprisoned in the State Reformatory at Pendleton for a term of not less than two years or more than twenty-one years."

A giant firecracker seemed to have exploded inside my head. It was all over. I didn't have to worry about what was going to happen to me anymore. Such were my thoughts.

Friends and well-wishers crowded around me. They congratulated me on what they thought was a fair sentence.[115]

Sheriff Bradley came forward, smiling like a little boy. He was actually jubilant!

"Jimmie, you have only two years to go and I know you can do them standing on your head," he told me.

---

[115] Not everyone felt this way about Jimmie's "light" sentence. Some white people in the Marion area talked about attacking Sheriff Bradley's jail and lynching Jimmie. This time, however, hundreds of Anderson's black citizens armed and organized themselves to "give the lynchers a really peppery time…," according to the *Indianapolis Recorder* (Madison, 2001, 108).

After the excitement had died down, I was taken back to the Madison County Jail to await transfer to the state Reformatory. My attorneys had tried to persuade the court to apply the time I had already spent in jail to my sentence. That way I would only have one year to serve, instead of two, before being eligible for parole. Judge Morrow overruled the plea.

Back in the Riverside Hotel, the prisoners wished me good luck. They staged an impromptu celebration in my honor. Old timers who had served time in various state prisons and other correctional institutions gave me all the advice they could think of. I made all kinds of mental notes.

CHAPTER FIFTEEN

Living with the Verdict

Whphen the time came for me to say good-bye, there was a lump in my throat. Sheriff Bradley called me into his office the day of my sentencing. There I said good-bye to my Mother and sisters Marie and Della. Mrs. Bradley and her children came forward and wished me good luck. All of them told me to be a good boy so that I could get out sooner. I promised them I would.

On the ride to Pendleton, which is twelve miles from Anderson, I rode up in the front seat with Sheriff Bradley. He drove his brand new Buick touring car. I sat between him and his chief deputy, Marion Fisher. One other car loaded with deputies and plenty of guns and ammunition followed us.

As we rode southward, Sheriff Bradley said: "Now don't let me down, Jimmie. Be a good boy. I am going to give you a good recommendation when we arrive at the Reformatory."

"I won't let you down, Sheriff Bradley." I meant every word of what I said to *that* man. People didn't come any finer than Sheriff Bernard Bradley.

In a few minutes the familiar gray walls of the state penitentiary began to loom ahead in all their gloominess. This was where I had been held for safekeeping. Now, I wondered what it would be like to have to stay in there as a prisoner for the next several years.

I hurried to finish eating a candy bar the sheriff had given me, just as the car came to a halt in front of the administration building. I followed the sheriff up the entrance steps. We stopped at the same window where I had registered as a safe-keeper. The same clerk who had signed me in then was on duty. Sheriff Bradley handed him my commitment papers and requested a talk with the Superintendent about me. The clerk nodded and wrote my name down on a form sheet. That's how I officially became a ward of the state of Indiana. My identity became a number, a vital statistic to be filed away.

Sheriff Bradley said good-bye to me. We shook hands warmly. And then, in front of everybody in the front offices, he gave me a fatherly hug, as guards and visitors stared with embarrassment. It was an emotional parting.

As the sheriff was ushered in to talk to the Superintendent, I was hustled through the large steel gates along with seven other new inmates. The grinding gears of the gate did not startle me as it did some of the new men. I felt a small sense of superiority having gone through the gate once before.

One of the men, "Tiger" Flowers, a black man, was a repeater. He was as mean a criminal as ever walked the face of the earth. He was back to pull a ten-year stretch for a part he had played in a hold-up. He had used a toy pistol, but the victim, an elderly white lady, dropped dead from fright. Tiger was homely enough to scare anybody to death even without a gun. Just one of his scowls would suffice.

We were then led through the same gate by three guards and lined up in front of a desk at the long end of a corridor, deeper inside the walls. A tall consumptive-looking, very wrinkled guard who looked like he had a Halloween mask on, greeted us. He was sixty or seventy years old and walked as if every bone in his body was creaking from the effort. He looked like the devil if ever I had seen one play the part.

Placing his hands on his side where his hips were supposed to be, he spoke to us in a sarcastic tone of voice:

"We didn't know that you were coming. But now that you are here, we are going to take real good care of you. Of course, we knew that Cameron here was coming. But we're going to take care and look out for all you boys. If you do what you are told and don't give us any back lip, you'll make out all right. Don't come in here with the idea that you are going to run this place. We ran it before you came here. We'll run it while you are here. And we'll still be running it after you're dead and gone!"

It was an impressive pep talk. I began thinking about all the countless prison stories I had heard, about how men were beaten up for no reason at all and no corrective action is ever taken about it. I prayed, silently, that such a thing wouldn't happen to me. Judging from the expressions on other faces around me, I wasn't praying alone.

The old guard's name was Henry Lictner. He had a reputation for being an ornery cuss, a real louse. Whenever he served as an interview officer in the visiting room, it was always a great delight to him to ask any one of the prisoners visiting with their loved ones some kind of demeaning question, such as "Hey, you! Stand up and tell all these people in here why you're in prison!" Whoever the prisoner was, he had to stop talking to his mother or sisters or friends, get to his feet, and tell everyone present what his crime had been. We knew just what to expect out of him—the worst in mankind. I found this out later.

"What are you in here for?" I heard him ask one of the white prisoners starting on his time the same time I was.

"For nothing," the boy snapped, sarcastically.

The words had barely left his mouth before Officer Lictner knocked him flat on his back with one hand and pulled out his blackjack with the other. It was a nasty-looking weapon with a weighted tip. From the looks of it one could easily surmise that it had been bounced off many heads.

"When you address an officer, always say 'sir.' Do you understand me?" he growled at the man.

"Yes, sir," the boy replied, as he was permitted to get up off the floor and resume his place back in line.

"That goes for all you rummies," Officer Lictner warned, waving his blackjack menacingly as if he could hardly wait for a chance to use it on one of us.

I made the first of a long list of mental notes for use inside those prison walls.

Officer Lictner walked over and stood in front of me. I stopped breathing. I looked him straight in the eyes. I saw before me poor white trash, glorying in what little authority he was allowed to wield.[116] Every black man knows the character of these little gods.

"Well, you sure were lucky," he told me. "The mob nearly lynched you and the jury nearly turned you loose!"

No question had been asked, so I remained rigid and quiet. I could feel his hateful, sneaky-looking, snake eyes raking me from head to foot. But, then again, maybe it was a

---

[116] "Poor white trash" is a demeaning term signifying low-income, generally uneducated white people who live on the fringes of white society. Under the plantation system in the South, low-income whites had to compete with enslaved blacks for enough work just to subsist. Some house slaves looked down upon white servants, many of whom lived in miserable conditions, and coined this term for them. This pejorative term continues to be used today by both blacks and whites.

look more of incredulity than spite. All I could make out of the instance was that Officer Lictner was trying to judge for himself whether I was innocent or guilty.

"All of you follow me," he ordered.

Tiger and I, another black man, and five whites fell in line and marched behind the guard. We were all led through the prison yard, past the guardhouse where I had been held for safekeeping for nearly four months to a large building in the rear. It was the bathhouse. There we were all given a shower and a delousing with kerosene and blue ointment. A black inmate, still in his teens, was in charge of the stalls. When the guard wasn't looking he whispered to me, "You're Cameron, ain't you?"

"Yes, I am."

"I thought so. All of us in here were hoping you would beat the rap."

"I thought so, too." I smiled at him. "I was kinda hoping that way."

"You're going to make it in here," he told me. "We're going to see to that. I'll let you talk to some of the boys when you come out of quarantine."

"That's all right with me," I told him.

A great, big, barrel-chested guard, appropriately named Two-Ton by the prisoners, came into the guardhouse. He had on a pair of the largest pants I had ever seen on a man. His waist was nearly as high as I was tall. His beefy body was supported on surprisingly thin legs. He weighed well over three hundred pounds. He was Clarance Delington, whom I grew to love as a friend and a confidante.

I didn't notice his six feet and eight-inch frame strolling around the horseshoe-shaped row of shower stalls. I turned my back and was stooping over to pick up a piece of soap that had fallen onto the floor when SMACK! Great day in the morning! The sound could be likened to a forty-five cap being exploded in the frame of a .357 Magnum revolver. The sound echoed through the whole building. He had dealt a stinging blow with his bare hands on my rump. It landed squarely and solidly on my buttocks, making me almost jump out of my stall.

Two-Ton roared and slapped his thigh in a frenzy of glee. I didn't know that this was a daily routine with him, that being in charge of the bathhouse, he religiously followed the new men around like a bum searching for stubs on a street. I didn't say a word to Two-Ton as my behind went into all kinds of contortions to ease the excruciating pain. I was afraid he would hit me again. But I made another mental note: NEVER TURN YOUR BACK IN THE SHOWER ROOM!

Still naked as a jaybird, we new inmates were led through the laundry to the clothes shop. The laundry was a steaming beehive, swarming with inmates in gray, postman-like uniforms washing, ironing and pressing clothes. They whistled and jeered at us new arrivals.

"You'll be sorrr-eee! Fresh meat! Fresh meat!"

I was glad when we got out of there. All that hollering made me very nervous. I already had some idea about what they meant when they called out "fresh meat!"

In the clothes shop, we were issued flour-sack undershirts, like my Mother used to make for the family, two pairs of gray, cotton socks, and one gray uniform. I was allowed to keep my black oxfords after they had been stamped with my number. Everything I received from the state had my number stamped on it somewhere. That place was numbers crazy.

After we dressed, a messenger inmate led me and Tiger and the other black man to H-cell house. All of us were placed in solitary, individual cells. This was the beginning of our two weeks quarantine period. We were vaccinated for every known disease and some that were not. It was tough to sit down after receiving some of those shots. We were given physical, dental and psychological examinations during this period.

I remember one of the last shots I received. It made everything and everybody, regardless of color, look snow white. I keeled over in a faint in the hospital corridor, and was a very sick young man for the rest of that day.

We were only allowed to leave our cells for those required examinations and, of course, for our meals. I tried to eat like some of the old-timers, but the steam-cooked food was way too hot for me at first. It was impossible for me to finish my food along with the rest of them. Extra time was always allowed to me to clean my plate. It was a "hole" offense to leave even a crumb on your plate.

But in two weeks time I had learned to wolf the meals down in the regular allotted time, no matter how hot, with the rest of the men.

Finally, quarantine was over. It was now time to be assigned to a regular job inside the walls. From the talk I had heard from the prison grapevine, one of the factories to stay out of was the shirt shop. Those inmates working there were the objects of pity and all the emotions that go with suffering mankind. All of the "tasks" there were said to be almost impossible. The scuttlebutt said it was a regular Devil's Island inside a brick and red building.

I was summoned to the Assistant Superintendent's office and assigned to the dreaded shirt shop. Dejectedly, I followed the messenger to the place I had hoped to avoid. The guard in charge of the department I was assigned was an old man with crusty features and bloodshot eyes. He never smiled and his jaws drooped, giving his face a sad, bloodhound look. With an ever-present wad of chewing tobacco in his mouth, he looked like a Hollywood make-up artist had fitted him out for some role in a horror movie. He never stopped chewing, it seemed. He was strictly business though.

"Old Droopy" as he was called behind his back, looked me over and copied my name and number down on a piece of paper. Without a word, he turned me over to the civilian in charge of the prisoners operating the various sewing machines. He was a tall, thin man of about sixty years of age or more. He could have passed for the twin brother of the consumptive-looking Officer Lictner, who had given me the entrance pep talk. Instinctively, I disliked the man. His name was Barwick.

" Know how to run one of these machines?" he asked me.

"No, sir."

"Well, you will learn to run one. You better learn how to run it real good, too, if you expect to stay out of the guardhouse on a fare of bread and water!"

I got the feeling that the man was deliberately picking on me, hoping for some trouble out of me.

"I'll do the best I can," I hastened to assure him.

"Your best may not be good enough," he said, flippantly.

He called one of the inmates over who seemed to be in charge of the line. He was a white man. "Make a side-seamer out of Cameron, here," he ordered, pointing his finger at me. "Give him three weeks to learn, then put him on task," he directed the prisoner.

The convict's name was Henry. He was a narrow-faced thirty-year-old man who looked like he was fifty. He had been on the penal farm, in the house of correction, served countless jail terms, and was a three-time repeater in the Reformatory. He was doing ten years for bank robbery. Over half of his life had been spent behind bars for various offenses. He was an extremely nervous sort of a fellow, but was awfully sure of himself around sewing machines.

He smiled at me when Barwick left us alone, flashing badly-stained tobacco-colored teeth. The bulge on the side of his jaw gave evidence that he had a large cud in his mouth at the time. "Nothing much to it," he told me. Then he placed two pieces of precut cloth between the folder on the machine and flicked the switch with the pressure of his foot on an electric pedal that resembled an automobile accelerator. Thus, I was shown how side seams are made on shirts and trousers.

Henry showed me over and over, again and again. Then he showed me some more. Finally he permitted me to try my hand as an operator. When I tried to imitate him, I gave up all hope of ever getting out of the Indiana State Reformatory. I could see myself in the "hole" on bread and water, jumping up and down and screaming like a raving maniac.

My exasperations and earnest gyrations amused Henry very much, but it sure was not funny to me. He doubled over in laughter. I failed to see one bit of humor in the situation. I was all tied up in knots deep down in my stomach.

"Don't worry, kid," he told me finally. "Everything's gonna be all right."

I didn't know it at the time but Henry was right. But it was a full six months before I could turn out eighteen dozen shirts in one 8-hour day, as required for task, or thirty-six dozen pair of pants.

A few days later, my first Sunday out of quarantine, I found myself marching with 2,100 other prisoners to the drill ground, as it was called,

Figure 36. Inmates in a prison sewing room, circa 1930. *State Archives of Florida*

where baseball games were held. There I met the men who actually ran the prison. It was my first meeting with them. Most of them were characters who had been in and out of prison as if trapped in a revolving door. They knew all about me, my whole life's story. Most of them were white men. They told me to let them know if anybody bothered me in any way. I was not to worry about making task in the shirt shop, or any other shop. I guessed they had decided to take care of me because of the publicity my case had received. But it turned out that I had become an object of pity and compassion to those men, the blacks and whites, who had a hand in everything that went on inside the prison. Many of the whites told me that they had a lot to make up to me for the things the mob had done to me and my people. They were really sorry the lynchings had taken place.

I felt at home, a little. I almost had the feeling of having big brothers, blacks and whites, to help me out of tight spots.

Then the thought struck me that it would, indeed, be a wonderful world in which to live if people on the outside, blacks and whites, would consider not only pity and compassion but respect in their race relations, if they would put into practice more understanding and tolerance and brotherhood, as these were inclined to do.

The best break of all was that I did not smoke. Each Sunday, after dinner in the mess hall, the prisoners were locked up in their cell houses and dormitories for the rest of the day. It was then that the Captain of the Guards, Captain Moore, would hand each prisoner, except those locked up in the guardhouse disciplinary cells, a five cent bag of Bull Durham smoking tobacco or a ten cent plug of Brown Mule chewing tobacco. That was it, the weekly allowance. That was why tobacco was the most valuable item in the Reformatory, more valuable than dollar bills!

Figure 37. A nickel bag of Bull Durham smoking tobacco: the currency of the Reformatory.

For a bag of Bull Durham, a prisoner could read the Indianapolis Star newspaper or the Anderson Herald or Bulletin, every day for a whole week, as fast as they were smuggled inside the prison. A single sack of tobacco could also pay your way out of a "hole" offense, or have someone knifed so that nobody would ever know who did the carving. Tobacco was the magic word. It ruled the inmates. It commanded the utmost respect and favors to those who had it to spare. There was nothing the men would not do for tobacco. The prison authorities made criminals out of the men by such a skimpy allowance of tobacco!

My "big brothers" told me to give my bag of Bull to a character named Jughead. Jughead was a black man, a sort of collector of men for Henry, my benefactor in the shirt shop, sort of like a runner in the numbers racket. This arrangement did not come any too soon, because after only two weeks instead of three, as Barwick had stated, I was assigned First Task: three dozen shirts or six dozen pants a day. The task could also be worked out with a combination of the two, such as one and a half dozen shirts and three dozen pants. Second Task would involve six dozen shirts and twelve dozen pants the following week. When that week was up, I was expected to turn out nine dozen shirts and/or eighteen dozen pairs of pants. The task would climb each week until the maximum quota was reached and maintained, from then on: eighteen dozen shirts or thirty-six dozen pairs of pants.

I had not learned to sew and could not turn out one dozen shirts that could stand inspection. Raw edges and crooked seams were making a nervous wreck out of me, killing me by degrees.

Henry watched me like a toddling infant. He would sit down at my machine and pretend something was wrong with it. He would "fix it" and then test it out by running five or six dozen shirts to proportionate pairs of pants in ten or fifteen minutes time. It was a known fact that he could turn out one hundred dozen shirts in one eight-hour day, or over three hundred dozen pairs of pants! I believed every word of it. I would have believed he could turn out twice that much work in one day. There was no doubt about his ability on one of those sewing machines. He was constantly blinding with his speed and dexterity. Dozens of shirts and pants tumbled from my machine as if they were being dumped from a chute whenever Henry operated my machine.

He had other routines which were just as effective. Sometimes, he would tamper with my machine so that it really wouldn't run. This would automatically exempt me from task for that day. Again, after a little talk with Henry, the shop mechanic, another white man (there were no black machinists in the whole prison), would give my machine a thorough check to determine the "cause" of the breakdown. The machine would then be completely dismantled. Parts would be replaced, rough edges replaced by a precision machine in the machine shop, new needles installed, belts tightened or replaced, pedals replaced, etc. Although I could not sew very well, I knew how to fix my sewing machine blindfolded! I had seen it torn down so many times and rebuilt.

I saved tobacco like an immigrant in America who had plans for visiting relatives in the Old Country and wanted to show how much money he had made in the New World. My very welfare depended on its proper distribution to those prisoners in positions to help me from time to time. I found out they were men who knew how to get things done, quickly, efficiently, and without any red tape.

After six months those men decided that I could be trusted. Gradually, I was taken into the group, which consisted of about fifty blacks and two hundred whites. Prison officials only thought they were running the place. The fact was the ruling inmates did just whatever they pleased. One of their best stunts was smuggling prostitutes into the prison for a few days.

On one of those occasions, they brought in, with the help of certain corrupt guards who could be bribed, a white girl barely out of her teens. They kept her in the laundry, in the bakery shop, and, sometimes, in the hospital. It all depended on which area they considered safest at the time. The girl worked three days and nights. When she left to return to her home in Indianapolis, she carried away twelve hundred and seventy dollars!

I discovered a strange thing about myself during her visit. Although I had tried several girls before being incarcerated, I was at a complete loss to explain my impotency when offered the chance to lay with that white girl. No clearly defined fears went through my mind to cause it. I simply was helpless, as soft as a marshmallow. This caused me a lot of concern until a few months later, when they smuggled in a black girl. I was able to rear like a bull! But when they brought in that white girl, I failed miserably. Jughead thought my impotency with the white girl only was real funny.

"Guess dem white folks is right," he teased me. "Only way to stop us black boys from gittin dat white stuff is to put a rope around our necks!" He laughed hysterically.

"Course you ain't missing much," he went on. "Dem ofay[117] bitches jist lak to lay dere on dere pretty little pink asses and dares yuh to show 'em a good time. Hell, I'll take a black gal every time, somebody who believes in wiggling her little ass until yuh is wrung out dry as a desert. When dey fights me back, I loves dat!"

One day the whistle blew for dinnertime. We prisoners lined up downstairs to be counted before marching off to the mess hall from the shirt shop. A tall, young black man rushed up to edge in alongside me as we assembled and waited for the guard to come down and count us before leading us off. I had noticed the man before in a casual way. He wore tailor-made uniforms, kept his nappy hair konked[118], moved about as if he thought himself better than anyone else. He had an air of superiority, of looking down on other people, of poking fun at them. This seemed to have been his passion. No one was as great as he fancied himself to be.

Nudging up to me, he asked me did I have a sister named Marie. I told him I did.

"I got a cell buddy who says he knows your sister Marie," he told me. "He said he had been out with her on several dates and that she sure is got some good pussy!"

I swung and hit the man in the mouth as hard as I could before he could get the words out of his mouth. Then, in a blind rage, tears of anger streaming from my eyes, I began pummeling the man, flailing away at him, trying to kill him in as short a time as possible. Six fellow inmates pulled me off of him as I tried to stomp the daylights out of him. Luckily for him, and for me, the guard had tarried awhile upstairs to look over

---

[117] Ofay: a demeaning term for a white person, used by black people.

[118] Straightened and oiled.

some papers and did not see the fight. By the time he got downstairs, a semblance of order had been restored.

In the meantime, I had knocked out the man's center front teeth, raised a goose egg alongside his right eye, and fractured one of his ribs.

That encounter with me resulted in a traumatic experience for that fellow. In a short while, prisoners soon forgot about how the guy used to act because he seldom had anything to say to anybody. Perhaps the main reason was that he had been spoken to by several of my big brothers. The error of his way had been pointed out to him as they whipped his ass real good. I was accused of paying two bags of Bull for a job well done!

Several days later, the guard in charge of the shirt shop called me up to the stand where he sat in a heightened position to enable him to see all over his department.

"Cameron, I know all about that fight you had with that fellow the other day. I just want you to know that you should have knocked his damn brains out. If I'd known that you were fighting him because of an insult to your sister, I would have stayed up here a long time to give you a chance to kill the son-of-a-bitch. We can do without those kind of people around us."

I just looked at the man. Since he hadn't asked any questions, I didn't volunteer any answers. Sometimes a member of the ruling gang would be thrown into the hole on what prison officials called "indefinite charges of investigation." It was a way they used to try to make him squeal about illicit operations inside the prison walls. He would be placed on bread and water and without any tobacco. But just the same, three meals a day would be smuggled in to him with factory-made cigarettes every day of his confinement. If he kept his mouth shut, he invariably came out of the hole looking much better than when he went in. He would be well rested. The penalty for an open mouth was death. It was always very difficult to organize a complete new underground system. But it could be done.

Only once during my stay in the prison did a prisoner spill his guts to the prison officials. The very next day he was released from the hole, he met with a fatal accident in the tin shop. A pair of tin snips were pulled from his chest. No one was able to ascertain whether he fell on them or just what did happen to him. At any rate, nobody squealed after that, even though the third degree was used and practiced more and more by prison officials in their desperation to find out what was going on in the prison. Several convicts were beaten to death with blackjacks by sadistic guards in attempts to force them to talk.

After six months on my sewing machine, I began turning out so many shirts and pants that I consistently went over task. I began making big money, by Reformatory standards: twenty cents a week! Now it was my turn to help new men make task. Occasionally I helped some of the old-timers, too. They were men who had come back from the grave (the hole) or from some guardhouse beating too weak to stand the pace. Such aid was a simple matter when all of us were working on the same order, the same series of shirts and pants. It was very difficult when the projects differed. Nearly all of the men who went over task would take their excesses and secretly place them in the hampers of the men needing the count.

Three or four times a week somebody would fail to make task. That meant three or four days in the hole. When released they came back to work pale and gaunt, cadaverous-looking, as if in the last stages of tuberculosis. Just the same, they immediately were placed back on task again, right where they had left off, which they invariably failed to meet because of their weakened condition. So, back to the hole. It was the worst kind of a vicious cycle.

The Assistant Superintendent decided whether you'd stand up for missing task or be thrown in the hole. The "stand-up" was really tougher than the hole. You had to take off your shoes and stand in your stocking feet on a piece of cloth one foot square. Your spine had to be straight as a rod. Sometimes, you stood for an hour, two hours, four hours. For one, two, or three days in a row. You'd miss all meals served during that time. The only time you could leave your pad was when nature called and then, only under guard for proof of the trip.

I saw many grown men crying like little children, like babies, when sentenced to the stand-up. Many of them begged the guard to allow them to see the assistant to ask permission to be thrown into the hole instead. The stand-up did not go against your record. The hole was a parole-blocking demerit.

The stand-up made your feet feel as if someone was sticking needles into the bottom of them. You could not bend over and message them with your hands. You could not vary your stance. It was like posing in the still for a great painter. To take either foot off the pad for a single moment, without permission, meant a cruel, bloody, head whipping with a blackjack.

Extra guards were always loitering around to see that you stayed in your place or they'd knock you into it. Even if an inmate got the blind staggers[119] and fell out, it made no difference to them. "There's not a goddamn thing wrong with you," they'd tell a standee. "Stand up there before we beat your fucking brains out!" Then, they'd proceed to do just that, while rough-handling you to your feet!

All the guards kept their eyes on the pads of cloth cut from a blanket, hoping for a chance to do some head-whipping whenever they noticed both feet were not squarely in place.

So you stood up. You thought your back would break in two or was already broken. You stood there with the picture of your crime or thoughtlessness being stamped indelibly on your mind. You cursed yourself for being such a damn fool, for being so stupid as to get in trouble in the first place. Then you formulate plans for getting even with the rotten, stinking guards for slandering your manhood, for being so sadistic. Later on, you change your mind. The thought occurs to you that all you want is out, away from so much human suffering, misery, and forgotten humanity.

I can recall when the Assistant Superintendent sentenced a one-legged prisoner to stand up for one hour!

Talking in the mess hall, possession of contraband, failing to show proper respect for a guard were the usual offenses. Most of the time, the stand-up section of the guardhouse was filled to overflowing. The little pieces of blanket cloths were placed about three feet apart, about twenty pieces lined up on each side of the corridor. Each man faced a small locked cell. The toilet was at the end of the aisle. The place was always hot, stifling, and the tension was nearly always unbearable. The monotony was relieved only by the cries of pain and anguish when one of the inmates collapsed and was beaten back up on his feet by the sadistic guards until he resumed his proper position. It was practically impossible to pull a long stand-up trick without suffering two or three head whippings.

One of the inmates, a white fellow, doing ten years for bank robbery, was in an enviable position. Because of his hulk, Big Ed was appointed as an assistant to the guard in charge of the guardhouse. He was a strapping, beetle-browed man of about twenty-five years of age. He stood nearly seven feet tall and weighed in the neighborhood of three hundred pounds. He was a giant of a man and there was not an ounce of fat on

---

[119] Blind staggers are the symptoms of several diseases affecting farm animals. The sick animal walks with an unsteady, staggering gait and appears to be blind.

him anywhere. He took great pleasure in whipping fellow convicts. The stand-up was tougher than ever with Big Ed around. He'd walk up and down the aisles, just looking for trouble, hoping to find a man's foot off the mat. He whipped me once during a two-day stand-up. I still have the scars to show for it.

When Big Ed's hitch was cut short by a governor's parole, the ruling inmates sent one of its members, Chick Brady, to pick a fight with him on the day of his release. Chick had been a sparring partner for Chuck Wiggins who had been a sparring partner for Jack Dempsey, the heavyweight-boxing champion of the world. Brady whipped Big Ed like a farmer whipping a horse when he is trying to get to the county fair before closing time. He gave himself a good workout at Big Ed's expense. Both men were thrown into the hole. The Superintendent, however, somehow got word of the plot and Big Ed was released as scheduled.

Three days after his release, Big Ed died in an accident on the outside. The "accident" had been arranged and cost certain men inside the Reformatory five hundred dollars. When word of Big Ed's death was confirmed to the men in the prison, there was great rejoicing inside the walls of the Indiana State Reformatory.

It was a relatively simple matter to arrange special accidents or anything else on the outside that could possibly affect the welfare of men on the inside. Messages could be sent by certain members of the baseball team, which played a certain number of games away from "home." Those men were also able to pick up much contraband from friends and well-wishers and bring it back inside the prison. This was, in fact, the way we obtained the necessary ingredients for making most of our corn whiskies and various wines. The rest of the stuff was stolen from the prison commissary.

Parts for the stills were made in the metal shop and set up in places like the bakery, laundry, bathhouse, and engine room. Every time a still was discovered by some nosy guard, another one sprang up the very next day. One of the largest stills, which turned out Raisin Jack, was discovered in the Chapel![120]

It was possible to get drunk every day! Many of the inmates lived in a mild stupor. The guards never knew they drank unless they caught them sober! It was impossible to tell if they were drunk because we never saw them sober! They said it was the only way they could make their time! The Reformatory baseball team was always losing games by

---

[120] A still is an apparatus used to make, among other things, alcoholic beverages from various fruits and vegetables. Raisin Jack is a wine distilled from raisins.

whopping margins just because the center fielder, the first baseman, or the shortstop was too drunk to catch a routine pop fly or an easy ground roller!

In the meantime, I had enrolled in school and continued studying during my entire period of confinement. I studied geometry, algebra, English, typing, shorthand, and world history, which turned out to be my favorite subject. I also read as many books as I could from the prison library.

At the end of a year's confinement, I had a pretty good idea of the kind of men living behind the walls. I was amazed to learn that they came from every walk of life, that doctors, lawyers, ministers, drug addicts, homosexuals, murderers, thieves, robbers, whore mongers, con men, the wise and the foolish, the rich and poor, saints and sinners, the well and the sick, all became just another number in the state Reformatory. Even more surprising to me was the fact that many of the people who had been convicted of the more violent crimes, such as patricide, matricide, brutal armed robberies, rapes, and plain cold-blooded murder, were kind and sensitive men.

The line between good men and bad men was extremely difficult to determine at times. Some of the men I never learned to trust. They were the blacks and whites who had spent most of their lives in and out of prison, men who never learned decency, honor, respect, and integrity. The prison was no temporary stop-over for them; it was a way of life! They no longer dreamed of the kind of life that I and the rest of the first offenders, for the most part, looked forward to with ever increasing hope and anxiety. They had given up all hope, the very essence of life. Many of them had their bodies warped as well as their minds because of savagely administered beatings by sadistic prison guards. That state of lawlessness, over which they had no control, was the only excuse for their many violations of laws governing human conduct and behavior patterns.

Toward the second year of my confinement, I had a cellmate only a year older than I. His name was Jabbo. He was a round-faced, friendly little fellow, with limpid brown eyes. Looking at him and talking with him, it was difficult to believe that he had shot a man to death. A much larger man had drawn a knife on him in a crap game. He had knocked the knife away, causing the big man to fall to the ground, and ran out of the house. He was followed, however, and fired three shots at the huge man closing in on him. The man was wounded and did not die. However, one of Jabbo's wild shots had hit a young man standing on a porch nearby, killing him instantly. Little Jabbo was in his second year of a one to ten year sentence for involuntary manslaughter. He brooded night and day over his mistake.

"I wish I hadn't hit that kid," he'd say over and over, as if that was the only sentence he knew how to speak. "Wish I hadn't hit that kid!"

"Worrying about it is not going to do any good now, Jabbo," I told him. "It don't bring the boy back to life. Why don't you get yourself a book and try to learn something while you're in here? Get your mind off your trouble."

Such advice did little good. Jabbo actually worried himself to death! He finally reached the stage in life where he stopped eating and just wasted away. He punished himself. When he died in the prison hospital, several days later, I sneaked over to view his body before it was shipped back to Indianapolis for burial. Jabbo appeared to be in a deep, satisfying sleep. And for the first time since I had known him, the little fellow had a smile on his face.

The man who replaced Jabbo in my cell was called South Bend. He was a large chested, dark-skinned man who could have easily been mistaken for a Latin. He had short, spindly legs, so short, in fact, that they looked like he was deformed. His mean looking, narrow face was heavily pock-marked, and there were heavy shadows under his evil looking eyes that were forever shifting about. He even looked the proverbial description of a crook. He had a pleasant enough sounding voice but he used it only to talk about crime. He was firmly convinced that crime did pay and that only fools worked for a living when robbery and burglary were so easy.

"What in the hell are you doing in here if you're so damn smart?" I asked him one day.

"If that knee-action hadn't broken down on our get-a-way car, it would have been the perfect crime," he blabbered to me.

He and four buddies had held up a string of filling stations. When their car broke down during their last hold-up, all of them had been caught and sentenced to from ten to twenty-five years in the Reformatory.

"Look at all the guys in here with us," I pointed out to him. "Think of all the fellows in prisons all over the world who thought they were so damn smart."

"Yeah, but they didn't know what it was all about," South Bend countered. "Listen, man, it's so easy. First you case the joint."

Then the fine points of casing a joint were laboriously counted off in South Bend style. "When you know everything there is to know about the place, you can knock it over anytime you want to. It's easy, man, I tell you, it's easy!"

I laughed at him. "Man, you must have a screw loose somewhere, right in the top of your head," I told him.

"Hell, there's plenty of money outside these old gray walls," South Bend rambled on. "I'm gonna get my share of it, too. You ought to see me crack a safe, man. I know how to blow one, too. Let me tell you ..."

With the arrest of South Bend and his gang, the police in South Bend, Indiana, where they had been apprehended, reported robberies and burglaries had taken a nose dive in their area.

It took just two days for me to become fed up with South Bend's one-man crime wave. I made arrangements to have that automatic mouthpiece transferred out of my cell. The very next day, I said good-bye to South Bend and good riddance. The deal had cost me six bags of Bull Durham smoking tobacco.

The thing I noticed most of all was not just the fact that the Reformatory was a crime school, turning out expert safe crackers and more polished thieves, but that it was also a bughouse, turning out permanently deranged men. Some of the men were quiet and went almost unnoticed. They simply wasted away. Others were very violent in their behavior, creating scenes frightening to watch. One day they would be working normally just like anybody else. Then, suddenly, their minds would snap under what to them had become a grueling mental strain.

That's how it had been with Big Stew. He was a husky black man standing six feet four inches tall. He weighed in the neighborhood of two hundred and seventy-five pounds. Nearly all of us were deathly afraid of him because he always walked around gnashing his teeth and talking to himself. Former cellmates of his said basically he was a fine fellow; that he just walked around gnashing his teeth and talking to himself, looking all the while like he was ready to kill somebody, just to keep people from messing with him! The scuttlebutt said that he had been thrown into the hole several times for wrapping a knife around some of his cellmates' throats in attempts to rape them–or have them rape him! He was one weird dude. All of us treated him with the utmost respect–and stayed out of his way. He had spent twenty years of his thirty-three years in and out of many places of confinement.

One day while Big Stew was sewing collars on the shirt assembly line, a messenger handed him a pink slip. The convicts called them "Pink Panties." A slip meant only one thing: the captain of the guards wanted to see you about some offense you had been accused of. Big Stew looked at the slip of paper that meant some kind of punishment. A look of a mixture of anger and bewilderment appeared on his clouded, dark, pockmarked face. Without a word to the messenger, Big Stew walked up to Officer Green, the guard in charge of the department that day.

"Did you report me for something?" Big Stew asked him.

"No," came the answer.

Big Stew followed the messenger to the Captain's office in the front of the guardhouse. Captain Moore told him to be seated. Presently, the Assistant Superintendent, Mr. Dowd, came in. He was accompanied by the sergeant of the guards, Big Hite. The captain informed Big Stew that he had been reported for talking in the mess hall, a major offense. Big Stew wanted to know who had reported him. They told him it was Officer Green, the same officer Big Stew had queried a few minutes earlier in the shirt shop. Big Stew became so angry, tears began to run out of his eyes. He denied talking in the mess hall and said Officer Green ought to be ashamed of himself for making up a story like that. Mr. Dowd told him to wait outside, in the corridor of the guardhouse, while he discussed the matter further with the captain and the sergeant. The captain and the sergeant wanted to throw Big Stew in the hole.

He did as he was told and went out of the office and sat on the long wooden bench lining the wall of the corridor. He sat there only a few minutes, though. The longer he sat there, the angrier he became. Abruptly, tears streaming down his cheeks, he stood up and smacked his fist into his hand. He had made up his mind. He knew what he had to do. His teeth commenced gnashing so loudly it sounded as if he was cracking walnuts with them. He took off for the shirt shop. Civilian contractors were in the process of building a new engine house or power plant near the shirt shop. That was the route Big Stew took on his way to the shop. Piles of bricks and heavy course gravel littered the route. Big Stew stopped and did some choice picking. He loaded his pockets and the inside of his shirt with bricks and baseball size rocks. The weight of all that ammunition would have ruptured the average man just to lift it off the ground.

No one questioned his actions along the way. He arrived back at the shirt shop hell bent on pure murder, premeditated murder. He bounded up the stairs to the second floor as if he had wings on. Suddenly, as if an enemy barrage had opened up with every description of artillery known to man, the air was filled with flying bricks and stones!

The frightening screams of Officer Green brought all work on the entire floor to a standstill. The first brick bounced off the shoulders of Officer Green. Then another one grazed his forehead with such force that it tore off the visor of his military-style cap. He dropped his oversized riot stick or forgot all about it and took off running to save his life. Big Stew was no more than fifteen or twenty feet behind him at any one time. He was pelting Officer Green all over the various departments. Officer Green kept screaming and begging Big Stew not to kill him, to have mercy on him. But bricks and stones and rocks and curse words I had never heard continued to find their mark. When Big Stew exhausted his ammunition, he grabbed chairs, tools, sewing machines, parts of machines, cuspidors,[121] anything that wasn't nailed down, and threw them at Officer Green. The man was bleeding profusely from wounds about his head and on his arms. His shirt looked like someone had taken a knife and methodically shredded it to pieces. Only the man's fear of the huge black man who had turned into a monster kept him for falling unconscious. Big Stew was on his trail like a hungry bloodhound.

Figure 38. A brass cuspidor.

Those of us in the other departments thought this was an extremely funny situation, like an episode from the lives of the Keystone Kops.[122] We ducked under our machines and laughed until we cried. There was no controlling the humor we found in what was taking place before our very eyes. A smart-alecky guard was getting his comeuppance! Officer Green was running so fast, if he had been running in a circle, and his bowels moved, it would have hit him smack in the face. He managed to duck a lethal blow from a heavy iron rod and maneuvered his way back through the shop. He was cornered again and for a moment contemplated jumping out of the window! Quickly, he changed his mind and showed no signs of tiring. He dropped to his hands and knees and crawled under two or three of the long worktables almost as fast as he had been running on his feet.

He had a clear shot now and made the most of it. He headed for the stairway leading down and out of the shirt shop. There was no way Big Stew was going to catch him unless he fell down and broke a leg.

Everything imaginable was being thrown at him and finding their mark on his sore body. When he reached the top of the stairway, the Assistant Superintendent, Captain,

---

[121] A cuspidor is an urn-like metal receptacle used by men who chewed or sniffed tobacco. Also called "spittoons," they were considered an advance in public health, because they encouraged users to spit into a receptacle instead of on the floor or sidewalk. Spittoons are uncommon now, except at wine tastings. However, by tradition, the U.S. Senate Chamber and the U.S. Supreme Court have cuspidors at each senator's and Justice's seat, where they serve as wastebaskets.

[122] The Keystone Kops were a comical fictional police force in the silent movies of the 1920s. While chasing criminals they ran in zigzags, bounced off walls, and drove in a speeded up jerky manner—but no one ever got hurt.

Lieutenant, and Sergeant met him. They were out conducting a search for Big Stew. Officer Green collapsed in their arms, sobbing like a baby. Big Stew froze in his tracks, a few feet away. One of his arms was upraised, poised to throw a cast iron cuspidor at any one of them.

"Put that cuspidor down!" the Lieutenant bellowed like a wild bull, walking slowly toward him.

Big Stew drew his arm back further for more potential energy. He started to hit the Lieutenant in the head but changed his mind when the man stopped walking toward him. Then, as ugly as he was, Big Stew started crying louder than ever. He swore his revenge on anybody who ever picked on him again.

"I haven't done anything," he shouted maniacally. "I'll kill the first white son-of-a-bitch who touches me!"

Not a man in the building doubted his word. He stood there a fearful figure, scowling, gnashing his teeth, tears running down his face. Spittle was running down his upraised arm from the cuspidor he held in his hand. That sight was enough to turn the most hardened stomachs.

Lieutenant Harold stepped forward again. He told Big Stew to put down his weapons and behave himself, that nothing was going to happen to him if he obeyed. That was the turning point. The roaring lion became a bleating sheep. The promise Big Stew had been wanting to hear was made. It was an offer he could not refuse. Every prisoner in the Reformatory knew that Lieutenant Harold never broke his word once it was given. Even the Captain and Mr. Dowd respected it and abided by it. All of us could swear by Lieutenant Harold because he was a real square shooter. Black and white were all the same to him. He didn't put out any stuff and he never gave anybody any.

Big Stew gave up and was led back to the guardhouse. He was put in the hole for one day with plenty of food and drink. While he was undressing to get into the guardhouse dungarees, he told Lieutenant Harold:

"You're the only one who understands me, Mr. Harold. The rest of the guards in here just pick on me for nothing at all. I like you. That's why I gave up. I know you ain't gonna let anything bad happen to me. You're a good man, Mr. Harold. Yes sir, you're a good man!"

When he was released from the guardhouse the next day, nothing further was mentioned about the matter. Officer Green was transferred to an outside detail after his release from the hospital. The Captain gave out strict orders that Big Stew was a "crazy nigger" and to leave him alone before somebody got killed!

CHAPTER SIXTEEN

A Promise to God

After I had served eighteen months of my sentence, my mother brought word that the governor had turned down a petition from Bailey and Brokenburr, my attorneys, for a governor's parole. That meant that I would have to serve the full two years of my sentence before being eligible for parole consideration by the Board of Trustees of the Reformatory. I was eighteen at the time. Six more months in that bughouse seemed like six years.

Time began to weigh heavier than ever on my hands. The hope of a parole after eighteen months had buoyed my spirits. With that hope shattered I somehow felt I had been betrayed. In the world of embittered men in which I lived it was easy to plot and plan revenge. Expert guidance and counseling was all around me. I spent many a night lying awake in my cell thinking and making lots of plans for getting even.

Someone on the outside was going to pay for my rotting away in that stinking cesspool of a dump called the Reformatory. They had never seen the number of killings and robberies that would terrorize the state when I finally got out. My actions would relegate the crimes of John Dillinger[123] to that of a kindergarten pupil. I would be the

---

[123] Dillinger was the most notorious of all the many Depression Era gangsters. The media made him out to be a very brave and colorful personality. He escaped from prison twice. An Indiana native, his Terror Gang robbed twenty-four banks and four police stations. Dillinger was incarcerated in the Indiana Reformatory, from 1924 to 1929–just two years before Jimmie would become an inmate there. Like Jimmie, Dillinger worked in the shirt shop. He was also on the baseball team.

black Jesse James, a grim and merciless avenger of the wrongs perpetrated on black people.[124]

Figure 39. John Dillinger with a pistol and a machine gun. *Indiana Historical Society*

It just hadn't paid off, that jazz about being a model prisoner. Maybe, I thought, I shouldn't wait. Breaks were being planned every week. Practically all of them failed but it was worth the effort. Something had to be done. Somebody was bound to break out one of these days. Why couldn't it be me? At the very least, I could be killed and put out of my misery.

But I never tried to break out of the penitentiary. I would like to say that the reason was my desire to make good my promises to Sheriff Bradley, Mother, my sisters, and others who believe in me. The truth was, however, I was afraid. Yes, afraid of being caught and having more years added onto my sentence. I was also afraid that even if I did get away I might fall into the hands of the mob that had not forgotten its plans for me. That thought always seemed to come back to haunt me.

Then, too, the thought came to me that man, through his own conduct and behavior patterns, has much to do with his own destiny. Days, months, even years might be added to his life or subtracted according to his good or bad works in association with other people. This, I still firmly believe and will die with that conviction.

---

[124] James was a legendary Wild West outlaw. A former Confederate guerrilla fighter, after the Civil War he turned to robbing banks, trains, and stage coaches. As with Dillinger, the national media exaggerated James' deeds. They called him the American "Robin Hood," even though there is no evidence he ever gave a penny of his ill-gotten gains to help the poor. In fact, he was a committed white supremacist who vowed to kill every free Negro in Missouri. Jimmie Cameron only knew the media-created heroic myths about Dillinger and James. Like many teenagers today who are angry about their situations, Jimmie imagined that his life would be better as a powerful "gangsta."

But the thought of that Marion mob still made me nervous. I knew that white mobs take it upon themselves to add much more punishment to the fate of others.

Hope returned on my parole hearing day. My record was clear. Not one mark had been chalked up against me. The full two years had been served, which was the first part of my sentence of 2 to 21 years. I had been a model prisoner all down the line, according to Reformatory standards. That day couldn't pass quick enough for me, for I knew that that night the Board of Trustees of the Indiana State Reformatory would hold their monthly meeting to consider the many requests for parole.

Shortly before the noon meal, the Assistant Superintendent and the Superintendent told me that they were going to give me their highest recommendation.

All that day in the shirt shop, and in lines leading to the mess hall, everybody was wishing me good luck. Bets were being placed as to whether or not I would make the grade. The odds were three to one in my favor.

The room where the five trustees met was located in the guard hall directly across from Baldy Stewart, the guard who turned the large wheel that controlled the sliding gates leading in and out of the prison.

I had my uniform cleaned and pressed, my hair cut and shoes spit shined. Other men scheduled to appear before the Board that night were similarly groomed.

Looking down the long line of chairs outside the board room, it was difficult to believe that we were a gang of misfits, murderers, thieves, robbers, muggers, dope addicts, whoremongers, pimps, cut-throats, bad associates, stupid individuals, and everything else. All of the rough edges on us had miraculously disappeared. If we had a best foot, it was put forward that night. We might have been, I thought, a group of applicants seeking employment in the civilian world. Some of us would be hired; others would be passed over.

We sat along the long white wall of the guards hall and were numbered accordingly. I was number nine. As I waited for my turn, I tried to think of all the good things that ever happened to me, with the number nine playing an important role in my life. I managed to find consolation in the fact that I had ninety-nine sacks of Bull Durham hidden in my cache, which put me in the "rich class" by Reformatory standards. I had surpassed task in the shirt shop for the last nine months. Actually, I had beaten task for the past fourteen months, but I was in no mood for quibbling or splitting hairs. I sat there anxiously, nervous, and just a little bit hopeful.

Number one didn't make it. His last six months were not clear of disciplinary marks. He was a picture of abject misery as he left the room. The Board had set him back ninety days. Numbers two and three made it. Paroled! As they walked down the corridor, they had a hard time keeping their elation under control. But they did, taking no chances on violating a rule at that late hour. They had made it! Their faces were picture book smiles.

Number four came out in tears. He had failed to give the Trustees a clear picture of just what he intended to do if granted a parole. They had given him another year to think the situation over.

That's how it is with those indeterminate sentences, such as one to ten years, or two to ten years, or five to ten years, or ten to twenty-five years. The Trustees could let you out in one year, two years, five or ten years, or keep you for the whole maximum number of years. The first part of the sentence was the least they could hold a man, unless, of course, the governor granted a parole before that time had been reached. The second part was the most they could keep you in prison. A prisoner never knew what to expect from an indeterminate sentence.

I wondered about my two to twenty-one years sentence. The governor had denied me a parole after I had done eighteen months. Was I really going to make it in two years, or three or four, or five or six, or would the Trustees keep me confined the whole twenty-one years? Hope did abound in me but I had no idea of what it was based on.

Finally, the door opened and number eight came out. His was the only smile I had seen since number five. I was next. Ten minutes passed, then twenty. Still they hadn't called me in. I wondered whether they were discussing my case. I would soon know.

"Keep your spirits up, Jimmie," number ten whispered to me. "They just might be talking up something good for you."

Another ten minutes passed in agonizing silence and bewilderment. I was squirming in my seat. Beads of perspiration stood out on my forehead the size of navy beans. The palms of my hands were moist. My breathing was labored and measured. I had no idea of what to expect, but whatever it was, it was tearing me up inside.

At last the door opened: "James Cameron, come in!" the guard called out.

I was all smiles as I entered the Board Room. The guard closed the door behind me. I found myself facing five strangers, all white, seated at a long conference table. I stood in front of the table. The Superintendent and his Assistant were sitting close by. Each member of the Board had a complete case history of the Cameron murder trial spread out before him.

"Cameron," the Board chairman commenced, "you're up for parole now. We know you deserve one. But the Board is undecided."

I strained to keep my facial features intact. My heart was doing strange gyrations and sinking to knee level.

"Yes," another Board member put in, "we've got three letters here protesting your release."

I noticed he had three pieces of paper in front of him that could have been letters. Then all of the members took turns questioning me about my part in the murder of Claude Deeter. I took my time and gave them the same answers that could be found in my packet.

"Are you guilty?" the chairman finally asked me.

"I am guilty of bad associates, sir, but not of murder," I told him.

"Cameron, we're going to set you back thirty days for investigation," the chairman concluded.

I had been too busy trying to make an impression, a good impression. Up until then I hadn't noticed the Trustees as individuals. Suddenly the Board chairman loomed before me as huge and ominous as a giant. His round, egg-shaped head seemed to be pressing against my chest. I wanted to cry out from pure instinct but I was confused.

"You'll come up for parole consideration again in a month," the chairman added. "Keep your record clean and be a good boy. That's all."

"Yes, sir," I managed to say. There was nothing else to say. I could have kicked myself all over that place. I had nobody but myself to blame for the fix I was in.

As soon as I stepped outside the Board Room, the remaining inmates began firing questions at me. Very quietly I answered all of them at once. "I got thirty days for investigation."

"You'll make it next time, Jim," somebody said.

"Yeah, next time," I commented, wondering whether I believed it.

In a few days, after I had recovered from the initial shock of disappointment, I began to feel confident about my next appearance before the Board. The days creeped along. Finally thirty days were a thing of the past.

Again the Board greeted me cordially and expressed sympathy. But the investigation was still on and would take another sixty days, I was told.

I went back to my cell, feeling that I would serve sixty years, and gladly, for about two hours alone with each one of the three people who were supposed to have written letters protesting my release.

I brooded over my two setbacks and kept to myself for the next sixty days. I was being extra careful to keep my record clean. There was no point in giving the Board any more excuses. They had enough already!

On my third trip to the Board, they told me the investigation was still on and "We'll let you know in ninety days," the chairman told me.

Thirty days, sixty days, and now ninety days. I began doubting the Board's sincerity. Maybe it was some kind of a game they were playing with me. Still, I had nothing to lose, everything was to gain by playing along with their rules. I kept out of trouble for the next ninety days.

On my forth attempt for parole I was told by the Board that, "The investigation is still on and we'll let you know in six months!"

For some strange reason, I was more confident than ever, but also angrier and more confused than ever when I emerged from that board room that fourth time. Surely, I reasoned, the investigation would be completed in six months. What in the hell could be wrong? That had to be my last setback.

I felt, too, that part of the delay could have been my fault. I still had not overcome my resentment completely and had crime on my mind. Maybe, I thought, the Board could tell that I wasn't ready to be released.

I pondered this problem many a night in my cell as I waited for the next six months to roll by. I stayed away from the stills and other hole traps and kept out of trouble. Reading the Bible became more frequent with me. I lived in the Psalms of David: "Oh Lord, deliver me from my enemies." I was trying, desperately, to get my thoughts in order for a life on the outside, in the civilian world. Surely, if my thoughts were right, with no thought of revenge or acts of crime lying dormant in the back of my mind, the Lord would help me to make the right impression on the Board.

Then a whole new field of thought opened up to me. It made me nervous to think about it but I couldn't erase it from my mind. The trustees had a tough job to do, I began to understand. It was a tricky business trying to determine exactly at what point in his life a convict is ready to assume normal and moral responsibilities of citizenship. Holy Smokes! Three of the men who had been granted parole on my first appearance before the Board were back behind the walls in the Reformatory as parole violators! Some of them were busy doing time in some other prison before they would be brought back to the Reformatory to answer as parole violators. Others released later were still on the outside but the odds were against them remaining there. The point of when to release a convict to return to society was a very difficult thing to judge. Maybe, I was not ready to be released!

Still, there was no doubt in my mind that someone on that Board, one of the members, or all of them, were making it pretty tough for me to gain freedom. For the stupid role I had played in the Deeter stick-up, they seemed bent on driving me out of my mind. Values were way out of line in the Board's consideration of paroles.

One eighteen-year-old white youth from Gary, Indiana, had been sentenced to one to ten years in the Reformatory for involuntary manslaughter. He had cold-bloodedly killed his sweetheart in a jealous rage. The jury hearing the case had meant to give him life imprisonment in the state prison at Michigan City, but had been confused in their degree of guilt and turned in the wrong verdict! The judge had polled the jury and each one of them said they had thought they were voting for life imprisonment for the killer, but now it was too late to change the verdict. The youth had been interned in the Reformatory after I had been admitted. He did his one year, was granted a parole, and left me still serving time!

Another white youth from the central part of the state had killed his wife with five shots from a revolver. Then he had held his eighteen-month old daughter in his arms and slit her little throat with a butcher knife. Jumping into his car, he drove downtown to the river where police found him trying to wash the blood off his hands! When he had finished, he decided to commit suicide by drowning himself. He found the water too cold for his sensitive skin. The police found him sitting on the bank still trying to wash the blood from his hands and arms. He had entered the Reformatory while I was still there, did his two years, was paroled and left me still doing time!

I could think of a score of cases like that of similar convictions of white youths who had entered the prison while I was still there. They all did their time, were paroled, and left me still doing time!

It didn't take me long to figure out that something was radically wrong with our criminal justice system. I found out that black people are arrested on flimsy or no evidence at all; are held longer in jail awaiting trial; are denied bail more often than others; when convicted are given much stiffer sentences for the same crime; are held in prison longer than others for the same type of crime; and, when finally paroled, have a longer commitment to a parole officer than other criminals. The list goes on and on![125]

At last, my latest setback of six months came to an end. This time I had to make it. This had to be it! But the investigation was still on, and it would be at least another year before the Board could come to a decision!

Five strikes meant I was completely out, I decided. I cried freely. I was now firmly convinced that I would never get out of the penitentiary until my full twenty-one years had been served. The Board would have to let me go then.

One of the first things I learned after my one-year setback was that hope dies hard in the young. Within a few weeks I was dreaming again. But this time my dreams were quite different than they had been. There was an intensity and passion and purpose connected with them. I spent many hours in prayer and meditation and vowed that if the Lord gave me strength to carry on for another year, I would put aside all thoughts of committing crime on the outside, I would never give the law any cause to question my honesty, integrity, ability, and character to abide by the rules and regulations of our society. I would be the kind of Christian I knew in my heart God wanted me to be. Those precious dreams were made in the forms of vows. I felt much better after those vows. They were full of meaning and I believed God heard my prayers.

That fifth setback of one year was the toughest, the slowest, and the most punitive 365 days I had ever spent in the prison. Every damn thing seemed to happen to me. I sweated out the stand-up fourteen times! On one of those occasions, after I had been caught with some contraband, the Captain and the Lieutenant wanted to throw me into the hole. That would have meant a disciplinary mark on my record.

"Throw him in the hole," they implored the Assistant Superintendent.

But, fortunately, I had only six more months to go before my next and sixth appearance before the Board of Trustees. For that reason Mr. Dowd let me stand-up instead of throwing me into the hole. My back felt as if it was breaking in two or was

---

[125] The differences between the treatment of blacks and whites in the criminal justice system began when Reconstruction ended just a dozen years after the Civil War. This inequality continues today. As of this writing in 2015, new attention is being paid to the injustices that Cameron pointed to in 1935. This attention is the result, in part, of citizens using camera phones to record the killings of unarmed African Americans and post them on social media. It also results from important studies published by scholars and journalists like Michelle Alexander (2012) and Douglass Blackmon (2008) and the work of such organizations as the Equal Justice Initiative (eji.org).

already broken. But throughout the two days I was forced to stand, and the meals I missed, I have been eternally grateful to Mr. Dowd.

My mother came down to see me a few days after that particular stand-up. She told me that she and several friends, including Sheriff Bradley, had visited the newly elected governor on my behalf. He was Paul V. McNutt.

"Now keep your record clean, son," she told me. "This time there is a real investigation going on, and the governor's office is handling it."

It took every bit of strength and will power I had to stay out of trouble those last few months, those last few weeks, those last few days.

Conditions at the prison went from bad to worse. The guards had become more brutal than ever. They seemed forever on the lookout for excuses to use their heavy, death-dealing blackjacks, and almost any excuse would do. In one week's time, three of the prisoners were bludgeoned to death by a gang of guards. The food got worse. Then the guards started wearing firearms.[126] They became even bolder and more sadistic, if that was possible. The medical treatment was "die and prove it." [127]

A break-out plan was on every tongue. More attempts were made than ever before. Nobody ever made it over those walls to safety. Four of my best friends were shot off the walls and roofs of the cell houses.

As if that wasn't enough, the prisoners rioted in an attempt to force prison officials to improve conditions inside the prison. A dozen guards were grabbed by the inmates and beaten nearly to death. The state police and the National Guard were called into service and restored order inside the walls. The guards who got beat up by the prisoners were the bad guys in the uniform of a guard. They were the ones who needed to be whipped good and proper! Prisoners, during such stressful periods of prison life, never harm the guards who are decent and respectful of another human being, because they need that kind of people to be guards. When the state stopped the whipping of

---

[126] In such a maximum-security prison nowadays, guards would always carry weapons.

[127] The worsening of prison conditions may have been a result of the Great Depression, which lasted through the 1930s. Cameron was held in the State Reformatory from 1931 to 1935. It is also possible that the prison's administrative leadership changed or that new policies were enacted.

prisoners, the bad guys quit in droves because there would be no more heads for them to bounce their blackjacks off of anytime they felt like having a little fun.[128]

More than half of the prisoners were locked up in their cells and put on bread and water. About two hundred men, considered by prison officials to be the ringleaders and incorrigibles, were transferred by special train to the state prison at Michigan City. Big Stew was one of them.

I was working as a messenger in the guards hall at the time of the riot. In the language of the Reformatory, I was one of the "Soup's boys." Even so, I was locked up for three days on bread and water right along with hundreds of other prisoners. It was difficult to tell which inmates had been in on the uprising. I was questioned and closed up like a clam. I didn't know "nothing!" Human suffering and misery was everywhere inside those gray prison walls.

Only when the Superintendent was fired by Governor McNutt and replaced by Mr. Dowd, the Assistant Superintendent, did conditions slowly but surely settle back to normalcy.

A few weeks after the riot, I appeared before the Board of Trustees for the sixth time. I spent very little time on my shoes and uniform. I just didn't give a damn how I looked. What was the use? I fully expected to play another round of the Board's depressing game of setbacks. If the Board followed true to form, the investigation would still be on and this time it would take another two years to complete it.

But this time the [Parole] Board was different. The new governor had made some sweeping changes. I later learned that one of the members of the group had been an editor of one of the newspapers in Marion, that he was a known member of the Ku Klux Klan, and a prime suspect in the writing of three letters protesting my release on parole. He was no longer a member of the Board. In fact, only one of the original five members remained.

The air in the room seemed to feel lighter to me even before I realized I was facing four white men I had never seen before. They actually seemed friendly to me. They only asked me two questions. One was, "Where would you go to serve your parole if we see fit to grant you one? We'd rather you go out of the state."

I told them I had an aunt, my mother's sister, Katherine Brown, in Detroit, Michigan, who would be glad to have me stay with her.

---

[128] Here we see that prison conditions are not only affected–for good or for ill–by the administrative leadership and economic conditions, but also by state policy and procedures.

The Board's other question was, "How long do you think you can stay out of trouble if we let you out of prison?"

I told them that if they let me out, they wouldn't ever be bothered with me again. The way I said it caused the Board members to laugh heartily. I smiled myself.

"Cameron, we are going to grant you a parole on the governor's recommendation, but it will have to be a five year parole."

If that's the way they want it, I thought, that's the way they can have it. Other prisoners, though, only had to pull a one year parole.

At last! Paroled! I felt as light as a breeze. I could not control myself. I kept jumping up and down with joy as if I had a built-in spring in my behind. Profusely I thanked the Board for their goodness to me. And I thanked God. Tears of happiness were running down my cheeks unashamedly.

One of the Trustees introduced himself as a Mr. George Phelan. He told me he was a real estate broker in Anderson. He knew Sheriff Bradley and my mother quite well. In fact, he said, my mother was working for him at the moment, washing and ironing clothes and doing domestic work.

I had received offers from some of the prisoners to join up with their old gangs still operating on the outside. I had been tried and proven, they said. They could fix it so that I could get in on some of the sweetest rackets in the country. I could make all the money I ever dreamed about. Since I intended to go to Detroit, Michigan, for my parole, I had a chance to join either the Purple Gang[129] or the River Gang.[130]

I thanked my buddies and big brothers for their offers and all the help they had afforded me. I told them I had decided to go straight. I had seen enough in my four years behind those gray, dingy walls to last a lifetime. I had even lived up a dozen lifetimes with the prisoners. I had seen murders, suicides, mental breakdowns, and bloody, merciless beatings by overbearing guards on inoffensive and defenseless prisoners. I had seen men suffer too much for nothing too long. For the past five years I had been under intense, excruciating mental and physical pressures. There had been few moments in my life in which the grim specter of pain, and even violent death, had not been my constant companion, my closest presence. The thought uppermost in my mind was thank you, dear God, for your goodness to me. Thank you very much!

---

[129] At that time co-headed by a Jewish mobster and an African American mobster.

[130] An Italian-run gang.

I realized I had reached and passed beyond the crisis between light and darkness, between good and evil. I understood, now, the full meaning of life and death. There was nothing for me to duck or fear anymore. I had dropped to the uttermost bottom of the pit in racial hatred, the most devastating of all hatreds, before love and kindness lifted me up into realms of reasoning, understanding and tolerance. This knowledge obligated me as a human being to return that love and kindness to others along the way of life who would need this human affection, this milk of human kindness. It would be proof to them that they are members of the human race, that they, too, belong in our world, that there are people who really care what happens to them, that they have value.

I felt I could do no wrong even if I wanted to. It was a cinch, no one was ever going to talk me into doing something against my will again! Those were the thoughts that would be beacon lights to flood my pathway through life. I would place my hand in God's hand and hold on for the peace and quiet it would entail. I would hold my head up high. God had given me a faith to live by. I had reached that point in life where I could see its worth, its value, its meaning to me.

I had been as frightened, broken-down, run-down, humiliated, insulted, frustrated, confused, sorry and ashamed and as miserable as any human being could be without losing my sanity. I had had enough! I had seen enough! Enough was enough!

I was thankful to God for everything: the trees, the grass, the flowers, the birds of the air; the beasts of the fields, for my worn and torn body, and a sick mind made whole again. I was thankful that no deaths had occurred in my immediate family during the five torturous years I had spent in confinement. I thanked God for my wonderful mother and my two faithful beloved sisters, and my many wonderful friends, both black and white. I was the most thankful young man in the world. I am still the most thankful *old* man in the world.

The ultimate value of prayer and faith was clear to me now. With that faith and a prayer on my lips forever, I was determined to keep my hands on the throttle and my eyes upon the rails. I knew what God had done for others. Now I knew what He had done for me. Those vows I had made would be kept. I would not shun my responsibilities. When the heartaches, disappointments, frustrations, confusion, pain, tears, and cares of this life are over, I would still, in the silence of my grave, continue to thank God in a never-ending dream of His goodness to me.

When the hour of my liberation had come, when I was able to walk out of the Indiana State Reformatory into the dawn of that day, into the blessed sunshine of freedom, my mother Vera and my two sisters, Marie and Della, were there, waiting for me at the gate.

I saw them as soon as I came out of the administration building. I had known they would be there. It was just like them. They had *never* failed me. My heart swelled with gratitude and deep appreciation. Suddenly my eyes were blurred with tears. I couldn't hold them back. I was surrounded with memories of how my mother and sisters had made that trip so many times before. One time Marie had been with Mother when they made a special trip together. They didn't have any money that time to pay bus fare. They had walked all the way down to the Reformatory at Pendleton from Anderson just to offer me words of encouragement. I was glad they would never have to make that trip again, walking twelve miles there and twelve miles back.

When I saw them I was a little boy again, a little boy who had been lost in the woods but found, at last. I ran as fast as my legs could carry me. They ran, too, and all of us were laughing and crying at the same time. The moment we slammed into each other and embraced in hugs and kisses, I felt free, really free, for the first time in my life.

I was free to think and reason and feel again. I was back where a young man of twenty-one years of age had time to pick up the loose ends of his life and weave them into something beautiful, worthwhile, and God-like.

Gee! It felt good to be back!

EPILOGUE

On February 3, 1993, 62 years after my conviction for being an accessory before the fact to voluntary manslaughter, I was issued a pardon by Indiana Governor Evan Bayh. On February 11th, I received a key to the City of Marion, Indiana. The following text is the acceptance speech I delivered that same day at the Marion-Sheraton Hotel after I was formally pardoned.

Before giving my acceptance speech in honor of this momentous and historical occasion, in which I have been presented a pardon for the indiscretion of my youth, I wish to preface my remarks with these words. The African American story has not been told. We are only beginning to learn that there is indeed something worthy to tell.

History tells me that a people without a story are a people with no name. Without a name, one is not respected or understood. Without a name or a story, the depth-regions of the heart will never be plumbed. You remain a stranger to yourself and to others. Stories give shape to our personal journey. Stories give a context to our collective pilgrimage. Outside the city of Jerusalem in Israel, there is a memorial (Yad Vashem) keeping alive the story of the Jewish Holocaust victims before the conscience of the world. An inscription there reads as follows: "To remember is salvation. To forget is exile." An oppressed people find their strength and identity in remembering their passages. For indeed these passages have made them a people.

Awakening is an experience of consciousness-raising, transformation and conversion. Awakening implies the whole range of growth possibilities. These growth experiences are largely concerned with a growing recognition of the beauty, goodness and power that is already present within each one of us but somehow frequently lies dormant. I have come here today to disturb that dormancy and fan its flames throughout our whole state of Indiana and hope it will spread throughout our whole nation. Through reflection on life-experience and participation in a healing community, the individual arrives at a new awareness, a new sense of self, a feeling of "I can" when others say "I can't." The ability to fly, even soar, has been revealed. Perhaps, if this newly discovered inner source of power is fully unleashed, the horizon for future growth toward liberation is suddenly available.

So I say to you, the equalization principles of the law of our land can be compared to light that gradually breaks upon our world after a night of restful repose. It is first seen in the gray streaks blended with the rosy hues of the rising sun. Then it gilds the mountaintops and the hills, the high places and the low places, until in its inexorable advances it shines upon every plain, penetrates every valley and ravine. These principles struggled through centuries to have their realization—on paper at least—in the organic laws of the United States of America. Step by step through the terrible centuries marched these great principles, these ideas about how a people could be free was advancing, and gradually weakening the despotic forces in our world, until the bonds of oppression and exploitation were snapped asunder in our great Revolutionary War. Peace and goodwill is supposed to prevail in our country.

Peace and goodwill failed to prevail in Marion, Indiana, on the night of August 7, 1930. The highest and most solemn duty of any government is to apply some prompt corrective measures to any increasing spirit of insubordination and non-obedience to law and order; the open and daring and bare-faced attempts and intentions by bad people to overthrow it. The operators on the machinery of government in Marion, Indiana, at the time of the double lynching, were careless operators, poor workers, to have stood by and watched a deliberate build-up of insubordination and non-compliance to law and order. They did not lift a hand to correct the situation, a statewide known condition. This is eternal history, and those sloppy government workers did it over a mountain of perjury with which their very souls were charged. They pretended to stand on the walls of the people's citadel of liberty—yours and mine, the black and white people—and their guardianship was to serve as a defense for all of us in Marion. Yet we know now that their purpose was fraught with destruction and loss of human life; that they indeed tore down the very temple of local liberty. Nobody can defend this charge. Nobody can deny this charge.

There was this numerous body of dangerous people belonging to our dominant society. They had gathered in such a manner as to endanger the peace and quiet of the city, the state, and the nation. They were determined to cause the lives of citizens of

Marion to be subjected to their particular forms of terror, violence and murder. The citizens, for the most part, had been mentally conditioned by Ku Klux Klan philosophy and demagoguery. Their minds were set on commotion, on extreme turmoil, on the agony and fury of racial passion and hatred that dethroned their reasoning, that destroyed all the charities of the human heart, that subverted patriotism and every duty of life, private and public. They wanted the mad frenzy and fanaticism of Ku Klux Klan lynching passions then raging unbridled throughout our whole nation, to continue in Marion, Indiana, and they expected their animalistic behavior patterns to be justified and excused by the power structure. It was.

Any violation of just and equal and righteous laws must of necessity be followed by evil consequences to the transgressor. There is no government either on earth or in Heaven, either human or Divine, that can long exist without the exercise of a power which shall vindicate its authority by inflicting some punishment upon those who violate the laws.

If one generation will not afford the solution to our baffling racial problems, the following one is most certainly expected to do so. But we still find people persisting, willfully, in the expedience of group domination, in beliefs of racial supremacy, just to become advantageous at the disadvantage of others. They still can't realize the duties of citizenship demand the obedience and subordination to a constant practice of equal rights, privileges and opportunities inside our borders.

On May 29, 1991, I sat down at my typewriter and composed a letter to the Honorable B. Evan Bayh, III, Governor of the State of Indiana, in which I asked consideration for a pardon from the State of Indiana.

I received communications from the Indiana Parole Board in regard to this matter, filled out the pardon request form and returned same to the Board. I made several trips to Indiana and appeared before the members of the Board and told them my story. These are the very words I used in stating my reason for clemency from the State of Indiana: I ask for this pardon because I know that God has forgiven me for the role I played in the initiation of a crime that resulted in the loss of three human lives. I ask for this pardon because I know where great crimes have been committed, parole boards have been the occasion of great charity. When the devil's envy had destroyed man, God's mercy restored him! Your pardon on this occasion will be more honorable to the State of Indiana than the most celebrated cases who have received your mercy. It will adorn your Parole Board with a far brighter diadem than it now wears, as it will be the fruit only of your own virtue. It is easy for a master to punish, but rare and difficult to pardon. When my request for a pardon is generally known, the State of Indiana, the whole country will have their eyes fixed on your Parole Board at this critical junction in my life. I ask for this pardon, because I know there is a God in Heaven who checks the anger of those who acknowledge no master upon earth, and who can transform men into angels so that they can and will embrace, as I have done, that faith in God which teaches such sublime morality.

Now that the State of Indiana has forgiven me for my indiscretion, I, in turn, forgive Indiana for their transgressors of the law in Marion on the night of August 7, 1930. I forgive those who have harmed me and Abe and Tom, realizing I can never forget the traumatic events that took place that night.

Dear Heavenly Father in Heaven, I ask that you shower grace and blessings upon Governor Evan Bayh for his goodness to me. I know that all goodness comes from you, Lord. I praise your name, I exalt you, I adore you, I love you. I give you thanks for your goodness to me.

Bless this state of Indiana with your graces and mercies. Let the City of Marion, Indiana, set a beacon light for the rest of the state to follow in asking God to be their Way; that the people, as a whole, may be welded into one single and sacred nationality. Be their Truth. Let those equalitarian principles of love and justice shine in all their neighborhoods, in palatial homes and tumble-down shacks, among the poor and needy, the hungry, the homeless, the unemployed, the people who have given up hope. Be their Life, dear Lord, as you have been my Way, my Truth, my Life.

I ask all this in the name of Jesus Christ, our Lord and Savior and give thanks to His Mother, Holy Mary, for her intercession prayers for me and my family, for the whole world, that we might be saved from the wrath of God!

As I conclude my remarks, I cannot think of anything more appropriate to say to the people of Marion, Indiana, and to the state of Indiana than to quote from my beloved Maya Angelou's *On The Pulse Of Morning*:

Here on the pulse of this new day

You may have the grace to look up and out

And into your sister's eyes, and into your brother's face, your country

And say simply

Very simply

With hope

Good morning!

AFTERWORD

The Amazing Afterlife of Dr. James Cameron

I can't remember the date, but I can clearly recall the day that my life changed. I was driving through segregated Milwaukee's African American community and noticed a small, nondescript building with an unusual name: America's Black Holocaust Museum. I decided to stop and go inside. An elderly gentleman opened the door and welcomed me in. His name was James Cameron and this was his museum.

Later I would come to know him as *Dr.* Cameron. He gave me a tour and told the fascinating story of how he survived a lynching. The museum had numerous images of lynchings, only one of which I'd ever seen before. I was studying to be a history teacher and recognized the value of the stories in this place, stories largely absent from history

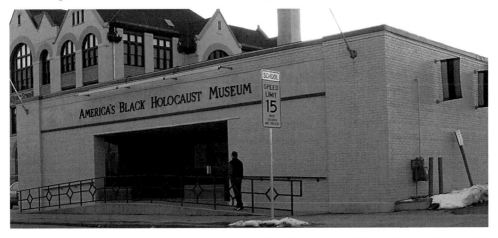

Figure 40. The museum in the building it occupied in Milwaukee's Bronzeville neighborhood from 1992 to 2008. *Fruit of the Tree Productions*

textbooks. Dr. Cameron had a natural gift as a storyteller. He was a griot[131] in the tradition of West Africa. Little did I know that I would one day join him in the pursuit of educating the public to injustices suffered by Africans and their descendants in America.

On that day I was fascinated to learn the stories of Mack Parker and other lynching victims. Parker was taken out of his jail cell, beaten and killed by a mob in Mississippi. However, none of the stories were as captivating as Dr. Cameron's. At that moment he and I were the only people there, so I had his full and undivided attention. He told me about his youthful naiveté, which almost cost him his life. I knew instantly that I would share this lesson with my public school students some day.

Over time I discovered that his childhood lynching was not the only amazing aspect of Dr. Cameron's life. I came to know what a brilliant, productive, and visionary man he had become as an adult. This is the story I want to share with you here.

James Herbert Cameron, Jr. was born on February 25, 1914. On that same day a lynch mob in Leland, Mississippi, killed a black man named Sam Petty. These two seemingly unconnected events–along with a solar eclipse–would foreshadow the dark day sixteen years later when young Jimmie came near to death.

As you have read, Jimmie spent a year in the county jail awaiting trial and four more in the state Reformatory. When he was finally released at age twenty-one, he was forced to leave his home in Indiana to serve five years parole in the custody of an aunt in Detroit, Michigan.

There he found work as a truck driver for Stroh's Brewing Company and attended classes at Wayne State University. During his spare time he continued to write this memoir, which he had begun in prison. Calling it *From the Inside Out*, Cameron would later change its name to *A Time of Terror: A Survivor's Story*. He was to spend more than forty years researching, revising, and searching for a publisher for the book.

While driving his truck route, he spotted a lovely young woman, Virginia Hamilton, who worked as a nurse. Their relationship would grow over the next several years. Married in 1938, they would spend the next 68 years together. That year they welcomed their first child, Herbert, into the world. In 1940 their second son, Walter, was born. Two years later Virgil became their third and final child born in Detroit.

---

[131] "Griot" (pronounced GREE-oh) is a French term used in West Africa for a traditional oral historian, a teller of history and news. ABHM docents and public speakers are called griots.

In 1943 Cameron moved back to Indiana with his wife and three sons. They settled just over thirty miles south of Marion in Anderson to be close to his mother and sisters. James and Virginia celebrated the birth of their daughter Dolores in 1944. It was a prosperous year for the Cameron family. They would open Cameron's Shoe Shining Parlor. It was the only black-owned business in downtown Anderson. Cameron's place also sold records by famous jazz and blues artists. The store served a mostly white clientele for shoe shines. Blacks came to buy records and other items.

Figure 41. James in his shoe shine parlor and store with his friend Vestor, circa 1943. *Cameron Family*

Cameron became active with the Anderson branch of the National Association for the Advancement of Colored People (NAACP). He would be instrumental in opening branches of the iconic civil rights organization in towns throughout the heavily Ku Klux Klan-populated state. While James traveled on behalf of the NAACP, Virginia and the children tended to the store.

James found it difficult to convince blacks to join the NAACP and set up chapters in their communities. Fighting for civil rights was still a dangerous proposition–not just in the Jim Crow South but in the segregated North as well. He often returned to Marion to interview eyewitnesses to the lynching he survived. He spent countless hours at the Grant County courthouse, where he had once stood with a rope around his neck, researching court transcripts and depositions related to his trial. He based his book's many revisions on this research.

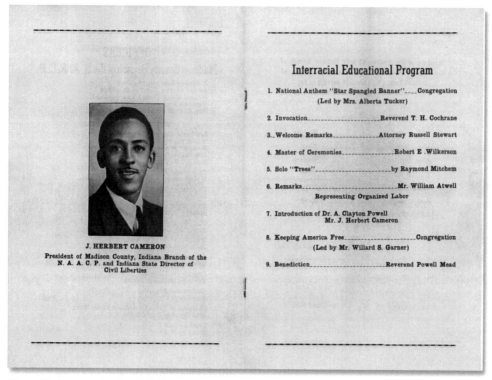

Figure 42. Program booklet, Madison County NAACP. By the time of this program on March 1, 1944, James Cameron had been appointed the Indiana State Director of Civil Liberties by the governor. *Cameron Family*

In 1946 the Camerons' last child, David, was born. They would become prominent members of the black community over the next several years. They raised their children to always challenge injustice, teaching these lessons with both words and deeds. The downtown Paramount Theater was segregated and disallowed black moviegoers. Virginia and James challenged this practice by taking their children to see a movie.

When an usher asked them to leave, they threatened to sue the theater's owner. The owner knew Cameron's fierce activism, so his act led to the theater's integration.

The Camerons lived in a racially integrated neighborhood, sent their children to integrated schools, and swam in an integrated swimming pool. Their status and work within the community offered them opportunities to challenge and overcome some of the obstacles of segregation. In 1942 Governor Henry F. Schricker would appoint Cameron to be the Indiana Director of Civil Liberties. He travelled all around the state investigating violations of the Indiana Public Accommodations Act until 1950.

In the end, Cameron was able to establish only four new NAACP chapters in Indiana. [132] Disillusioned by the lack of support of blacks in the state and facing multiple death threats to his family, in 1952 Cameron

Figure 43. James and his children in their backyard in Anderson, Indiana, circa 1948. The children, left to right, are Virgil, Herbert, Dolores, David, and Walter. *Cameron Family*

decided to move to Canada. On the way to Canada, the family stopped and stayed in Milwaukee, Wisconsin. He found work in this city where aspiring black migrants from

---

[132] The modern civil rights movement would not become an active force until the Brown v Board of Education decision in 1954 and the murder of Emmett Till in Money, Mississippi, in 1955.

the South and neighboring states had already established a substantial community.[133] They moved into a neighborhood in Milwaukee's Third Ward on the edge of downtown. A newly integrating area still predominately Italian, the Third Ward had about fifteen black residents in 1950.

In 1954, James, Virginia and the children converted to Roman Catholicism and joined the Blessed Virgin of Pompeii Church. James' conversion was inspired by his relationship with Sheriff Bernard Bradley, who had cared for and mentored him during his year in Bradley's jail. The two kept in contact and maintained a friendship until Bradley's death at fifty-two in 1946. This religious conversion would be a major factor in the lives of James and Virginia. James was a devout and active member of his parish until his death.

Cameron found work at the Pabst Brewery. He also worked at Inland Container Company while beginning his studies in electrical engineering at Milwaukee Area Technical College (MATC). At the same time, he sent all five of his children to college. All graduated. Walter and Virgil joined the Marine Corps.

Figure 44. Cameron at his job as the HVAC system manager at Mayfair Mall, Wauwatosa, Wisconsin. *Cameron Family*

---

[133] Milwaukee's black population had grown from just 862 in 1900 to 21,772 by 1950. Many of the first migrants had been sharecroppers (tenant farmers) from the South. They came north to escape Jim Crow and build a better life. Later the city became a magnet for blacks due to the growth of manufacturing and brewing after World War II. Most settled around a 12-block area known as Bronzeville, a thriving residential, business, and entertainment community. Barbershops, restaurants, drugstores, and funeral homes were started with a little money saved from overtime pay at factory jobs or extra domestic work taken on by the women. Nightclubs, taverns, and restaurants catered to a racially mixed clientele. Bronzeville is remembered by African American elders as a good place to grow up. Times were hard, but the community was close-knit. (Geenan, 2006.)

During this time, Cameron continued to search for a publisher for *A Time of Terror*.

The early 1960s brought Cameron medical problems related to the Marion lynching. One of his kidneys had calcified due to the terrible beating he endured and had to be removed.

The 1960s also saw the rise of Milwaukee's civil rights movement. Cameron traveled to the 1963 March on Washington where Dr. King gave his famous "I Have a Dream" speech. He joined Father James Groppi and the NAACP Youth Council in challenging segregated housing in our city. The Milwaukee Open Housing marches were instrumental in leading the federal government to pass the 1968 Fair Housing Act.[134]

In 1979, after retiring from his job as an HVAC system manager at a suburban shopping mall, Cameron became a fulltime advocate for black people in Milwaukee. He wrote numerous letters to the Milwaukee Journal and Milwaukee Sentinel newspapers. These addressed issues of race and racism, such as police brutality and killings of unarmed black men. The death of an unarmed black man, Ernest Lacy, who died in 1981 while in police custody, became one of his primary subjects of protest.

Cameron began to spend more time closely reading and studying American and Black Holocaust history, making numerous trips to the National Archives and Library of Congress in Washington, D.C. He became a brilliant, self-taught historian and lecturer. He gave many interviews on national television, including on Larry King Live, the Oprah Winfrey Show, and the 700 Club, retelling the story of the lynching he'd survived as a teenager. The British Broadcasting Corporation (BBC), a Dutch film company, and several public television stations featured him in documentary movies made about the lynching.

---

[134] The Open Housing marches were organized by the NAACP Youth Council and Alderwoman Vel Phillips, the first woman and first African American member of Milwaukee's Common Council. In 1962 Phillips proposed a city ordinance barring housing discrimination. Frustrated by the Common Council's repeated refusal to pass the ordinance, Alderwoman Phillips and hundreds of Milwaukee citizens took to the streets for 200 consecutive days in 1967-1968 to press for its passage. The NAACP Youth Council, led by its advisor, Father James Groppi, a white priest, joined them. The Commandos, the Youth Council's all-male security unit, formed a protective cordon around the marchers. Despite the Commandos' protection, the marchers, including Dr. Cameron, faced thousands of belligerent whites along their route, who pelted them with racial epithets, eggs, glass bottles full of urine, and rocks. They were also confronted and arrested by armed police.

In the tradition of pamphleteers from David Walker to Ida B. Wells-Barnett, Cameron began to write and sell booklets related to American history and race relations to educate the Milwaukee community. The questions he tackled ranged from American history ("What was the condition of Black Labor in America at the end of our Civil War?") to analyses of local race relations ("An Open Letter to the Milwaukee Fire and Police Commission Regarding the Earnest Lacy Complaint"). He still searched for a publisher for his memoir.

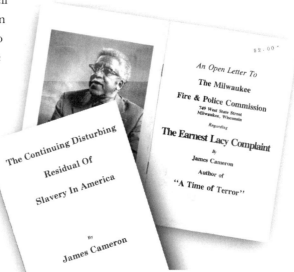

Figure 47. Dr. Cameron wrote dozens of these booklets and sold them at speaking engagements and, eventually, at his museum. The Milwaukee Public Library has a complete digitized collection available to researchers. *Cameron Family*

After retirement, he traveled with Virginia on a long-awaited, church-sponsored pilgrimage to the holy city of Jerusalem. This trip included a visit to Yad Vashem, the Jewish people's living memorial to the *Shoah*, the holocaust they suffered in Europe. James and Virginia spent hours touring the museum. He saw pictures of the ovens and gas chambers where Hitler destroyed millions of Jews. Standing with tears in his eyes before a huge pile of murdered children's shoes, he told his wife, "We need a museum like this in America, to tell the stories of blacks and their freedom loving white friends." The seed was planted for what would become America's Black Holocaust Museum.

In 1982 he gave up the dream of finding a publisher after hundreds of rejection letters. He took out a second mortgage on his home to cover the cost of self-publishing *A Time of Terror*. Cameron sold that 5,000-copy run of the book out of the trunk of his car and at speaking engagements in schools and universities around the Midwest–

including in Marion, Indiana.[135] To support his travels Cameron bought a Rug Master carpet and furniture cleaning franchise and truck, running the business from home.

Having collected Jim Crow and other historical objects in his study, Cameron began exhibiting them in a series of storefront museums. On June 19, 1988, in honor of Juneteenth Day[136], he opened his first formal museum on the second floor above the Masjid Sultan Muhammad. He used $5,000 of his personal savings. It was

Figure 48. Dr. Cameron in his office at America's Black Holocaust Museum in 1993. *Cynthia Carr*

not a big hit. He went days without a single visitor. Still, he persisted in pursuing his vision and eventually found a new home for the museum. He purchased an old boxing

---

[135] Cameron told journalist Cynthia Carr that the 200 lynching spectators he interviewed while writing *A Time of Terror* were all happy to see him and to learn that the rumor–that he had died of the injuries from the beating–was false. "But," as Carr noted, "none had lifted a finger to help him, and no one apologized." Even so, Cameron was glad of Marion's response to his continued existence: "In the spring of 1980, when the people of Marion found out that I was alive and well…and that I had written a manuscript relating in minute detail the shame and disgrace that befell their city on the night of August 7, 1930, I received and accepted numerous invitations to visit Marion to tell my story. I made appearances on television talk shows, call-in radio programs, and interviews in the local press. I also spoke to thousands of school students." (Carr, 2006, 25.)

[136] June 19th has been celebrated as Juneteenth Day since that date in 1865, when the enslaved blacks in Texas were freed. Because no Civil War battles were fought in that state, these were the last slaves to hear from Union troops about the Emancipation Proclamation. From the first public celebrations organized by freedmen in Texas, the custom spread across the United States. Forty-three states now recognize June 19th as a state holiday or a day of observance.

gym in the Bronzeville neighborhood for $1 from the city of Milwaukee in May of 1992. He formed a nonprofit organization to run the museum. After extensive repairs, many of which Cameron did himself, the Bronzeville location became the home of the America's Black Holocaust Museum (ABHM) on November 9, 1994.

Cameron built the museum into a valued part of Milwaukee's cultural life. He would work there almost every day until his late 80s. Cameron used the museum to tell the untold stories of African-American suffering and resilience. He gave tours of the museum, mopped the floors, and cleaned the toilet. For some time, he would be a one-man museum.

The early ABHM included a "Chamber of Horrors" featuring graphic "souvenir" photos of lynchings and eventually a diorama depicting his two friends in Marion hanging on the tree in 1930. He had a "Young Writers Corner" which showcased the work of 5-16 year-olds. The museum was designed as an educational institution to promote understanding and dialogue about those parts of American history that are typically left out of the history books.

Figure 49. Carrying his customary protest sign, Cameron marched against the KKK in Beloit, Wisconsin, in winter 1974. *Troy Freund*

In addition to running the museum, he traveled around the Midwest speaking about his book, telling his story to school and college groups, and others. Dr. Cameron's lifework focused on raising Americans' consciousness and conscience about the atrocity of lynching. He did this by publicly and tirelessly retelling his personal experience. He believed that hatred was a poison that corrupted the hater from within. He taught, by word and example, how to "forgive but never forget." He dreamed of our nation as "one single and sacred nationality" and fought to hold Americans to our ideals of freedom and equality for all. Cameron wanted his museum to "prick the conscience of America, to raise the moral sensitivity of the American people."

Cameron closely watched the activities of the Ku Klux Klan in the Midwest and would often attend their rallies in protest. He persisted in this practice well into his 80s, when he staged his last protest in a wheelchair.

While fighting for changes in America's race relations, Cameron was constantly reminded of that night in Marion where he alone survived the triple lynching. He had for many years hoped to receive forgiveness.

In 1991 he wrote to Indiana Governor Evan Bayh asking for a pardon for "the foolish role I played in the commission of a crime that resulted in the loss of three precious lives." In September 1993 the pardon was approved and signed by Governor Bayh. Cameron cried when he received the phone call from the parole board commissioner. On February 11, 1993 the city of Marion formally presented Cameron with his long awaited pardon and gave him a key to the city at a ceremony attended by 75 friends, family members, and officials. "Now that the state of Indiana has forgiven me for my indiscretion, I, in turn, forgive Indiana for their transgressions of the law in Marion on the night of August 7, 1930," Cameron stated. "I forgive those who have harmed Abe and Tom, realizing I can never forget the traumatic events that took place that night…you have no idea what this means to me. The slate has been wiped clean," he said, wiping tears from his eyes.

The following year brought joy and pain for Cameron. Black Classic Press published *A Time of Terror.* Five thousand of its 15,000 copies were sold in the first week and another 7000 in less than a year.[137] However, a diagnosis of multiple myeloma, an incurable blood cancer, at the age of 80 dampened the joy. He underwent months of

---

[137] "The publicist hired by Black Classic Press described media interest around the book as a 'feeding frenzy'" (Carr, 2006, 29). This second edition of his book would go out of print in 2003.

chemotherapy and the cancer went into remission. Though weakened by the cancer, Cameron continued to share his story.

In 1995, the BBC filmed Cameron for their documentary, *Unforgiven: Legacy of a Lynching*. He was once again able to travel, and he and Virginia visited Ireland, England, and other European countries with a church group. Cameron continued to develop the museum and traveled again to schools to tell his story to the young.

On Cameron's 82nd birthday, February 25, 1996 a large painting called "The Lynching" by Massachusetts painter Michael Russo, was donated to ABHM after the painter read about the museum in the New York Times. The painting depicts a lynching with a single victim hanging from a tree with a crowd milling in the foreground, some hooded KKK members, and the form of Christ in the distance. It became a treasured part of ABHM's collections.

In May of 1999, Cameron and the museum welcomed a national exhibit, "A Slave Ship Speaks: The Wreck of the Henrietta Marie." As part of a twenty-city tour, the artifacts discovered thirty-five miles off the coast of Florida provided a firsthand account of slavery. A $1 million construction project, including a 5,000 square foot expansion to the museum, was built to house the exhibit. Along with the exhibit the museum sponsored a six-week course entitled "Africans in America–The Middle Passage and Slavery" for Milwaukee Public School teachers, to prepare them to teach this history to their students.

Figure 50. In 2006, a young visitor stops and listens to the creaking of the ship and the groans of the kidnapped Africans inside the cargo hold of the slave ship exhibit. *Fruit of the Tree Productions*

Cameron continued to attract countless numbers of volunteers to become griots who gave tours at the museum. ABHM now displayed professionally curated exhibits in a series of galleries. Griots began their tours at the African village, discussing the ways of life shattered by the kidnapping of Africans from their homes. They then led visitors to the Middle Passage exhibit. In the simulated slave ship's cargo hold, packed into the claustrophobic din, they would hear the creaking of the ship, footsteps of the captors, and moans of the captives. Visitors would emerge to stand on an auction block, surrounded by replica posters advertising men, women, and children for sale.

From there griots escorted them through an exhibit about life on the plantation. They then explained the Jim Crow era by showing "collectible" racist memorabilia[138] and the lynching exhibit. An exhibit about Cameron's life and various traveling exhibits from other museums completed the tour. The trained griots, both black and white, made the museum a safe place for visitors to learn about and discuss issues of race relations. People from around the world visited the museum in hopes of meeting the lynching survivor.

In May of 1999, the University of Wisconsin-Milwaukee awarded Cameron an honorary degree for a lifetime of work exhibiting materials of uncommon merit, moral, and intellectual value to the city and state. From that time forward, museum visitors, staff, volunteers and the greater Milwaukee community would call him Dr. Cameron

In June 2005 Dr. Cameron traveled with family and friends to Washington, D.C. With hundreds of others, he had been invited to witness the historic signing of a public apology by the U.S. Senate for never passing a federal anti-lynching bill. Eighty Senators sponsored the resolution that apologized for the inaction of the Senate despite the passage of three anti-lynching bills by the House of Representatives between 1920 and 1940. "It's a hundred-something years too late, but I'm glad they're doing it," Cameron said that day. Senator Barack Obama, the only black member of the Senate, stated, "I do hope that this chamber also spends some time doing something concrete and tangible to heal the long shadow of slavery and the legacy of discrimination so that 100 years from now we can look back and be proud and not have to apologize again."

---

[138] These Jim Crow objects – saltshakers, greeting cards, porcelain figurines, games, and the like – depict negative stereotypes of African Americans, such as "mammies," "pickaninnies," and "Sambos." People bought (and still buy) them to display on walls and shelves in their homes. Among ABHM's collection of such objects was a tin of Niggerhair Tobacco, snuff processed in Milwaukee. Its can sported the profile of a black woman with exaggeratedly full lips.

Figure 51. Dr. Cameron and his wife Virginia during an interview at their home on their sixty-eighth wedding anniversary, a month before his passing. *Fruit of the Tree Productions*

Following a long battle with illness, Dr. James Cameron passed away quietly at the age of ninety-two on June 11, 2006. Virginia, his wife of sixty-eight years, survived him, along with three of his children Walter, Virgil and Dolores. He had been preceded in death by sons James Herbert and David Cameron, and great-grandson Zaire Cameron. Four grandchildren, a niece, great-grandchildren, great great-grandchildren and a host of other loving relatives and many friends also survived Dr. Cameron.

His funeral was held in Milwaukee's St. John Cathedral, attended by more than five hundred friends and relatives from Milwaukee and Marion, Indiana. State and national elected officials eulogized him. His pastor, Father Carl Diederichs of All Saints Catholic Church, described him as "a giant of a man, great in vision, and a man of deep, yet humble faith." The funeral was held on June 19th–Juneteenth Day–the eighteenth anniversary of the opening of America's Black Holocaust Museum. Alderman Michael McGee Jr. delivered on a promise to have a portion of the street in front of the museum renamed in Dr. Cameron's honor.

Two years later the museum building closed its doors due to financial difficulties during the Great Recession. On November 30, 2010 Virginia Cameron peacefully passed away.

In 2012 members of the museum's former board of directors and community activists joined to form the nonprofit Dr. James Cameron Legacy Foundation to maintain and build upon his legacy. Working with other volunteers, the group launched an entirely online version of America's Black Holocaust Museum at www.abhmuseum.org.

This *virtual* museum now attracts thousands of visitors weekly from more than two hundred countries. The Legacy Foundation also runs public programs, including film screenings, speakers, and interracial dialogues around the city and region. This book is one of its initiatives. At this writing, planning has begun to reestablish ABHM's physical presence in Milwaukee in the coming years.

Dr. Cameron and his work touched the hearts and minds of thousands of people. His legacy lies in the work that these people continue in his honor. He lives in those of us dedicated to the mission of educating the world about the long shadow of slavery and opening hearts to repair and reconciliation. Dr. Cameron's true impact can be seen in the faces of the children and adults who shed a tear hearing his story, just as he shed a tear that first day that we met.

I've been fortunate enough to know a legend. He will always be my friend and mentor. I will continue to follow in his broad footsteps. Dr. Cameron was a selfless fighter and teacher. I strive to carry those same traits. My short years being friends with him changed the trajectory of my life, as he changed the lives of many others. His mission has become my mission. I can't thank him enough.

Reggie Jackson
Milwaukee, Wisconsin
April 15, 2015

BIBLIOGRAPHY

Print

Alexander, Michelle. *The New Jim Crow: Mass Incarceration in the Age of Colorblindness.* New York: The New Press, 2010, 2012.

Allen, James, John Lewis, Leon F. Litwack, and Hilton Als. *Without Sanctuary: Lynching Photography in America.* Santa Fe, NM: Twin Palms Publishers, 2000.

Barnes, Harper. *Never Been a Time: The 1917 Race Riot That Sparked the Civil Rights Movement.* New York: Walker Publishing Company, 2008.

Blackmon, Douglas A. *Slavery by Another Name: The Re-Enslavement of Black Americans from the Civil War to World War II.* New York: Anchor Books, Random House Publishing, 2008.

Carr, Cynthia. *Our Town: A Heartland Lynching, a Haunted Town, and the Hidden History of White America.* New York: Crown Publishers, 2006.

DeGruy Leary, Joy. *Post Traumatic Slave Syndrome: America's Legacy of Enduring Injury and Healing.* Portland, OR: Uptone Press, 2005.

Dray, Phillip. *At the Hands of Persons Unknown: The Lynching of Black America.* New York: The Modern Library, 2002.

Fedo, Michael. *The Lynchings in Duluth.* St. Paul, MN: The Minnesota Historical Society Press, 2000.

Feldman, David B. and Lee Daniel Kravetz. *Supersurvivors: The Surprising Link Between Suffering and Success.* New York: HarperCollins Publishers, 2014.

Geenan, Paul H. *Milwaukee's Bronzeville, 1900-1950,* Charleston, SC: Arcadia Publishing, 2006.

Ginzburg, Ralph. *100 Years of Lynching.* Baltimore, MD: Black Classic Press, 1996.

Goldsby, Jacqueline. *A Spectacular Secret: Lynching in American Life and Literature.* Chicago: University of Chicago Press, 2006.

Gregory, James. *The Southern Diaspora: How the Great Migrations of Black and White Southerners Transformed America.* Chapel Hill, NC: The University of North Carolina Press, 2007.

Ifill, Sherrilyn A. *On the Courthouse Lawn: Confronting the Legacy of Lynching in the Twenty-First Century.* Boston: Beacon Press, 2007.

Kwitny, Jonathan. *Endless Enemies.* New York: Congdon and Weed, 1984.

Lafferty, R. A. *Okla Hannali*. Garden City, New York: Doubleday, 1972.

Lane, Charles. *The Day Freedom Died: The Colfax Massacre, the Supreme Court, and the Betrayal of Reconstruction*. New York: Henry Holt and Company, 2008.

Lichtenstein, Alex. *Twice the Work of Free Labor: The Political Economy of Convict Labor in the New South*. New York: Verso, 1996.

Litwack, Leon F. *Trouble in Mind: Black Southerners In The Age of Jim Crow*. New York: Vintage Books, 1998.

Loewen, James W. *Lies My Teacher Told Me: Everything Your American History Textbook Got Wrong*. New York: Touchstone, 1995, 2009.

——. W. *Sundown Towns: A Hidden Dimension of American Racism*. New York: New Press, 2005.

Madison, James. *A Lynching in the Heartland: Race and Memory in America*. New York: Pelgrave Macmillan, 2001.

Margolick, David. *Strange Fruit: The Biography of a Song*. New York: HarperCollins Publishers, 2001.

Muhammad, Khalil Gibran. *The Condemnation of Blackness: Race, Crime, and the Making of Modern Urban America*. Cambridge, MA: First Harvard University Press, 2011.

Oshinsky, David. *Worse Than Slavery: Parchman Farm and the Ordeal of Jim Crow Justice*. New York: Free Press, 1997.

Quillen, Frank U. *The Color Line in Ohio*. Ann Arbor: Wahr, 1913.

Raper, Arthur F. *The Tragedy of Lynching*. New York: Dover Publications, Inc., 2003.

Rice, Anne P., ed. *Witnessing Lynching: American Writers Respond*. Rutgers, NJ: University of Rutgers Press, 2003.

Royster, Jacqueline Jones, ed. *Southern Horrors and Other Writings; The Anti-Lynching Campaign of Ida B. Wells, 1892-1900*. Columbus, OH: Bedford/St. Martin's, 1996.

Smith, Shawn Michelle and Dora Apel. *Lynching Photographs*. Berkeley: University of California Press, 2007.

Stevenson, Barbara J. *An Oral History of African Americans in Grant County*. Charleston, SC: Arcadia Pubishing, 2000.

Waldrep, Christopher. *African Americans Confront Lynching: Strategies of Resistance from the Civil War to the Civil Rights Era*. Lanham, MD: Rowman & Littlefield Publishers, Inc., 2009.

——. *The Many Faces of Judge Lynch: Extralegal Violence and Punishment in America*. New York: Palgrave Macmillan, 2004.

Washington, Booker T. *Up From Slavery: An Autobiography*. (1901).

Washington, Harriet A. *Medical Apartheid: The Dark History of Medical Experimentation on Black Americans from Colonial Times to the Present*. New York: Doubleday, 2006.

Wells-Barnett, Ida B. *The Red Record*. Echo Library, 2006.

White, Walter. *Rope and Faggot*. New York: Alfred A. Knopf, Inc., 2001.

Wilkerson, Isabel. *The Warmth of Other Suns: The Epic Story of America's Great Migration.* New York: Vintage Books, 2010.

Wood, Amy Louise. *Lynching and Spectacle: Witnessing Racial Violence in America, 1890-1940.* Chapel Hill, NC: The University of North Carolina Press, 2009.

Online

——. "100 Years of Jim Crow," America's Black Holocaust Museum. http://abhmuseum.org/category/galleries/one-hundred-years-of-jim-crow/

——. "Anthony Crawford," Entry in the *Memorial to the Victims of Lynching.* America's Black Holocaust Museum. http://abhmuseum.org/2012/01/anthony-crawford/

——. "Ending the Schoolhouse to Jailhouse Track," Advancement Project. http://safequalityschools.org/pages/understanding-the-school-prison-pipeline.

——. "Hate and Extremism Blog," Southern Poverty Law Center, 2015. http://www.splcenter.org/what-we-do/hate-and-extremism

——. "The Castle," Castle Property. Accessed July 4, 2015. http://castleproperty.net/home.html

Boston, Nicolaus and Jennifer Hallom. "The Slave Experience: Freedom & Emancipation," PBS. http://www.pbs.org/wnet/slavery/experience/freedom/history.html.

Ferraro, Anthony and Fran Kaplan. *Sweet Messenger* video, *"Dr. James Cameron: Museum Founder and Lynching Survivor,"* America's Black Holocaust Museum. http://abhmuseum.org/2012/01/dr-james-cameron-museum-founder-and-lynching-survivor/

Ghandnoosh, Nazgol. "Race and Punishment: Racial Perceptions of Crime and Support for Punitive Policies," The Sentencing Project, 2014. http://www.sentencingproject.org/doc/publications/rd_Race_and_Punishment.pdf.

Harp, Stephanie. "John Carter: A Scapegoat for Anger," America's Black Holocaust Museum. http://abhmuseum.org/2012/08/the-lynching-of-john-carter/

Jim Crow Museum of Racist Memorabilia. Ferris State University. http://www.ferris.edu/HTMLS/news/jimcrow/who.htm.

Kaplan, Fran. *Video: Carl Deeter Jr. talks about his grandparents' forgiveness.* "Freedom's Heroes During Jim Crow: Flossie Bailey and the Deeters," America's Black Holocaust Museum. http://abhmuseum.org/2012/01/freedoms-heros-during-jim-crow-flossie-bailey-and-the-deeters/

——. "Tour: Racial Repair and Reconciliation," America's Black Holocaust Museum. http://abhmuseum.org/2014/07/tour-racial-repair-reconciliation-and-redemption/.

——"An Iconic Lynching in the North," America's Black Holocaust Museum. www.abhmuseum.org/2012/01/an-iconic-lynching-in-the-north/

King, Jr., Martin Luther. "Letter from Birmingham Jail, April 16, 1963." Stanford University. http://mlk-kpp01.stanford.edu:5801/transcription/document_images/undecided/630416-019.pdf.

Kochnar, Ramesh and Richard Fry. "Wealth inequality has widened along racial, ethnic lines since end of Great Recession," Pew Research Center, 2014. http://www.pewresearch.org/fact-tank/2014/12/12/racial-wealth-gaps-great-recession/.

Loewen, James W. "Sundown Towns." http://sundown.afro.illinois.edu/sundowntowns.php

Lowery, Wesley. "85 years after infamous lynching, another noose stirs tension in Indiana town," The Washington Post. March 31, 2015. http://www.washingtonpost.com/news/post-nation/wp/2015/03/31/85-years-after-infamous-lynching-another-noose-stirs-tension-in-indiana-town/

Onion, Rachel. "Take the Impossible 'Literacy' Test Louisiana Gave Black Voters in the 1960s," Slate: The Vault. http://www.slate.com/blogs/the_vault/2013/06/28/voting_rights_and_the_supreme_court_the_impossible_literacy_test_louisiana.html

Potok, Mark. "The Year in Hate and Extremism 2013," Intelligence Report, Issue 153. Southern Poverty Law Center, Spring 2014. http://www.splcenter.org/get-informed/intelligence-report/browse-all-issues/2014/spring

Read, Warren. "Shaking the Family Tree," America's Black Holocaust Museum. http://abhmuseum.org/2014/07/shaking-the-family-tree-my-journey-of-recovery-repair-and-renovation/

Scott, Jennifer. "Stories Behind the Postcards," America's Black Holocaust Museum. http://abhmuseum.org/2012/04/stories-behind-the-postcards-paintings-and-collages-of-jennifer-scott/

Film

Adelman, Larry. *Race: The Power of an Illusion.* California Newsreel, 2003.

Sapin, Paul. *Unforgiven: Legacy of a Lynching.* British Broadcasting Service (BBC), 1995.

Image Sources & Credits

Please note: Every effort has been made to contact all rights holders for all images. If you are a rights holder for an image and have not been reached, please contact LifeWrites Press.

Figure 1. Map of Indiana in the US (*Wikimedia Commons/Creative Commons Attributions-Share Alike*) and Locations in Indiana (*Fran Kaplan*)

Figure 2. Ku Klux Klan parade, 9/13/26. LC-F8- 40558. National Photo Company Collection. (*Library of Congress*)

Figure 3. Group of Negroes picking cotton. LC-USZ62-12511. (*Library of Congress*)

Figure 4. [Untitled] (Guard and convicts, 1941). Jack Delano, photographer. LC-USF33- 020861-M3. Farm Security Administration–Office of War Information Photograph Collection (*Library of Congress*)

Figure 5. Negro entering theater, Belzoni, MS, 1939. Marion Post Wolcott, photographer. LC-DIG-ppmsca-12888. Farm Security Administration–Office of War Information Photograph Collection (*Library of Congress*)

Figure 6. Negro drinking at "Colored" water cooler, Oklahoma, 1939. Russell Lee, photographer. Farm Security Administration–Office of War Information Photograph Collection (*Library of Congress*)

Figure 7. Family just arrived in Chicago. b11588545. Photographs and Prints Division. (*Schomburg Center for Research in Black Culture, The New York Public Library, Astor, Lenox and Tilden Foundations*)

Figure 8. Will Brown, circa 1919. RG2467-08. (*Nebraska State Historical Society*)

Figure 9. The burning of Will Brown's body. RG2281-69. (*Nebraska State Historical Society*)

Figure 10. 1929 covenant. Restrictive Covenants Database. (*Seattle Civil Rights and Labor History Project*)

Figure 11. 1944 program booklet, Anderson NAACP. (*Cameron Family*)

Figure 12. Lynching of circus workers in Duluth, 1920. (*Minnesota Historical Society*)

Figure 13. Rubin Stacey, lynched victim, 1935. Psnypl_scg_311. Photographs and Prints Division. (*Schomburg Center for Research in Black Culture, The New York Public Library, Astor, Lenox and Tilden Foundations*)

Figure 14. Lynching of Smith and Shipp, Marion, Indiana, 1930. Lawrence Beitler, photographer. (*Indiana Historical Society*)

Figure 15. Baby James with relatives, La Crosse, Wisconsin, 1914. (*Cameron Family*)

Figure 16. Frankenstein trestle 80 feet high, 500 long. LC-USZ62-27959. (*Library of Congress*)

Figure 17. Class photograph, D.A. Payne School in Marion, circa 1928. (*Cameron Family*)

Contributors

Reggie Jackson chairs the board of the Dr. James Cameron Legacy Foundation, the parent organization of America's Black Holocaust Museum (ABHM). He is also the museum's Head Griot (lead docent). Reggie first volunteered with ABHM in 2002. He led hundreds of tours during the last six years that the brick-and-mortar museum was open. He joined Board in 2005 and helped developed ABHM's Virtual Museum.

As an independent public historian, Reggie has been a much sought-after speaker on Black Holocaust topics locally and regionally for over a decade. He presents little-known stories in African-American history at schools, libraries, churches, and businesses. He also conducts diversity and race relations training. In 2015 the YWCA of Southeastern Wisconsin presented Reggie with their Eliminating Racism Award, and the First Unitarian Society honored him with their Courageous Love Award.

Reggie taught Contemporary Social Problems and Introduction to Sociology at Concordia University. He currently works as a special education teacher in a middle school in Milwaukee, Wisconsin.

Dr. Fran Kaplan serves as coordinator of the America's Black Holocaust *virtual* Museum. She has been an educator, social worker, writer, and racial justice activist for nearly five decades. Fran has created and run nonprofit and for profit organizations that address issues from women's health and farmworker rights to nurturing parenting, early childhood education, and peace-building.

Fran is also a published writer and the producer of award-winning short and feature films. Her co-authored screenplay, *Fruit of the Tree*, about the life of James Cameron has won awards in national and regional competitions. The international trainer-consultant for a global parenting education program, Fran authored and co-produced its Spanish-language videos, books, and games. With Dr. Robert Smith, Dr. Kaplan curated and edited *Lynching: An American Folkway*, a digital transmedia anthology distributed by Biblioboard, Inc. to libraries across the country.

Fran has been recognized by various organizations in Milwaukee and Wisconsin for promoting racial justice and providing leadership in children's and human rights.

Dr. James W. Loewen's gripping retelling of American history as it should be taught, *Lies My Teacher Told Me*, has sold more than 1.3 million copies and inspires K-16 teachers to help students challenge, rather than memorize, their textbooks.

Jim taught at the University of Vermont and Tougaloo College in Mississippi. He now lives in Washington, D.C., continuing his research on how Americans remember their past. *Lies Across America: What Our Historic Sites Get Wrong* came out in 1999. *Sundown Towns* was named Distinguished Book of 2005. In *Teaching What Really Happened* (2009), he gives teachers solutions to the problems described in his earlier works.

Loewen has asked thousands of Americans what caused the Civil War. Concerned by their replies, in 2010 he published *The Confederate and Neo-Confederate Reader*, setting the record straight in the Confederates' own words.

Dr. Loewen's honors include the American Sociological Association's Spivack and Cox-Johnson-Frazier Awards for scholarship in service to social justice; the American Book Award; the Oliver Cromwell Cox Award for Distinguished Anti-Racist Scholarship; and, the National Council for the Social Studies "Spirit of America" Award. He is a Distinguished Lecturer for the Organization of American Historians, Visiting Professor of Sociology at Catholic University in Washington, DC, and Visiting Professor of African-American Studies at the University of Illinois in Urbana/Champaign.

Dr. Robert Samuel Smith is Associate Vice Chancellor for Global Inclusion & Engagement, the Director of the Cultures & Communities Program, and Associate Professor of History at the University of Wisconsin-Milwaukee. He teaches courses on African American History, Multicultural America, African Americans and the Law, and U.S. Legal History.

Dr. Smith's research considers the intersection of race and law. In his book *Race, Labor and Civil Rights: Griggs v. Duke Power and the Struggle for Equal Employment Opportunity*, Rob chronicled the efforts of grassroots civil rights activists who used Title VII of the Civil Rights Act of 1964 to garner better jobs and long overdue promotions. Currently, he is exploring the relationships forged between civil/human rights attorneys in the United States and South Africa during the latter stages of apartheid and into the new millennium.

Rob is also a writer and speaker on contemporary race relations to both academic and general audiences. He currently contributes a regular monthly column on these issues to Milwaukee Magazine.

ACKNOWLEDGEMENTS

Bringing out this third edition of Dr. Cameron's memoir has been a long labor of love by a large group of hardworking volunteers backed by a crowd of individual donors and pro bono professional advisors. Words are inadequate to describe my gratitude for their generosity of spirit, persistence, and belief in the importance of returning this unique literary and historical work to the public forum.

In 2010, Dr. Cameron's son Virgil and I began exploring republication. We turned for advice to Dr. Sandra A. Adell, professor of Afro-American Studies at the University of Wisconsin. She drafted a preliminary scholarly introduction to the manuscript and connected us with editor Raphael Kadushin at University of Wisconsin Press. We ultimately decided to publish the book for a general–not academic–audience, but their encouragement and guidance gave this project its start.

Dr. Robert S. Smith, Reggie Jackson, Brad Pruitt, and I began collaborating on this and other projects for America's Black Holocaust Museum in 2011. It has been my great good fortune to be part of this amazing team. Each of these men is indefatigable, patient, wise, caring and supportive, fun to be with–and skillful. Along with his excellent historical scholarship, Rob has an abiding commitment to and talent for making academic scholarship accessible to the general public. Reggie's long close relationship with Dr. Cameron, his work as an educator at the museum and in the community, his in depth research about this lynching and racial terrorism in general provide intimate background knowledge and critical perspective. Behind the scenes, Brad is keeper of the fire and vision, the dreamer of ABHM's possibilities and advisor on such practicalities as how to crowd-fund and market a book.

I feel very honored that Dr. James Loewen volunteered to pen the Foreword. Dr. Cameron would be so pleased to know that a best-selling scholar/author champions this book as valuable, especially for young Americans. My gratitude goes out, as well, to other national figures who reviewed this edition: U.S. Congresswoman Gwen Moore, a longtime supporter of the museum; anti-racism educator/author Tim Wise; and Dr. Stephen Small, who is introducing Dr. Cameron's legacy to an international audience.

Many people contributed to making this edition beautiful and a pleasure to read. ABHM's graphic designer, Anthony Ferraro, guided us in envisioning an initial cover concept. Then, in the spirit of community, assisted by graphic design professor Michelle Quinn, we reached out to emerging and established professionals for their ideas. Nancy DuPont, Amy Kleinhans, Nate Pyper, and Jane Wodarczyk volunteered to create a variety of designs. We asked our social media community to select their favorite and comment. Based on over one hundred sixty responses, Michelle finalized our beautiful cover, using Tony Ferraro's as the primary concept and adopting influences from the others. Tony also lovingly optimized all fifty photographs in this book, some of which required a lot of work to look their best.

No one is more deserving of our gratitude than my friend Amy Stone, the lead copyeditor for the book. She was deeply respectful of and careful with Dr. Cameron's manuscript, suggesting only those edits in punctuation and wording that would enhance readability without altering his voice. Amy also read closely for content, asked perceptive questions, and suggested some of the annotations that enhance the text. I also appreciate the help of my sister Dr. Nancy Kaplan and intern David Nichols, whose initial editing improved our Introduction and Afterword, and of my friend Maureen Rosenblum, who meticulously proofed the final galley.

This project benefitted from the intellectual property services of Attorney Jeffrey Peterson at Michael, Best & Friedrich and the accounting expertise of Anick and Associates. Both firms donated thousands of dollars worth of work to support this project, without which this book would not have been published. We are very indebted to Dan Gronitz, web developer extraordinaire, who has generously provided many pro bono hours to ABHM over the years and is responsible for the silent smooth running of our virtual museum and this book's website. Thanks, too, to the staff of our local independent bookseller, Boswell Books, and its owner Daniel Goldin for helpful publishing, design, and distribution advice.

Then there's millennial artist, Jenna Knapp, who ably led our successful crowd-funding campaign. She created great promo videos, tweeted often, and assembled a small but mighty crew of social media-savvy young people to do outreach: Bryn Cooley, Tawana Ferraro, Brandon McGee, and Monica Miller. Thanks to them and to all of the generous donors listed here below, we could afford the upfront publishing expenses: the absolute necessities, like ISBN numbers, and the good stuff, like licenses for the many vintage photos that enrich this book.

Here is our "crowd," those who ensured that Dr. Cameron's story got into print:
- *Visionary Level:* Russell G. Brooker, PhD; Lanetta N. Greer, PhD; Michael and Ellie Kaplan; Dr. Nancy Kaplan; and Red Brown Kle´ Marketing Communications.

- *Beloved Teacher Level:* Shelley B. Fagel and Robert Perlis.
- *Social Justice Activist Level:* Karen Branan; Phyllis Mensch Brostoff; Virgil Cameron; Barbara J. Dineen; Chip Duncan; Hibbie and Jerrianne Hayslett; Reggie Jackson; Fran Kaplan; Catherine Knapp; Kevin Kuschel; Beth Lange; and William F. White.
- *History Scholar Level:* Kenneth Cooley; Aaron Greer; Ralph and Margaret Holman; Dr. Stuart Moulthrop; Brian Nigus; and Eilene Stevens.
- *Witness to History Level:* Iyalosha Adekola Adedapo; Adam Carr; Coming To The Table, LLC, and Tom DeWolf; Mary Dally-Muenzmaier; Barbara Federlin; Jean Honig; Venus Lewis-Jackson; Brad Lichtenstein; Louise W. Lindsey; Mark Metcalf; Ellen W. Miller; and Ms. Maureen Rosenblum.
- *Freedom Lover Level:* Chinedu Amaefula; Marcus S. Beebe; Bruce Brewer Jr.; Rhonda Brown; Janet A. Buchler; Tanya Dhein; Emily Franco; Robert Lange; John G. McDaid; Jennifer Nagle; and Chelsea Alison Wait.

I also wish to gratefully recognize the keepers of history in Indiana who have helped this project along for years: the librarians at the Indiana Historical Society, the Anderson Public Library, and, especially, the Marion Public Library and Museum. There are other Indiana-related people to thank as well. Carl Deeter, Jr. spoke with me several times about his uncle's murder and the lynching, and his aunt Faith kindly provided Deeter family photos for use on the ABHM site and in this book. In authoring the Introduction to this volume, Rob and I depended heavily on the thorough research of historian James Madison and of journalist Cynthia Carr, who also allowed us to use her photos. I wish Tom Wise, Dr. Cameron's cousin, could see this edition, but sadly, he is no longer with us. Tom helped Dr. Cameron self-publish the first edition of this book. Interviews I conducted with him and the tour of Marion he gave my film team in 2006 contributed immeasurably to my understanding of the context of Dr. Cameron's story.

Finally, I want to appreciate Virgil Cameron for our many, many hours of discussion about his father's life and works; for searching out and providing photographs, manuscripts, and other materials; and for his friendship and patient faith in the fruition of this and other projects that we are endeavoring in his dad's name.

Fran Kaplan, Editor
Milwaukee, Wisconsin
October 15, 2015